THE ANGLO-SCOTTISH BALLAD

The Anglo-Scottish Ballad and its Imaginary Contexts

David Atkinson

http://www.openbookpublishers.com

© 2014 David Atkinson

This work is licensed under a Creative Commons Attribution 4.0 International license (CC BY 4.0). This license allows you to share, copy, distribute and transmit the work; to adapt the work and to make commercial use of the work providing attribution is made to the author (but not in any way that suggests that she endorses you or your use of the work). Attribution should include the following information:

Atkinson, David, *The Anglo-Scottish Ballad and its Imaginary Contexts*. Cambridge, UK: Open Book Publishers, 2014, http://dx.doi.org/10.11647/OBP.0041

Further details about CC BY licenses are available at http://creativecommons.org/licenses/by/4.0/

Digital material and resources associated with this volume are available at http://www.openbookpublishers.com/isbn/9781783740277

ISBN Paperback: 978-1-78374-027-7
ISBN Hardback: 978-1-78374-028-4
ISBN Digital (PDF): 978-1-78374–029–1
ISBN Digital ebook (epub): 978-1-78374-030-7
ISBN Digital ebook (mobi): 978-1-78374-031-4
DOI: 10.11647/OBP.0041

Cover image: Henry Robert Morland (1716–1797), *The Ballad Singer* (*circa* 1764). http://commons.wikimedia.org/wiki/File:Henry_Robert_Morland_-_The_Ballad_Singer_-_Google_Art_Project.jpg

Every effort has been made to identify and contact copyright holders; any omissions or errors will be corrected if notification is made to the publisher. Please see the list of illustrations for copyright relating to individual images.

All paper used by Open Book Publishers is SFI (Sustainable Forestry Initiative), and PEFC (Programme for the Endorsement of Forest Certification Schemes) Certified.

Printed in the United Kingdom and United States by Lightning Source for Open Book Publishers

For Catherine, Francis, and Jennifer

Contents

References and Abbreviations		ix
List of Illustrations		xi
Preface		xiii
1.	Where Is the Ballad?	1
2.	On the Nature of Evidence	25
3.	Textual Authority and the Sources of Variance	49
4.	The Material Ballad	69
5.	Sound and Writing	89
6.	Agency, Intention, and the Problem of Version (with a brief history of ballad editing)	119
7.	Palimpsest or *texte génétique*	149
8.	Afterword: 'All her friends cried out for shame'	173
Select Bibliography		183
Index		203

References and Abbreviations

The following abbreviations are used throughout for standard editions and reference works:

CSD: *Concise Scots Dictionary*, ed. Mairi Robinson (Edinburgh: Polygon at Edinburgh, 1999).

DSL: *Dictionary of the Scots Language / Dictionar o the Scots Leid*, available at http://www.dsl.ac.uk/dsl/ [*DSL-DOST*: *Dictionary of the Older Scottish Tongue* entries; *DSL-SND*: *Scottish National Dictionary* entries].

EDD: *The English Dialect Dictionary*, ed. Joseph Wright, 6 vols (London: Henry Frowde, 1898–1905).

ESPB: Francis James Child, ed., *The English and Scottish Popular Ballads*, 5 vols (Boston: Houghton, Mifflin, 1882–98).

ESTC: English Short Title Catalogue, available at http://estc.bl.uk

OED: *Oxford English Dictionary*, available at http://www.oed.com

Child numbers: refer to items in *ESPB*.

Roud numbers: refer to items in the Roud Folk Song Index and Broadside Index, available at http://vwml.org.uk/search/search-roud-indexes

Bodleian Library broadside ballads are available at http://ballads.bodleian.ox.ac.uk

All web addresses cited, and Digital Object Identifiers (DOIs) in the Select Bibliography, were accessed prior to publication on 12/13 February 2014 and were valid at that date.

List of Illustrations

1.1	Enos White and his wife, outside Crown Cottage, Axford, Hampshire. Provenance unknown.	2
5.1	Carpenter Collection, Photo 101, James Madison Carpenter sitting in his Austin Roadster. Courtesy of the American Folklife Center at the Library of Congress, Washington, DC, USA.	102
5.2	Carpenter Collection, MS p. 08356. Courtesy of the American Folklife Center at the Library of Congress, Washington, DC, USA.	106
5.3	Joseph Taylor, 'Lord Bateman', transcribed by Percy Grainger, *Journal of the Folk-Song Society*, 3.3 (no. 12) (1908), 192–93. Courtesy of the English Folk Dance and Song Society.	114–115
6.1	Carpenter Collection, MS p. 04267. Courtesy of the American Folklife Center at the Library of Congress, Washington, DC, USA.	143
7.1	Carpenter Collection, MS pp. 04384–04387. Courtesy of the American Folklife Center at the Library of Congress, Washington, DC, USA.	156–157
8.1	Carpenter Collection, MS pp. 04403–04404. Courtesy of the American Folklife Center at the Library of Congress, Washington, DC, USA.	176

Preface

The 'imaginary' in the title of this volume is quite deliberate. The ballad and its *imagined* contexts, with its echoes of Benedict Anderson's imagined communities, Georgina Boyes's imagined village, and Eric Hobsbawm and Terence Ranger's invented traditions, might have evoked an oral, ballad-singing community of a kind that owes as much to the broad thrust of Romanticism as it does to a historical back-projection from (limited) evidence drawn from the folk song revivals of the twentieth century. The *imaginary* contexts of the title, in contrast, refer to the abstract ideas that are the necessary counterpart of any attempt to describe the ballad – be it at the level of genre or of the individual literary/musical item in its social and historical context – in terms either of ontology or of textual constitution.

Conceptually, there is a danger that 'the ballad as abstract idea' might appear perilously close to the sort of conflationary, 'idealist' notion of ballad editing that characterized publications of a much earlier period. Editions such as Thomas Percy's *Reliques of Ancient English Poetry*, Walter Scott's *Minstrelsy of the Scottish Border*, and William Motherwell's *Minstrelsy: Ancient and Modern* drew on and compounded different texts in order to achieve a comprehensive and complete, 'ideal' version of each individual ballad. They have been much reviled for doing so, although as an exercise in 'best-text editing', duly described and documented, this could still be a defensible approach. However, it is certainly true that it falls foul of the ethnographic turn that ballad studies have taken since that time.

Both Scott and Motherwell came to reject their own editorial practices and instead to laud the discrete integrity, and poetic and musical value, of each separate ballad instance, or 'version'. Subsequently, mediated by the practice of the Danish editor Svend Grundtvig, this insight provided the theoretical basis for Francis James Child's standard edition of *The English and Scottish Popular Ballads*. The 'type/version paradigm' embodied therein represents the distinctive contribution of ballad studies to editing theory. In short, the ballad 'type' is identified as the abstract sum of all actual and possible manifestations, or 'versions', of what is recognizably the 'same' thing. The definition is notably circular – but it does mostly work in practice because there turns out to be a high level of seemingly inherent stability in ballad narratives and melodies, which makes it possible, most of the time, to recognize quite intuitively which items belong together.

Since it is frequently possible to ascribe individual versions to individual sources, this type/version paradigm lends itself very neatly to the ethnographic orientation. In what has been rather grandly termed 'the post-Child era of scientific folklore', a premium attaches to the precise recording, attribution, and presentation of the collected item. And yet there is already a paradox here, because the type/version paradigm has also, almost uninvited, introduced an abstract dimension into the discussion. For the 'version' cannot exist without inherent reference to the 'type' – and so while on the one hand the item's uniqueness is being identified, on the other it is simultaneously being absorbed. Just as the 'version' is a constituent part of the 'type', so the 'version' itself derives from the 'type'.

This 'imaginary context' then goes to the heart of ballad representation, for the type/version paradigm has to incorporate *all* possible manifestations and not just a chosen few. 'Ballad representation' impinges on many of the critical dimensions that have dominated (some might say, bedevilled) ballad research: ballad origins; oral and printed transmission; sound and writing; agency and editing; textual and melodic indeterminacy and instability; and the premises and purposes that lie behind collecting, editing, publishing, and research. Some of these issues are addressed in the chapters that follow.

While the focus here is mostly on ballad texts (words), and a good deal of the argument draws on theories of textual editing, it is to be hoped that several of the main ideas that can be extracted from the discussion will turn out to have a bearing on ballad melodies. Nevertheless, it is unwise to press too far the idea that the ballad comprises an indivisible textual and melodic whole. Not least because the two things are inherently separable: the same words can go to different tunes, and vice versa; and the words can exist without the melody (in broadside print, for example), just as the melody can exist without the words. While there is the possibility for melody to impact upon versification, and the two things can certainly interact associatively – collectors like Cecil Sharp have commented on the difficulty singers sometimes experience in recalling words in the absence of a tune (and there is some evidence from neuroscience for the synergy of the two things in human memory) – there is still an absence of a critical vocabulary that would convincingly facilitate the discussion of an integrated whole. Ballad words belong ultimately to the domain of language, and ballad melodies to the domain of music, yet it remains unclear to what extent those two domains really can be thought of as precisely equivalent – as both belonging, as it were, to a single grand domain of Saussurean *langue*.

Versions of some of these chapters have been aired as published articles or as presentations, but all have been rewritten for this volume in order to integrate them into the book, to bring them up to date, and, as far as possible, to avoid unnecessary repetition. Versions of chapters one, five, six, and seven, respectively, appeared in the journals *Lied und populäre Kultur/Song and Popular Culture*, *Twentieth-Century Music*, *Variants*, and *Folklore*, and I am very grateful to their editors and copyright holders for permission to reuse the material (full bibliographic details are cited at the beginning of the respective chapters). A version of chapter four was to have been published in *Estudos de Literatura Oral* but has not appeared at the time of writing.

I am especially grateful for the insights and enthusiasms of members of the European Society for Textual Scholarship, the Folklore Society, the Kommission für Volksdichtung, the Traditional Song Forum, and the Editorial Board of *Folk Music Journal*, who have all indirectly contributed to this volume. Likewise the readers for Open Book Publishers, who made some valuable suggestions which I have incorporated. This is the place, too, to thank Alessandra Tosi and Bianca Gualandi at Open Book Publishers for their professionalism and enthusiasm. Special thanks go to the J. M. Carpenter project team – Julia Bishop, Elaine Bradtke, Eddie Cass, Tom McKean, and Bob Walser; Malcolm Taylor and everyone at the Vaughan Williams Memorial Library; my co-editor on *Street Ballads in Nineteenth-Century Britain, Ireland, and North America*, Steve Roud; and Brian Peters, for the late nights and ballad discussions. It is a privilege and pleasure to work in a field where people still uphold the human values of friendship and cooperation. All of them have done their best to keep me from straying too far from the scholarly straight and narrow. All errors that remain are, of course, my own stupid fault.

East Finchley, February 2014

1. Where Is the Ballad?

Empirically, the English-language ballad comprises a genre of narrative verse and melody, of largely (or effectively) anonymous origin, examples of which have been in existence in one form or another since at least the fifteenth century. The combination of perceived anonymity with multiplicity, with the concomitant possibility (frequently enhanced by considerable depth in time) of variation during the course of transmission, has then allowed conflicting principles of organization to attach to discussion of the ballad. Some of those that come to mind are: (*i*) the individual rendition, and the various ways in which it might be reproduced; (*ii*) the psychology and personality of the contributor from whom the ballad was collected; (*iii*) any ideological agenda brought to the exchange by the collector; (*iv*) the synchronic context, with reference to political, social, cultural, literary, and musical history; (*v*) the diachronic complex of different 'versions' that constitute the 'same' thing, and the dual but separable nature of the ballad as literature and as music; (*vi*) the quality of being 'traditional', as opposed to 'literary' or even 'fabricated'. Whilst the seeming contradictions that arise from this situation often reflect first and foremost the particular orientations of the researcher – towards ethnography, historicism, or comparative textual and musicological analysis, for example – they can also encourage the conviction that the ontology of ballads is somehow distinct from that of more canonical works of literature and music. 'Ontology', as the term and the idea are being used here, refers to the whole range of conditions that are considered (or have been considered) as either necessary or sufficient to identify the ballad – either the individual item or the genre at large – as

http://dx.doi.org/10.11647/OBP.0041.01

a distinct literary and musical phenomenon, and to the consequences that might appear to flow from those conditions.[1]

In July 1955, Bob Copper, working for the BBC Folk Music and Dialect Recording Scheme, recorded the ballad 'George Collins' from the singing of Enos White, of Axford, Hampshire, a seventy-year-old carter, who could recall Ralph Vaughan Williams collecting songs in the area some fifty years before.[2]

Fig. 1.1 Enos White and his wife, outside Crown Cottage, Axford, Hampshire. Provenance unknown.

An earlier version of this chapter was published as 'Where is the ballad, and why do we want so many of them? An Essay in Ontology', *Lied und populäre Kultur/Song and Popular Culture*, 54 (2009), 11–32, and the material is reused with permission.

1   It is perhaps as well to state that ontology is not at all a mere synonym for a genre definition, and while scholarly tradition means that *ESPB* has provided the point of departure for the study of the English-language ballads, the discussion here and in the chapters that follow is not concerned with drawing the boundaries of a canon of narrative song.
2   BBC RPL 21857 [archival CD copy in London, Vaughan Williams Memorial Library, BBC CDA 12].

Later, Bob Copper published the words and music notation, together with a short appreciation of Enos White, in the *Journal of the English Folk Dance and Song Society*, and again in his book *Songs and Southern Breezes*.³ Enos White's 'George Collins' was included, in abbreviated form, on one of the Child ballad volumes of the Folk Songs of Britain series of LPs issued in the 1960s by Caedmon in the USA and Topic in Britain, and much later, still abbreviated, on the Child ballad CDs issued by Rounder based on those LPs.⁴ The ballad was presented in its entirety on the Topic LP *Songs and Southern Breezes*, and later in Topic's CD anthology The Voice of the People.⁵ The now-defunct Folktrax label (audio cassettes and then CDs issued by Peter Kennedy) also listed Enos White's 'George Collins'.⁶ Bob Copper himself sang 'George Collins' as he had learned it from Enos White and recorded it on CD, and the ballad is still sung in the Copper family.⁷

Where, then, is Enos White's 'George Collins'? The Hampshire carter is no longer living, and his social environment and way of life are likewise long gone. Bob Copper, to whom he passed on the song and who was himself instrumental in passing it on again, died in 2004. Yet the music and words are still in print and the recording exists in various forms and formats. It is still possible for people to say that they know and admire the ballad sung by Enos White. And there is a further reason for choosing this particular example – though any favourite ballad might have done – for we can pose another question: where is 'George Collins'? Is it, for instance, in the influential *Penguin Book of English Folk Songs*, which includes a tune and words, attributed to Henry Stansbridge, of Lyndhurst, Hampshire, in 1906, but in fact conflated from at least three different copies collected in Hampshire in 1906?⁸ In fact, some half-dozen copies of 'George Collins'

---

3 *Journal of the English Folk Dance and Song Society*, 9.2 (1961), 72–73; Bob Copper, *Songs and Southern Breezes: Country Folk and Country Ways* (London: Heinemann, 1973), pp. 108–13, 246–47.

4 *The Child Ballads 1*, The Folk Songs of Britain, vol. 4, 12-inch LP (Caedmon TC1145, 1961; Topic 12T160, 1969); *Classic Ballads of Britain and Ireland*, vol. 1, CD (Rounder 11661-1775-2, 2000).

5 *Songs and Southern Breezes: Country Singers from Hampshire and Sussex*, recorded by Bob Copper, 12-inch LP (Topic 12T317, 1977); *O'er his Grave the Grass Grew Green: Tragic Ballads*, The Voice of the People, vol. 3, CD (Topic TSCD653, 1998).

6 The Folktrax archive lists Enos White's 'George Collins' on two CDs: *Three Maidens a-Milking: Songs from Hampshire* (FTX-426); *The Baffled Knight: Classic Ballads 2* (FTX-502), available at http://www.folktrax-archive.org.

7 *When the May Is All in Bloom: Traditional Singing from the South East of England*, CD (Veteran VT131CD, 1995). My thanks to Jon Dudley for this last piece of information.

8 R. Vaughan Williams and A. L. Lloyd, eds, *The Penguin Book of English Folk Songs* (Harmondsworth: Penguin, 1959), pp. 44–45, 114–15; R. Vaughan Williams and A. L.

collected by George B. Gardiner in Hampshire in the first decade of the twentieth century are similar to that sung half a century later by Enos White (the words follow a similar pattern and most, though perhaps not all, of the tunes are related in some degree).[9] Together, these Hampshire copies are sufficiently distinctive to be considered as comprising a localized form of the ballad, or *oikotype*.

Or is 'George Collins' rather to be located in the 'definitive' ballad source, *The English and Scottish Popular Ballads* – though there is nothing there under the title 'George Collins' and something only vaguely similar under that of 'Lady Alice' (Child 85)? A further body of ballad scholarship, drawing initially on the Hampshire ballads like that which Enos White once sang, would conflate Child's 'Lady Alice' with the Scottish 'Clerk Colvill' (Child 42).[10] Where do folk revival performances, often drawing on sources like the Enos White recording and/or the *Penguin Book of English Folk Songs*, belong? And what about a burlesque parody, 'Giles Collins and Lady Alis', printed in *The Universal Songster* in the early nineteenth century?[11] Ballad scholarship has been dominated by the quest for an organizing principle that would lie behind such evident disparity – an urge to identify a single 'location' for the ballad. Child, for instance, found it in a 'condition of society in which a truly national or popular poetry appears [. . .] a condition in which people are not divided by political organization and book-culture into markedly distinct classes, in which consequently there is such community of ideas and feelings that the whole people form an individual'.[12] For Phillips Barry, influenced by Cecil Sharp, the organizing

---

Lloyd, eds, *Classic English Folk Songs*, rev. Malcolm Douglas (London: EFDSS, 2003), pp. 25, 90–91. (It is not in *The New Penguin Book of English Folk Songs* published in 2012.)

9 London, EFDSS Archives, George Gardiner Collection, GG/1/6/327 [George Blake, Southampton, Hampshire, 17 July 1906], GG/1/7/419 [Henry Stansbridge, Lyndhurst, Hampshire, 27 September 1906], GG/1/8/439 [Henry Gaylor, Minstead, Hampshire, 27 September 1906; Philip Gaylor, Minstead, Hampshire, 16 July 1906?], GG/1/11/658 [George Hiscock, Minstead, Hampshire, November 1906], GG/1/19/1193 [Henry Blake, Bartley, Hampshire, September 1908].

10 Barbara M. Cra'ster, 'George Collins', *Journal of the Folk-Song Society*, 4.2 (no. 15) (1910), 106–09; Samuel P. Bayard, 'The "Johnny Collins" Version of "Lady Alice"', *Journal of American Folklore*, 58 (1945), 73–103; Harbison Parker, 'The "Clerk Colvill" Mermaid', *Journal of American Folklore*, 60 (1947), 265–85. Currently, Child 42/85 is listed as Roud 147. For a counter-argument, see David Atkinson, '"George Collins" in Hampshire', in *The Flowering Thorn: International Ballad Studies*, ed. Thomas A. McKean (Logan: Utah State University Press, 2003), pp. 193–204.

11 *The Universal Songster; or, Museum of Mirth*, 3 vols (London: John Fairburn; Simpkin and Marshall; Sherwood, Gilbert, and Piper, 1825–26), III, 16.

12 F. J. Child, 'Ballad Poetry', in *Johnson's New Universal Cyclopædia*, eds-in-chief Frederick A. P. Barnard and Arnold Guyot, 4 vols (New York: A. J. Johnson, 1881 [1874]), I, 365–68 (p. 365).

principle was a process – one of 'individual invention plus communal re-creation'.[13] Others have sought to locate the ballad in the moment of re-creation by an orally improvising singer;[14] or in the ambience of 'cultural knowledge', the 'common assumptions and associations that singers and their audiences share'.[15]

F. W. Bateson can be credited with having, indirectly, posed a question that has become iconic in certain kinds of textual discussions: if the *Mona Lisa* is in the Louvre, where are *Hamlet* and *Lycidas*?[16] Or, as Leo Treitler has rephrased it: if the *Mona Lisa* is in the Louvre, where is the Bach *Toccata and Fugue in D minor*?[17] Thomas Tanselle asks the same question when he contrasts the physicality of the Grecian urn with the incorporeality of Keats's poem – do we ever know where a poem is?[18] The foregoing brief consideration of 'George Collins' has, in a modest way, posed it once more. Bateson's question, while predicated upon the apparent difference between art works of different kinds, is also predicated upon the assumption of two points of essential similarity:

(*i*) Both the *Mona Lisa* and *Hamlet* exist both within and outside of the various reactions they evoke in visitors to the Louvre or audiences at the theatre.

(*ii*) Accordingly, the *Mona Lisa* and *Hamlet* both have an 'objective' existence, against which the individual reactions of visitors and audiences can be measured, and for this reason it is useful to describe both art works as 'artefacts' – objects made by human beings.

The seeming difference in nature between the *Mona Lisa* and *Hamlet* as art works, however, stems from the fact the former is visible and the latter is not, in consequence of the different physical dimensions they occupy

---

13 D. K. Wilgus, *Anglo-American Folksong Scholarship since 1898* (New Brunswick, NJ: Rutgers University Press, 1959), p. 69.

14 David Buchan, *The Ballad and the Folk* (London: Routledge & Kegan Paul, 1972).

15 Barre Toelken, *Morning Dew and Roses: Nuance, Metaphor, and Meaning in Folksongs* (Urbana and Chicago: University of Illinois Press, 1995), p. 157.

16 F. W. Bateson, 'Modern Bibliography and the Literary Artifact', in *English Studies Today*, 2nd ser., ed. G. A. Bonnard (Bern: Francke, 1961), pp. 67–77 (p. 74); F. W. Bateson, 'The New Bibliography and the "New Criticism": A Lecture at Lausanne', in *Essays in Critical Dissent* (London: Longman, 1972), pp. 1–15 (pp. 9–10). See also René Wellek and Austin Warren, *Theory of Literature*, 3rd edn (Harmondsworth: Penguin, 1963), pp. 142–57 ('The Mode of Existence of a Literary Work of Art').

17 Leo Treitler, 'History and the Ontology of the Musical Work', in *With Voice and Pen: Coming to Know Medieval Song and How It Was Made* (Oxford: Oxford University Press, 2003), pp. 298–316 (p. 298).

18 G. Thomas Tanselle, *A Rationale of Textual Criticism* (Philadelphia: University of Pennsylvania Press, 1989), pp. 11–13.

– spatial in the case of the *Mona Lisa*, temporal in that of *Hamlet*. The temporal nature of *Hamlet* is evinced by the sequential nature of its lines and sentences, reflected in the time the play takes to perform in the theatre.

One might add that there is a more fundamental difference in that art works like the *Mona Lisa* are essentially unique, inherently non-repeatable, whereas *Hamlet*, or the *Toccata and Fugue in D minor*, is inherently repeatable – and repetition necessarily brings with it the possibility of variation, so that repeatable works are in a fundamental way multifarious. It has frequently been pointed out that a literary work would not be lost through the destruction of every known copy, provided a text of it were to remain in someone's memory.[19] One might doubt the accuracy of the memory – but equally one might doubt the accuracy of a particular written, printed, or recited text. Precisely the same can be argued in relation to musical works and their performances, written notations, or sound recordings. It is very much more doubtful that it could be argued in any meaningful way about the *Mona Lisa*.

Nevertheless, the identification of *Hamlet* as an 'artefact' seems to presuppose that it is embedded in a medium of some kind. While drama provides a particularly clear instance, it is the case that any literary artefact can be apprehended either by eye (reading) or by ear (listening), and so the medium for literature cannot be intrinsically either visual or auditory, either writing or sound. Instead, the medium is usually described as being language per se.[20] Certainly, on one view, language is not tied to a mode of sensory perception. As Tanselle states, 'arrangements of words according to the syntax of some language (along with such aids to their interpretation as pauses or punctuation) can exist in the mind, whether or not they are reported by voice or in writing'.[21] Bateson, however, rejects this explanation, on the ground that language is itself also an artefact, albeit an exceptionally elaborate one – to the extent that 'no even approximate parallel to it can be found in the media of the other fine arts'.[22] This is worth quoting, because Treitler's example of the Bach *Toccata and Fugue* (and the present investigation of the ballad) immediately prompts the observation that, on the contrary, a fairly exact parallel can be found in the medium of music. Music, like literature, can be apprehended by ear (listening) or by

---

19 Tanselle, *Rationale*, p. 17; Wellek and Warren, *Theory of Literature*, p. 142.
20 Tanselle, *Rationale*, pp. 16–17.
21 Tanselle, *Rationale*, p. 17.
22 Bateson, 'Modern Bibliography', p. 74; Bateson, 'New Bibliography', p. 10.

eye (reading). Its medium can then be described by analogy as 'musical language' or, in view of the cumbersome nature of the phrase and the problematic nature of the concept, simply as 'music'.[23]

Instead, Bateson identifies the medium of the literary artefact with what he calls 'human articulations', a substratum of 'articulated sound', or the 'oral drama of the mind' – 'brute matter' anterior to language.[24] While conceding that these 'articulations' need sound only to the 'inner ear', it is apparent that this position does in fact privilege sound, as a reference back to an earlier discussion of the role of rhyme in determining the text of a poem makes clear.[25] Bateson's 'oral drama' may therefore be an example of 'phonocentrism', the general precedence that, Derrida argues in *Of Grammatology*, has consistently been afforded to speech over writing in Western metaphysics.[26] Yet while the 'oral drama of the mind' is an immensely seductive phrase (for the student of the ballad especially), if the adjective were to be removed, leaving the formulation 'drama of the mind', then that would seem to offer a more universally applicable (if not especially informative) identification for the non-sensory medium of art works of all kinds – though whether that would really represent a level of ontological generalization beyond that of language and music is perhaps debatable. (Lest it be objected that all such ideas – language, 'musical language', the 'drama of the mind' – are too far removed from the putative physical basis for art works, it can be observed that in neuroscience creativity and memory are thought to have physical bases, though one would not wish to venture too far into that field.)

---

23 An analogy can be, and has often been, drawn between music and language. See Joseph P. Swain, *Musical Languages* (New York: W. W. Norton, 1997). Yet it is very difficult to comprehend what 'musical language' might actually be, in part because it is difficult to envisage what might be the nature of the information that (all) music can convey. Christopher Small, *Musicking: The Meanings of Performing and Listening* (Middletown, CT: Wesleyan University Press, 1998), addresses music as something like a system which can be apprehended in multiple ways: 'To music is to take part, in any capacity, in a musical performance, whether by performing, by listening, by rehearsing or practicing, by providing material for performance (what is called composing), or by dancing' (p. 9). Nevertheless, 'musicking' ties music more to action than to its imaginary presence. Mostly, I will simply use the term 'music' here, but with the language analogy always in mind.

24 Bateson, 'Modern Bibliography', pp. 72, 74; Bateson, 'New Bibliography', pp. 7, 8, 10. For a counter-argument, see James McLaverty, 'The Mode of Existence of Literary Works of Art: The Case of the *Dunciad Variorum*', *Studies in Bibliography*, 37 (1984), 82–105.

25 Bateson, 'Modern Bibliography', pp. 74, 71; Bateson, 'New Bibliography', pp. 10, 7.

26 Jacques Derrida, *Of Grammatology*, corrected edn, trans. Gayatri Chakravorty Spivak (Baltimore: Johns Hopkins University Press, 1997).

Having identified the medium of literature as something other than language itself, Bateson was then left with the necessity of explaining the role of language in literature. It is worth following his line of thought because it leads indirectly to a consideration of one of the ways in which the ballad can be thought of as distinctive, when compared with canonical literature (and music). For Bateson, the role of language in literature is explained by reference to, and extension of, Saussure's elemental distinction between *langue* and *parole*.[27] The literary artefact is equated with *parole* 'extended and elaborated' into a memorable, literary form. The corresponding *langue* is elaborated to incorporate not just the elements of language and the rules for their combination, but also a set of specifically literary devices and rules. These include such things as metre and rhyme, diction and figures of speech, and the themes and conventions (*topoi*) of literature and specific genres of literary writing (the characteristic subjects and styles of, say, Elizabethan drama or Romantic poetry). Again, it is not difficult to envisage a similar argument distinguishing canonical music from less strictly organized sound, also by reference to Saussurean *langue* and *parole*.

Other theorists, too, have endeavoured to apply the analogy of Saussure's division between *langue* and *parole*, or Chomsky's similar distinction of linguistic 'competence' and 'performance', to the literary realm. Jonathan Culler, for example, has developed the idea of 'literary competence' to denote knowledge of the system of conventions that is required for reading or writing texts as literature, rather than simply as a concatenation of phrases in a particular language.[28] Tzvetan Todorov proposes the term 'literariness' to embrace the abstract property that characterizes literature *in potentia*, an abstract and general structure of which a particular literary work is but one of many possible concrete realizations.[29] Note, however, that while both 'literary competence' and 'literariness' equate to *langue*, for Todorov the literary work itself equates with *parole*, while for Culler *parole* equates with something more like the act of reading or writing.

---

27 Bateson, 'Modern Bibliography', pp. 74–77; Bateson, 'New Bibliography', pp. 10–12.
28 Jonathan Culler, *Structuralist Poetics: Structuralism, Linguistics and the Study of Literature* (London: Routledge, 2002 [1975]), pp. 131–52. See also Jonathan Culler, 'Prolegomena to a Theory of Reading', in *The Reader in the Text: Essays on Audience and Interpretation*, ed. Susan R. Suleiman and Inge Crosman (Princeton: Princeton University Press, 1980), pp. 46–66.
29 Tzvetan Todorov, *Introduction to Poetics*, trans. Richard Howard (Brighton: Harvester, 1981), pp. 6–7.

Gérard Genette has a further take on the linguistic analogy: 'literary "production" is a *parole*, in the Saussurian sense, a series of partially autonomous and unpredictable individual acts; but the "consumption" of this literature by society is a *langue*, that is to say, a whole the parts of which, whatever their number and nature, tend to be ordered into a coherent system'.[30] Thus the translation from linguistics to literature is not transparent or uncontested. Moreover, 'literary competence', or a system of literature or poetics, however conceived, is something that must be learned or culturally acquired, by the individual or by society at large. Saussure's *langue* or Chomsky's 'competence', in contrast, is something that is assumed to be unconsciously assimilated or generated, and that has a probable innate, biological basis. The application to literature of these fundamental linguistic distinctions must therefore be made with caution, not as extrapolation but as analogy – which has the additional benefit of inviting the consideration of similar ideas in relation to other art forms, such as music.

Needless to say, it is not especially difficult to equate the specific verbal and musical vocabulary, grammar, and generic rules that can be empirically extracted from ballads and folk songs to a particular instance of *langue*, in much the same way that Bateson posits for canonical literature and its generic conventions and devices. W. P. Ker, for example, conceived of the ballad as a poetic 'form', a quasi-platonic idea which has as its essence, along with the intrinsic lyrical beauty of ballad language, 'the power of taking up new subjects, and treating them according to the laws of the Ballad'.[31] In rather more down-to-earth style, W. J. Entwistle states: 'Any one could compose a ballad who knew how to express events in the ballad manner.'[32] Albert Lord directly compares the 'method' of oral poetry with that of language, 'substitution in the framework of the grammar', so that '[i]n studying the patterns and systems of oral narrative verse we are in reality observing the "grammar" of the poetry, a grammar superimposed, as it were, on the grammar of the language concerned'.[33] Thus oral poetry per se would equate with *langue*, and the production by the individual

---

30 Gérard Genette, *Figures of Literary Discourse*, trans. Alan Sheridan (Oxford: Blackwell, 1982), pp. 18–19.
31 W. P. Ker, *Form and Style in Poetry: Lectures and Notes*, ed. R. W. Chambers (London: Macmillan, 1966 [1928]), p. 41.
32 William J. Entwistle, *European Balladry* (Oxford: Clarendon Press, 1939), p. 10.
33 Albert B. Lord, *The Singer of Tales*, 2nd edn, ed. Stephen Mitchell and Gregory Nagy (Cambridge, MA: Harvard University Press, 2000), pp. 35–36.

'singer of tales' with *parole*.³⁴ Lord's account of South Slavic oral poetry then led David Buchan in *The Ballad and the Folk* to a similar position, expressed in language that closely echoes the preceding quotations: 'In the Scottish Northeast, and presumably elsewhere, ballads were once composed in traditional fashion by local singers of tales who had mastered the patterns and systems of their poetic language.'³⁵

Elsewhere, scholars of both structuralist and behaviourist persuasions have sought to identify 'folklore' or 'tradition' itself with an abstract system of knowledge that then generates actual performances.³⁶ In an important article from 1929 titled '*Die Folklore als eine besondere Form des Schaffens*' ('Folklore as a Special Form of Creativity'), Peter Bogatyrëv and Roman Jakobson of the Prague linguistic circle state: 'A fundamental difference between folklore and literature is that folklore is set specifically toward *langue*, while literature is set toward *parole*.'³⁷ The rules and conventions found in the domain of folklore, unlike those that can be identified in the domain of canonical literature, comprise a generative system in their own right. The performer of a ballad or folktale, therefore, is not to be identified with the author, reader, or performer of a literary work. Even allowing for some invention and variation, 'the work [ballad, tale, etc.] is a fact of *langue*, i.e., an extra-personal, given fact, independent of this performer', not a fact of *parole*.³⁸ Presumably this situation accounts for an element of conservatism in the reproduction of ballads and so forth. In practice, this generative system is said to operate through a process of 'censorship' by the (putative) community.³⁹ Seemingly, the mechanism envisaged is something very similar to that which Cecil Sharp proposed, whereby selection by the community acts as a constraint on the transmission, preservation, and development of folk songs.⁴⁰

---

34 Elsewhere, Lord suggests that oral epic performance equates with something that is both *langue* and *parole* at the same time: 'a third form of communication, or of relationship, peculiar to oral verbal art' (*The Singer of Tales*, pp. 279–80 n. 7).

35 Buchan, *The Ballad and the Folk*, p. 61 (Buchan specifically quotes Ker, Entwistle, and Lord).

36 Dan Ben-Amos, 'The Seven Strands of *Tradition*: Varieties in its Meaning in American Folklore Studies', *Journal of Folklore Research*, 21 (1984), 97–131 (pp. 121–22); Mary Ellen Brown and Bruce A. Rosenberg, eds, *Encyclopedia of Folklore and Literature* (Santa Barbara: ABC-CLIO, 1998), pp. xxxvi–xxxvii.

37 Peter Bogatyrëv and Roman Jakobson, 'Folklore as a Special Form of Creativity', trans. Manfred Jacobson, in *The Prague School: Selected Writings, 1929–1946*, ed. Peter Steiner (Austin: University of Texas Press, 1982), pp. 32–46 (p. 39).

38 Bogatyrëv and Jakobson, 'Folklore as a Special Form of Creativity', p. 38.

39 Bogatyrëv and Jakobson, 'Folklore as a Special Form of Creativity', p. 39.

40 Cecil J. Sharp, *English Folk-Song: Some Conclusions* (London: Simpkin; Novello, 1907), p. 29.

Bogatyrëv and Jakobson's article is still cited (in European scholarship especially) and their qualitative distinction between folklore and literature remains influential, so that the repetition of ballads, folktales, and so forth can be envisaged as being constrained by an encompassing, collective, cultural system, in a manner that is simply not applicable to conventional literature – be it either canonical literature or 'popular' literature – which is an individual pursuit. However, ideas such as Bateson's literary *langue* or Culler's 'literary competence' now pose a very substantial challenge to this claim to exceptionalism – to the idea of folklore as a *special* form of creativity. The ready analogy between *langue* and a culturally based system of knowledge that enables the repetition of ballads and tales holds just as well for the creation and reception of literary works. And the fundamental objection to the extrapolation from linguistics remains the same for both: the practice either of literature or of folklore is always culturally learned; neither can be argued to have a biological basis comparable to that which is thought to underlie language (and perhaps music as well).

If that is so, then the ballad should be conceived as the equivalent of the literary 'work', equating to *parole* in its own right. The difficulty, though, lies in identifying where the boundaries of the work might fall: Enos White's 'George Collins' (which recording? which transcription of words and tune?), with or without Bob Copper's continued singing of it; the Hampshire *oikotype*, with its assumed, though unproven, genetic continuity; 'Lady Alice' (Child 85) at large, or a 'Lady Alice'/'Clerk Colvill' (Roud 147) complex? Here it is necessary to draw on the distinction between 'text' and 'work' that underpins much of modern textual criticism.[41] 'Text' can be defined as the actual order of signs contained within a single physical form. The most familiar kind of text consists of words and punctuation in a particular order, but texts may equally be comprised, for example, of sequences of music notation, or variations in the magnetic coating of recording tape or a computer disk, or the sequence of pits and lands on a CD. In principle, precisely the same text – exactly the same sequence of words and musical notes that comprise a ballad, say – can exist in several different places, held in different storage media – in print on paper, etched on a CD, or within the sound waves of a live performance. In practice, it is

---

[41] Peter L. Shillingsburg, *Scholarly Editing in the Computer Age: Theory and Practice*, 3rd edn (Ann Arbor: University of Michigan Press, 1996), pp. 42–47; James Grier, *The Critical Editing of Music: History, Method, and Practice* (Cambridge: Cambridge University Press, 1996), pp. 20–24. (This paragraph and the next draw particularly on Shillingsburg's concise account.)

extremely difficult to conceive of a text in isolation from the physical form, the 'document', that it inhabits.

The idea of the 'work', in contrast, is essentially an abstraction, which can be considered from a number of different perspectives: (*i*) the standpoint of the producer, as a dynamic product of the imagination, growing and changing until it reaches – if it ever does – a fullness and stasis; (*ii*) the point of view of audience and editor, as something represented more or less well and more or less completely by any one of the various texts that are available – manuscript, print, performance, sound recording, and so on; (*iii*) the perspective of aesthetic reception, in the minds of readers/ listeners, as an imagined whole implied by all the differing texts that can be conceived of as standing for a single entity. The literary or musical work, while still an artefact in Bateson's sense, is invisible, temporal, and infinitely reproducible, with (unlike an individual text) a capacity for variation and no single circumscribed form. The redundancy of possible documents and texts testifies to this condition. It testifies, too, to the ever present possibility not only of deliberate revision but also of falling short – at every stage of text production, from the making of documents (performance, manuscript, print, sound recording) through to reception by listener or reader – of the producer's presumed intention. Only an 'imaginary' work can be pinned down in the manner of a text, and such a form is always necessarily subject to conjecture.

These summary definitions apply readily enough to literary and musical works, and also to works in other sequential arts, such as dance and film, the media of which are likewise intangible.[42] For works in the non-sequential, plastic arts (painting and sculpture, pottery and textiles, architecture, and the like), the media of which are permanent and tangible, there is a readier sense in which the physical artefact – the 'text' in its documentary form – does equate with the work.[43] Unlike the texts of a poem

---

42 The distinction between intangible and tangible media is closely based on Tanselle, *Rationale*, pp. 20–33; G. Thomas Tanselle, 'The Varieties of Scholarly Editing', in *Scholarly Editing: A Guide to Research*, ed. D. C. Greetham (New York: Modern Language Association of America, 1995), pp. 9–32 (pp. 10, 12–13).

43 This is not to say that a painting or a pot cannot also be conceived of as an imaginary 'work', in much the same manner as a literary or musical work, taking account, for instance, of the creator's known or perceived intentions. But the distinction can be further illustrated by reference to the work of the scholar who wishes to recover a form that the work might have had at some point in the past. The art restorer can achieve this only by physically and permanently altering a painting, an intervention that will unavoidably change the experience of the work for everyone who subsequently views it. The literary editor, however, can produce a new text – or, heaven forfend, alter an

or a piece of music, the 'text' of a painting (arguably) cannot be preserved in different storage media. A painting or a pot, which is present in its entirety at any one moment, can be handed down through time. In contrast, a work comprising a sequential arrangement of language and/or music can be preserved and transmitted only by means of 'sets of instructions' for its reconstitution and repetition, which are themselves potentially variable. In brief, in a tangible medium, the text equates to the physical artefact and is the only possible representation of the work; in an intangible medium, the text is merely one of many possible 'translations' (Bateson's word) of the work.[44] We can 'know' what a painting or a sculpture consists of with a degree of confidence that we simply cannot enjoy in relation to a literary or a musical work. This is the difference between the *Mona Lisa* on the one hand and *Hamlet* or the *Toccata and Fugue in D minor* on the other, between the Grecian urn and Keats's poem.

Faced with all the documentary evidence in the world – performances, manuscripts, print, sound recordings – the constitution of the literary or musical work remains a matter of conjecture. It is not just that documentary texts may be faulty witnesses, as in the case of classical or biblical texts created long after the date of the work they purport to transmit, or conflicting witnesses, as in the case of the quarto and folio texts of *Hamlet*. Nor is it even that works of art are never quite realizable just as they were imagined by their human creators. The point is rather one of theoretical principle. Even if a work of art has been perfectly realized, there is no way of knowing for certain from the documentary evidence that this is the case. The great cruxes of literature and music – Hamlet's 'too too solid' or 'sallied' or 'sullied' flesh; the A-natural or A-sharp in the first movement of the *Hammerklavier* Sonata – are only illustrations of this all-pervasive principle. Cruxes serve as a sort of necessary evil to remind readers, performers, listeners, and editors alike of the unreliability that runs through all texts. For this reason, the individual ballad text does not serve to locate the ballad any more than does an individual text of *Hamlet* or of the *Toccata and Fugue*. It is fair to say that the 'work' is what both scholars and laypersons mean when they refer to Shakespeare's *Hamlet* or Bach's *Toccata and Fugue*. It remains, then, to identify what we mean by the ballad as a literary and musical work.

---

existing manuscript! – without bringing about any permanent alteration in the literary work itself, and subsequent readers can choose whether or not to take account of the editor's intervention. See Tanselle, *Rationale*, pp. 29–30.

44 Bateson, 'Modern Bibliography', p. 72; Bateson, 'New Bibliography', p. 7.

By and large, it is mostly textual editors who worry themselves about intractable discrepancies between quarto and folio texts of *Hamlet*, first and last editions of novels of Henry James, differing written notations and performances of medieval chant or of piano pieces by Chopin.[45] One reason for this is that (in at least three out of the four cases just mentioned) it is possible to impose a unifying label, in the shape of the name of the author or composer, which conveniently lumps together all the textual options in a manner that will satisfy most readers or listeners. Recent approaches to the sociology and materiality of texts have drawn attention on the one hand to the various kinds of collaborators (editors, readers, printers, performers, and so on) involved in the production of texts, and on the other to the material qualities of documents, which are capable of signifying in their own right. Nevertheless, the shorthand of identifying a work by reference to its primary, named author persists, even among the most committed materialist critics – to indicate, for example, that the folio and two quarto *Hamlet*s have something to do with each other, more so than with the non-Shakespearian *Ur-Hamlet,* possibly written by Thomas Kyd. The work thus identified is a means of defining – subjectively, no doubt – the amount of variation that is tolerable before one thing becomes something else.[46]

It was not always thus. With much of medieval vernacular literature and music, the named author is the exception rather than the rule. The modern conception of literary authorship is generally understood to have developed only gradually, over a long period of time from the late Middle Ages to the late eighteenth century, as the product of various interconnected factors, including the growth of a marketplace for works of the imagination, the gradual lessening of the book industry's monopoly over intellectual property rights, and an emerging idea of the autonomy of the creative artist.[47] Michel Foucault's famous essay 'What Is an Author?' sketchily outlines the process whereby over time, 'literary discourses came to be accepted only when endowed with the author function. We now ask of each poetic or fictional text: From where does

---

[45] For the musical examples, see Treitler, 'History and Ontology'.
[46] Paul Eggert, 'The Way of All Text: The Materialist Shakespeare', in *Voice, Text, Hypertext: Emerging Practices in Textual Studies,* ed. Raimonda Modiano, Leroy F. Searle, and Peter Shillingsburg (Seattle: Walter Chapin Simpson Center for the Humanities in association with University of Washington Press, 2004), pp. 162–76 (pp. 171–72).
[47] William St Clair, *The Reading Nation in the Romantic Period* (Cambridge: Cambridge University Press, 2004).

it come, who wrote it, when, under what circumstances, or beginning with what design?'[48] Yet it remains the case that there are other ways of envisaging both music and literature, in which an author figure is not invoked to assert authority over the limits of the work, and where instead such things as subject matter and generic devices chart its (generally much more fluid) boundaries. Middle English romances, chronicles, and saints' lives are good literary examples; the corpus of medieval chant provides a broadly comparable musical instance. The work is merely an organizing principle for texts; it is not ineluctably tied to external ideas of authorship, genre, or anything else.

Howbeit, students of the ballad have developed a strong tendency to label their object of study using the name of the source performer as organizing principle: Enos White's 'George Collins', and so forth. Often, this simply reflects an ethnographic, performer/performance-based orientation to the research.[49] If one wishes to study aspects of an individual singer's style, for example, a very good way of doing so is to compare their performance of a particular ballad with someone else's, even (indeed, especially) if the two ballads are all but identical in words and tune. Yet this hypothetical situation also brings out the ontological problem. On the one hand, the two renditions – the two singers' performances, comprising separate documents, even if their verbal and musical identity were such as to make it possible to speak of just a single text – clearly represent no more than instances of a single work, and they could quite reasonably be collated in the preparation of an edition. On the other hand, the application of the singer's personal name as organizing principle, capable of consolidating many potential renditions (texts) and/or different documentary formats (as in the initial 'George Collins' example described above), is well-nigh equivalent to equating the performer with the author or composer of a conventional literary or musical work. Editorial collation with texts from another source would then appear to be a violation of the integrity that implies.

---

48 Michel Foucault, 'What Is an Author?', in *The Foucault Reader*, ed. Paul Rabinow (Harmondsworth: Penguin, 1984), pp. 101–20 (p. 109).

49 Ian Russell, 'The Singer's the Thing: Individual and Group Identity in a Pennine Singing Tradition', *Folk Music Journal*, 8.3 (2003), 266–81, the title of which confronts D. K. Wilgus, 'The Text Is the Thing', *Journal of American Folklore*, 86 (1973), 241–52. However, some folklorists seemingly want to do away with the idea of texts altogether. See Jeff Todd Titon, 'Text', in *Eight Words for the Study of Expressive Culture*, ed. Burt Feintuch (Urbana and Chicago: University of Illinois Press, 2003), pp. 69–98.

That this equivalence is intended is apparent in a number of studies of variation in ballads and folk songs which emphasize the importance of conscious acts of creation on the singer's part, summed up in Phillips Barry's description of 'the passionate individualist folk-singer'.[50] Modern ballad editors have indeed generally reinforced this impression through the separate transcription and publication of words and music from each of the individual sources they had to hand (though in practice sometimes circumscribed by constraints imposed by their publishers). Conversely, editors like Arthur Quiller-Couch, who, in the (first) *Oxford Book of Ballads*, sought to edit not each text of a ballad but the work in its generality, collating texts to arrive at a representative text, which may not ever have actually been sung in quite that form, have attracted opprobrium.[51] Sound recordings of different performers, of course, have their own very immediate rationale, for they carry additional, usually quite distinctive, information in the form of vocal quality, style, individuality of expression and interpretation. Ironically, these are just the things that suggest a direct comparison not between ballad singer and author/composer, but between the ballad singer and the reciter of poetry, the actor in a play, or the performer of art music.

The ballad singer, too, is almost invariably *not* the author or composer – never, in the case of the Child ballads and the tunes generally associated with them. And despite the 'passionate individualism', while variations certainly do arise between ballads deriving from different sources (or the same source on separate occasions), in many cases what is more evident is a strong element of conservatism, so that the degree of variation is certainly no greater than can be found among texts attributable to a single author – the quarto and folio *Hamlet*s and *King Lear*s, the sketches and scores of Chopin's *Nocturne in B major*, op. 62, no. 1, the variant endings of *Great Expectations*, the

---

50 Phillips Barry, 'The Part of the Folk Singer in the Making of Folk Balladry', in *The Critics & the Ballad*, ed. MacEdward Leach and Tristram P. Coffin (Carbondale: Southern Illinois University Press, 1961), pp. 59–76 (p. 76). See also Roger D. Abrahams and George Foss, *Anglo-American Folklsong Style* (Englewood Cliffs, NJ: Prentice-Hall, 1968), pp. 12–36; Tom Burns, 'A Model for Textual Variation in Folksong', *Folklore Forum*, 3 (1970), 49–56; Eleanor R. Long, 'Ballad Singers, Ballad Makers, and Ballad Etiology', *Western Folklore*, 32 (1973), 225–36; Ian Russell, 'Stability and Change in a Sheffield Singing Tradition', *Folk Music Journal*, 5.3 (1987), 317–58.

51 Arthur Quiller-Couch, ed., *The Oxford Book of Ballads* (Oxford: Clarendon Press, 1910), pp. ix–xi. For a discussion, see E. David Gregory, 'In the Shadow of Child: Other Victorian Perspectives on Ballad Editing', in *Ballad Mediations: Folksongs Recovered, Represented, and Reimagined*, ed. Roger deV. Renwick and Sigrid Rieuwerts, BASIS, vol. 2 (Trier: WVT Wissenschaftlicher Verlag Trier, 2006), pp. 69–77.

multiple revisions in Joyce's *Ulysses*. Indirectly, the type/version paradigm of ballad scholarship goes some way to square this circle, tacitly acknowledging the anonymity of ballads while retaining a sort of equivalence between performer and author/composer. It does so effectively by introducing an additional ontological layer in the concept of 'type', which is similar to, but not identical with, the literary or musical 'work'.

Following the practice of the Danish ballad editor Svend Grundtvig (1824–83), who was in turn influenced by the Scottish collector William Motherwell (1797–1835), Francis James Child classified the individual texts in his *English and Scottish Popular Ballads* (1882–98) into 305 different types.[52] Stith Thompson defines type as a narrative 'capable of maintaining an independent existence in tradition' – that is to say, across time and space.[53] The individual instance is then identified by the (problematic) designation 'version' (or sometimes 'variant').[54] The corresponding categorization of ballad tunes involves grouping them into 'tune families'.[55] This type/version principle is widely applied to genres of folk literature – and is sometimes used, implicitly or explicitly, to define folk literature and music, and to distinguish these from canonical literature and music by their amenability to grouping into 'type sets' on the basis of similarities with other examples documented from elsewhere in time and space.[56] The type concept is embodied in the standard numbering system for English-language ballads and folk songs provided by the Roud indexes (even while its limitations in relation to genres with less

---

52 Flemming G. Andersen, '"All There Is . . . As It Is": On the Development of Textual Criticism in Ballad Studies', *Jahrbuch für Volksliedforschung*, 39 (1994), 28–40; Mary Ellen Brown, 'Mr. Child's Scottish Mentor: William Motherwell', in *Ballads into Books: The Legacies of Francis James Child*, ed. Tom Cheesman and Sigrid Rieuwerts (Bern: Peter Lang, 1997), pp. 29–39.

53 Stith Thompson, 'Type', in *Funk & Wagnalls Standard Dictionary of Folklore, Mythology, and Legend*, ed. Maria Leach, 2 vols (New York: Funk & Wagnalls, 1949–50), pp. 1137–38.

54 Confusingly, some scholars use 'version' and 'variant' interchangeably, while others maintain a distinction and prefer the latter term where a degree of apparently deliberate variation is apparent. See [Stith Thompson], 'Variant', in *Funk & Wagnalls Standard Dictionary of Folklore, Mythology, and Legend*, ed. Maria Leach, 2 vols (New York: Funk & Wagnalls, 1949–50), pp. 1154–55. Ballad scholarship currently tends to favour 'version' for all instances (but see chapter 6 below).

55 Samuel P. Bayard, 'Prolegomena to a Study of the Principal Melodic Families of British-American Folk Song', *Journal of American Folklore*, 63 (1950), 1–44; reprinted in *The Critics & the Ballad*, ed. MacEdward Leach and Tristram P. Coffin (Carbondale: Southern Illinois University Press, 1961), pp. 103–50; Bertrand Harris Bronson, *The Traditional Tunes of the Child Ballads*, 4 vols (Princeton: Princeton University Press, 1959–72).

56 Robert A. Georges and Michael Owen Jones, *Folkloristics: An Introduction* (Bloomington and Indianapolis: Indiana University Press, 1995), pp. 112–20.

narrative content, such as sea shanties and certain kinds of lyric songs, are readily acknowledged).

Yet it is questionable whether 'type' really does impart a distinctive ontology to folk music and literature. Treitler raises instances such as Leopold Stokowski's orchestral transcription for the Disney film *Fantasia* of the Bach *Toccata and Fugue* which was actually composed for the organ, a rendition by the Swingle Singers, Wendy Carlos's electronically synthesized recording on the CD *Switched-On Bach 2000*, or a performance that introduces a virtuoso obbligato violin part into the fugue.[57] Equally, we might pose the reported text contained in the first, 'bad' quarto of *Hamlet*, or the Reduced Shakespeare Company's 25-minute *Hamlet*. We might go on to add passages in the *Historiae Danicae* of Saxo Grammaticus and the *Histoires Tragiques* of François de Belleforest, the Elizabethan *Ur-Hamlet*, the German play *Der bestrafte Brudermord*, Franco Faccio's opera *Amleto* with libretto by Arrigo Boito, Tom Stoppard's *Rosencrantz and Guildenstern Are Dead*, John Wain's poetic cycle *Feng*, and Adam McNaughtan's song in vernacular Scots, 'Oor Hamlet'. By the same token, we could cite prosimetric *cantefables* that include the stanzas of the Child ballad 'The Maid Freed from the Gallows' (Child 95) in what are in effect folktales,[58] other ballad narratives retold by storytellers, and the operas *Lord Bateman* (the story of Child 53) by Arnold Foster to a libretto by Joan Sharp (daughter of Cecil Sharp) and *The Two Sisters* (the story of Child 10) by Cyril Rootham with libretto by Marjory Fausset. All of these are, of course, arguable instances, dependent simply upon the degree of variation, both thematic and generic, that one is prepared to allow within the boundaries of the 'same' work. They serve, however, to illustrate the general point that both 'type' and 'work' are subjective abstractions, organizing principles, constructed upon actual instances of texts.

Robert Georges maintains that 'the construct which is identifiable as the *tale-type* is based upon a concept which is itself a manifestation of the human abilities to conceptualize reality phenomenologically and to engage in the two seemingly contrastive, yet actually complementary, processes of distinguishing among phenomena, on the one hand, and grouping

---

[57] Treitler, 'History and Ontology', p. 298.
[58] See David Atkinson, 'The English "Maid" and the Ballad Idea', in *Singing the Nations: Herder's Legacy*, ed. Dace Bula and Sigrid Rieuwerts, BASIS, vol. 4 (Trier: WVT Wissenschaftlicher Verlag Trier, 2008), pp. 298–308.

phenomena together, on the other'.⁵⁹ Georges conceives of the activity of type classification as a behaviour that is innate, biologically based, rather than learned.⁶⁰ If that is so, then the type/version idea cannot in principle be confined to folk music and literature, even if empirically those are the genres that particularly and characteristically invite its application (largely because of the sheer volume of texts available to be compared). Rather, if the innate impulse towards type classification is analogous with *langue*, then type itself must equate with *parole* and is really not distinguishable from modern conceptions of the literary or musical work. The individual ballad version, then, equates simply with text – that is to say, a 'translation' or 'set of instructions', or 'exemplification' (Treitler's word),⁶¹ permitting a reconstitution and repetition, but only one of many conceivable such reconstitutions and repetitions, of a work.

Such a perspective does indeed accord with the mostly unknown authorship of ballads and the presumed ultimate genetic interdependence of all their known instances (even if those exact connections are no longer recoverable and the attempted reconstruction of a hypothetical archetype might be a largely futile exercise when one is faced with inordinate numbers of potential variables). But that is not the primary reason for pursuing this ontological inquiry into the ballad – for asking, what is the state of its being? The inquiry begins, rather, with the implicit insistence that the ballad is an aesthetic artefact, capable of existing both within and outside of the reactions it provokes among its readers and listeners (the latter including singers themselves), and worthy of the repetition that is intrinsic to works of art in sequential media. Like other such artefacts, the ballad cannot be located in a single place, but demands instead an organizing principle, which is what the concept of the work provides.

Yet, (*i*) the nature of the work is always a matter of conjecture, so that only a 'postulated work' can be advanced in any given situation, founded

---

59 Robert A. Georges, 'The Universality of the Tale-Type as Concept and Construct', *Western Folklore*, 42 (1983), 21–28 (p. 28).
60 See also George Lakoff, *Women, Fire, and Dangerous Things: What Categories Reveal about the Mind* (Chicago: University of Chicago Press, 1987); David V. Newman, 'Chaos, Classification, and Intelligence/Caos, classificazione e intelligenza', in *Origine della vita intelligente nell'universo/Origin of Intelligent Life in the Universe*, ed. Roberto Colombo, Giulio Giorello, Gioachino Rigamonti, Elio Sindoni, and Corrado Sinigaglia (Como: Edizioni New Press, 1999), pp. 93–106; Keith Thomas, *Man and the Natural World: Changing Attitudes in England, 1500–1800* (London: Allen Lane, 1983), pp. 51–70; and Jorge Luis Borges's essay 'The Analytical Language of John Wilkins'.
61 Treitler, 'History and Ontology', p. 312.

on the evidence of available texts; and (*ii*) texts themselves, at every stage of their production, can fall short of the works they endeavour to represent. To cite a concrete example, imagine conjecturing the play *Hamlet* with only the evidence of the first quarto to hand. A musical example, which comes closer to the ballad situation, is that of medieval chant, where the 'same' chant could be sung with a large variety of introductory and interpolated tropes, so that a single surviving notation alone could not possibly give an impression of the potential whole; it is not a question of the text being 'faulty' (as can perhaps be charged against the reported text of *Hamlet*), but of its being simply one possible exemplification out of many that could represent the same work.[62] Then it becomes a simple mathematical principle that the conjectured work can be refined by a proliferation of the available exemplifications, even if this means that the resultant postulated work is one that encompasses an increasing degree of fluidity. This is more than an adequate description of the ballad situation, where a proliferation of renderings, accessible through what Roger Renwick terms the 'data banks and databases' of Anglo-American folk song,[63] permits the refinement and amplification of an idea of the ballad as work.

It might be objected that to cast the individual rendering of a ballad as an exemplification of a larger, abstract concept that is the work appears to deprive the performer of agency. That is not the case, though, for two related reasons. The first is that the work concept does not in any way seek to negate the integrity of individual texts, which, indeed, provide its ontological foundations. Rather, the work provides a background against which the distinctive features of individual texts can appear in sharper relief, highlighting characteristics such as style and variation. The work provides the framework within which the individual text can represent a particular set of artistic, aesthetic choices made at a particular place and time. The second reason is that modern textual criticism, in the form of

---

[62] Treitler, 'History and Ontology', pp. 309–12. Lydia Goehr, *The Imaginary Museum of Musical Works: An Essay in the Philosophy of Music*, rev. edn (New York: Oxford University Press, 2007), argues cogently that the 'work concept' in Western art music, exemplified by the music of Beethoven, is a product of the history of musical practice and aesthetics which only emerged *c.*1800, and so the more fluid conception described by Treitler might well be the more representative case in relation to music at large. It would no doubt be possible to think of further examples from popular music genres such as blues and jazz. Treitler, 'History and Ontology', p. 312, explicitly compares his example of medieval chant with the tune family concept as it applies to 'Barbara Allen' (Child 84).

[63] Roger deV. Renwick, *Recentering Anglo/American Folksong: Sea Crabs and Wicked Youths* (Jackson: University Press of Mississippi, 2001), p. x.

the 'social theory of text', is highly conscious of the multiple agencies that contribute to the creation of texts.[64] Such agents might include editors, printers, readers, actors, even censors; performers in the Western art music tradition; scribes working in medieval scriptoria – all of whom have historically had various kinds of input into the received texts of literary and musical works. No longer are these agents perceived as potentially hostile mediators of the originating intentions of authors and composers – or at best as a necessary evil – but instead they are acknowledged as essential collaborators in the creation of aesthetic artefacts.

From the collaborative nature of much Elizabethan playwriting (even in the case of Shakespeare), through Edward Bulwer Lytton's role in the altered ending of *Great Expectations,* and Smith, Elder, and Company's in-house punctuation of *Jane Eyre,* to Ezra Pound's contributions to *The Waste Land* – not to mention Karlheinz Stockhausen's *Klavierstück XI,* a composition comprising eleven segments, the order of which is determined only by the performer at the moment of performance – the collaborative, social nature of text-making is more than apparent. This remains the case even when the author's name continues to be perceived as the dominant organizing principle, and may to the lay person be more or less coterminous with the very idea of the work. Where authorship is largely unknown – for much of medieval literature and music, and for the ballad – then the agency of contributors who are not the prime authors or originators of the texts in question seems incontestable.

In the absence of a controlling idea of unitary authorship, the ballad has fallen prey to competing and sometimes restrictive organizing principles, which seemingly seek to reinstate that missing 'author function', asking, in Foucault's words, 'From where does it come, who wrote it, when, under what circumstances, or beginning with what design?'[65] So approaches to the ballad variously defer to process, ethnography, text, geography, genre – emphasizing such things as method of production, singer and occasion, ballad type or tune family, concentration of texts and tunes found in a region, or the wider practice of telling stories in song to strophic melodies. In practice, of course, all of these approaches contribute to the interdisciplinary richness of ballad scholarship – but it can be difficult to

---

64 The *locus classicus* for the social theory of text is Jerome J. McGann, *A Critique of Modern Textual Criticism* (Charlottesville: University Press of Virginia, 1992 [1983]). The social theory informs Grier's *Critical Editing of Music* (see pp. 16–19) and, less explicitly, Treitler's 'History and Ontology'.

65 Foucault, 'What Is an Author?', p. 109.

maintain the broad-mindedness necessary to conceive of the ballad in all of these ways simultaneously, at all of its possible levels of ontology.

We cannot now know Enos White, though he can be heard briefly talking about his life and work on the BBC recording (cited above), and we have Bob Copper's bucolic pen-portrait, which is worth quoting in full:

> Enos will always be one of my favourite singers. A slight man of 70 years (at that time – now deceased), face and arms tanned to the colour of old oak by the sun of nearly as many harvests. He had been a carter for the whole of his working life, working on the farms in the immediate surroundings. I took all his recordings in the front parlour of his tiny cottage at the back of the 'Crown Inn', Axford, and afterwards spent the remainder of many long summer evenings on a rickety wooden bench under a gnarled apple tree in his garden. There we would sit while he recalled many of the old singers, sipping our ale until the last of the light had faded. He remembered Ralph Vaughan Williams's visit to the area some 50 years before. 'He used to come up with another gentleman from the station at Micheldever, in a horse and fly', he said, 'Black coats and hard-hats they had on and one was the "song-getter" and the other the "music writer".'[66]

But equally it cannot be said that Enos White's 'George Collins' no longer exists, for we have the sound recording (with its limitations) in various formats (with their limitations), as well as the transcribed words and music (with their limitations, too).[67] We have, moreover, the additional evidence of similar forms of 'George Collins' collected in Hampshire, and in North America (as 'Johnny Collins'), and rather less similar forms in *The English and Scottish Popular Ballads* – though we do not have the evidence of all the texts and tunes that were not recorded (the existence of such a lost multiplicity being suggested by the appearance of the parody in *The Universal Songster*). So the ballad – both 'George Collins' and the English-language ballad at large – cannot be located in one place, for while each documentary text is complete in itself, it also stands in relation to the work of which it is an incomplete realization. The ballad is both physical document and imaginary conjecture.

It may be that it has always been thus, and that the folk revival that gathered pace in Europe from the late eighteenth century onwards, which came to identify the individual ballad with the individual contributor,

---

66 *Journal of the English Folk Dance and Song Society*, 9.2 (1961), 73. See also Copper, *Songs and Southern Breezes*, pp. 108–13.
67 In each case, the printed words of 'George Collins' differ slightly from what can be heard on the sound recording.

thereby elevated to the status of an 'author-equivalent', has obscured a fundamental ontology that is much closer to that of pre-modern literature and music. As Treitler argues, understanding(s) of the ontology of works changes with the progress of history, and it is necessary to recognize the transience of any current perspective. The ballad should be seen not as a closed, original, and seminal utterance, but as constant and multiple production, like the constant reworkings of anonymous medieval texts.[68] It may be uncomfortable, but the appropriate organizing principle is precisely one of proliferation, and of multiple sets of instructions or exemplifications for the reconstitution and repetition of a work which, like *Hamlet*, like the *Toccata and Fugue in D minor*, can never be wholly represented by a single exemplification – but which, for so long as it remains in someone's memory, can never be altogether lost, either.

---

68 This sentence adapts remarks of Bernard Cerquiglini, *In Praise of the Variant: A Critical History of Philology*, trans. Betsy Wing (Baltimore: Johns Hopkins University Press, 1999), p. 39.

2. On the Nature of Evidence

At the end of the previous chapter, reference was made to the evidence of all the texts and tunes that were not recorded. The burlesque 'Giles Collins and Lady Alis' provides evidence of a kind for the currency of the 'George Collins' ballad at an earlier date, because parody makes little sense without some knowledge of what is being parodied. But the nature of that currency is uncertain (there is no earlier printed record for 'George Collins'). The heyday of folk song collecting in Britain falls into two distinct periods: the end of the eighteenth century and beginning of the nineteenth;[1] and the last decade or so of the nineteenth century up until the First World War.[2] The later period of collecting is very much the better documented, and it is now generally allowed that the collectors achieved rather more social depth than some revisionist critics have liked to make out.[3] Even so, their work was mostly compressed into a period of some thirty years (though the inter-war period also saw a certain amount of collecting), and it was

---

1   For the intellectual underpinnings of the Romantic period revival, see Matthew Gelbart, *The Invention of 'Folk Music' and 'Art Music': Emerging Categories from Ossian to Wagner* (Cambridge: Cambridge University Press, 2007).
2   For the origins of the Victorian/Edwardian revival, see E. David Gregory, *The Late Victorian Folksong Revival: The Persistence of English Melody, 1878–1903* (Lanham, MD: Scarecrow Press, 2010).
3   Revisionist accounts, which present the folk song movement as a bourgeois appropriation of proletarian culture, include Dave Harker, *Fakesong: The Manufacture of British 'Folksong', 1700 to the Present Day* (Milton Keynes: Open University Press, 1985); Georgina Boyes, *The Imagined Village: Culture, Ideology and the English Folk Revival* (Leeds: No Masters Co-operative, 2010 [1993]); Richard Sykes, 'The Evolution of Englishness in the English Folksong Revival, 1890–1914', *Folk Music Journal*, 6.4 (1993), 446–90. For trenchant criticism of their position, see Christopher James Bearman, 'The English Folk Music Movement 1898–1914' (unpublished doctoral thesis, University of Hull, 2001); C. J. Bearman, 'Who Were the Folk? The Demography of Cecil Sharp's Somerset Folk Singers', *Historical Journal*, 43 (2000), 751–75; C. J. Bearman, 'Cecil Sharp in Somerset: Some Reflections on the Work of David Harker', *Folklore*, 113 (2002), 11–34. A balanced account is provided by David Gregory, 'Fakesong in an Imagined Village? A Critique of the Harker–Boyes Thesis', *Canadian Folk Music/Musique folklorique canadienne*, 43.3 (2009), 18–26.

mostly concentrated in southern England, though there are important exceptions such as Frank Kidson's collecting in Yorkshire and the Greig–Duncan collection from the north-east of Scotland. For these reasons, the ballads and songs recovered at this time do not really provide much of a clue to their wider currency. The methodology of collecting, moreover, was directed to recovering the maximum possible numbers of songs and tunes – which, the collectors feared, were in imminent danger of dying out – and not towards a scientific sampling of the population of even a small area or locale.

For the earlier centuries, historians have found it necessary to adopt a range of 'oblique approaches'.[4] These include a 'regressive method', which takes the experience of the years around 1900, with all its limitations, as a starting point to interpret evidence, such as it is, that the same or similar things existed at a much earlier date. In the hands of cautious historians, that is all very well; but it is easy to see the temptation, for instance, to link Dorothy Osborne's description of ballad singing in the seventeenth century with something at a much later date. In a letter of 1653, Osborne wrote to her lover, William Temple, 'about six or seven o'clock I walk out into a common that lies hard by the house, where a great many young wenches keep sheep and cows, and sit in the shade singing of ballads. I go to them and compare their voices and beauties to some ancient shepherdesses that I have read of, and find a vast difference there; but, trust me, I think these are as innocent as those could be.'[5] Perhaps a suitable equivalent from a more recent time is the famous description of Cecil Sharp's first encounter with folk song when, sitting in the vicarage garden in Hambridge, Somerset, in 1903, he overheard the gardener, John England, singing 'The Seeds of Love' (Roud 3) as he mowed the lawn.[6] Yet Dorothy Osborne's description – and she almost admits this herself – seems to belong as much to arcadian literature as to real life. At least it can be confirmed that John England actually was the gardener at Hambridge, but the Sharp story, too, has a suspicious neatness to it.[7] Perhaps what is really most evident across the centuries is the persistence

---

4   Peter Burke, *Popular Culture in Early Modern Europe* (Aldershot: Wildwood House, 1988 [1978]), pp. 77–87.
5   Edward Abbott Parry, ed., *The Love Letters of Dorothy Osborne to Sir William Temple, 1652–54* (New York: Dodd, Mead, 1901), p. 107.
6   A. H. Fox Strangways, in collaboration with Maud Karpeles, *Cecil Sharp* (London: Oxford University Press, 1933), p. 33.
7   Derek Schofield, 'Sowing the Seeds: Cecil Sharp and Charles Marson in Somerset in 1903', *Folk Music Journal*, 8.4 (2004), 484–512.

of a tendency to myth-making around the idea of ballad singing. To cite just one more example, the introduction to a recent volume of essays about printed ballads observes in passing, 'ballads were originally an oral genre dating back to medieval times'.[8] It is a throwaway remark, but it is made without the support of bibliographic citation, let alone any actual evidence that ballads were circulating orally before, say, 1450.

The single overriding reason for this cavalier approach to evidence appears to lie with the fact that the entire edifice of ballad collecting, editing, and research has, at least since the eighteenth century, been predicated upon the idea of continuity over a long period of time. Whether they thought they were recovering the roots of a national literature or of a native musical style, revivalists were driven by the idea that what they were collecting and preserving was poetry and music of considerable antiquity, which had remained current among (largely) rural working men and women of their own day. Ballads and folk songs seem to *require* a diachronic continuity that is simply not demanded of other kinds of music and literature. The idea of (perceived) diachrony is absolutely inherent in the idea of 'tradition' so commonly attached to such items.[9]

That diachrony, however, would require evidence not just that the same pieces had existed at a significantly earlier date, which was often not particularly hard to find, but that there was a direct continuity between that earlier point in time and the Romantic or Victorian/Edwardian present, which could be very much more difficult to demonstrate. However, once collectors observed that their sources knew many of their ballads and songs from memory, without direct recourse to written or printed copies, it took little imagination to identify in this superficially non-literate aspect of folk song a mechanism that could provide the desired continuity – a mechanism readily elevated to iconic status as a theory of oral tradition. With the benefit of hindsight, the fact that working people would sing or recite songs from memory, learning them and repeating them with varying degrees of accuracy, scarcely seems worthy of special mention. Nevertheless, oral tradition lent to the folk revivals an intellectual framework, which was eventually (with some exceptions) wholeheartedly embraced.

---

8 Patricia Fumerton and Anita Guerrini, eds, *Ballads and Broadsides in Britain, 1500–1800* (Farnham and Burlington, VT: Ashgate, 2010), p. 1.
9 On 'tradition', see Raymond Williams, *Keywords: A Vocabulary of Culture and Society*, rev. edn (London: Fontana, 1988), pp. 318–20. For the *perception* of diachrony, see Eric Hobsbawm and Terence Ranger, eds, *The Invention of Tradition* (Cambridge: Cambridge University Press, 1983).

This theoretical underpinning frequently remains more implicit than explicit, but William Motherwell, for example, in the introduction to *Minstrelsy: Ancient and Modern*, explicitly invokes oral tradition as the guarantor of ballad continuity.[10] For the Victorian/Edwardian revival, the primary work of theory is Cecil Sharp's *English Folk-Song: Some Conclusions*. Sharp identifies the carriers of folk song as the 'unlettered, whose faculties have undergone no formal training whatsoever, and who have never been brought into close enough contact with educated persons to be influenced by them'.[11] He then goes on to describe oral tradition as the principal dynamic within a social Darwinist framework of continuity, variation, and selection.[12]

Collectors were, however, aware that oral tradition was not the only means of ballad transmission, and Sharp in particular attempted to incorporate printed ballads into his account, although he did so primarily by treating them as a degenerate manifestation of tradition.[13] But in any case, the important point is that the existence of written or printed copies would do nothing to negate the theory of oral tradition. And therein lies its beauty: it is non-falsifiable. Nowhere is this more evident than in the institutionalized definition of folk song that the International Folk Music Council built upon Sharp's model in the 1950s:

> Folk music is the product of a musical tradition that has been evolved through the process of oral transmission. The factors that shape the tradition are: (i) continuity which links the present with the past; (ii) variation which springs from the creative impulse of the individual or the group; and (iii) selection by the community, which determines the form or forms in which the music survives.[14]

The definition is entirely self-contained. Folk music is the product of oral transmission, and if an item were transmitted in another way – through print, for example – it would not be folk music. Similarly with the three descriptive riders: a break in continuity, variation for some other reason (say, a quirk of typography), or selection by someone else (a ballad printer

---

10 William Motherwell, *Minstrelsy: Ancient and Modern* (Glasgow: John Wylie, 1827), pp. ii–iv.
11 Cecil J. Sharp, *English Folk-Song: Some Conclusions* (London: Simpkin; Novello, 1907), pp. 3–4.
12 Sharp, *English Folk-Song: Some Conclusions*, pp. 16–31.
13 Sharp, *English Folk-Song: Some Conclusions*, pp. 101–02.
14 'Definition of Folk Music', *Journal of the International Folk Music Council*, 7 (1955), 23. For some of the problems of this definition, see Gelbart, *Invention of 'Folk Music' and 'Art Music'*, pp. 2–10.

or even an individualistic singer), would simply place the item outside of the definition. A negative instance has no power to challenge the definitional premise.[15]

The point here is not to argue about the definition of folk music, or even the possibility of oral transmission, but to address the nature of evidence. This is perhaps best illustrated by considering a couple of ballad examples. 'Lord Thomas and Fair Ellinor' (beginning 'Lord Thomas he was a bold forester') (Child 73 D) survives in printed copies – primarily broadsides and chapbooks, but also collections such as *A Collection of Old Ballads* and Thomas Percy's *Reliques of Ancient English Poetry* – from 1677 through to the mid-nineteenth century, after which it started to be collected from singers in England, Scotland, and North America.[16] Dating the broadsides and chapbooks can be difficult (though, somewhat unusually, the earliest extant broadside printing of this ballad carries a date), but it looks from the extant items as if 'Lord Thomas and Fair Ellinor' was printed in just about every decade (with a few possible gaps in the first half of the eighteenth century and the second quarter of the nineteenth). It is also listed in William Thackeray's stock list of *c*.1689, which is thought to represent the stock of the Ballad Warehouse at that time, and again in the Dicey firm's catalogues of 1754 and 1764. Print runs in the eighteenth century have been estimated at a minimum of 2,000–4,000 for broadsides and 1,000–2,000 for chapbooks.[17] William Chappell, writing in the mid-nineteenth century, noted that 'Lord Thomas and Fair Ellinor' was still kept in print in Seven Dials.[18] One can reasonably interpret these data as indicating that the ballad was more or less continually available in print, for distribution and purchase, throughout the period in question.

Here, then, is something approaching, not proof, but strong circumstantial evidence that the print trade provided continuity for this particular traditional

---

15 A later version of the same sort of manoeuvre is in David Buchan, *The Ballad and the Folk* (London: Routledge & Kegan Paul, 1972), where ballads are divided into 'the oral tradition', 'the tradition in transition', and 'the modern tradition'. Counter-evidence, such as printed transmission, would not challenge the basis of definition but merely shift the item from one category to another.

16 Note that for the present purpose, the Scottish 'Lord Thomas and Fair Annet' (Child 73 A, etc.) – which, *pace* Child, is quite possibly a deliberate reworking of 'Lord Thomas and Fair Ellinor' – needs to be considered as a separate ballad, as does the broadside *The Unfortunate Forrester; or, Fair Elener's Tragedy*, which is known in just a single printing.

17 William St Clair, *The Reading Nation in the Romantic Period* (Cambridge: Cambridge University Press, 2004), p. 340.

18 W. Chappell, *The Ballad Literature and Popular Music of the Olden Time*, 2 vols (London: Chappell and Co., [1859]), p. 145.

ballad over the best part of two centuries. For much of this time, there is precious little evidence that anyone actually sang it. Fortuitously, Joseph Ritson, at the end of the eighteenth century, did record that '[a minstrel] was within these two years to be seen in the streets of London; he played on an instrument of the rudest construction, which he, properly enough, called a *hum-strum*, and chanted (amongst others) the old ballad of *Lord Thomas and Fair Eleanor*'.[19] Later commentators, notably Flemming Andersen, have observed just how closely copies collected in the twentieth century correspond textually with the printed broadsides.[20]

The musical evidence is less conclusive. Chappell identified the tune he knew for 'Lord Thomas and Fair Ellinor' as a version of 'Who list to lead a soldier's life', attested in the late sixteenth/early seventeenth century and printed in editions of *The Dancing Master* from 1650 to 1725.[21] It was printed again in the early nineteenth century in William Sandys's *Christmas Carols*, under the title 'Lord Thomas', which is the copy Chappell reprinted.[22] The earliest broadsides are given 'To a pleasant new tune, called, Lord Thomas', and later 'To a pleasant tune, call'd, Lord Thomas, &c.', or else are without a tune direction. Claude Simpson, not finding any further instances, writes of this 'Lord Thomas' that it 'has survived only in tradition', thus equating it with the ballad tune collected at a later date.[23] That is, of course, possible, but it is not unequivocally so. Bertrand Bronson writes: 'Whether it [the collected tune] is actually the same as that sung to the early broadsides there is nothing to show.'[24] The designation 'new' in the tune direction is perhaps promotional, but one might still ask why, if the ballad were indeed to be sung to an established and apparently popular tune – namely 'Who list to lead a soldier's life' – should the broadside carry a tune direction that seemingly points in a different direction? Conversely, if 'Lord Thomas'

---

19 [Joseph Ritson], *Ancient Songs, from the Time of King Henry the Third, to the Revolution* (London: J. Johnson, 1790), p. xvii.
20 Flemming G. Andersen, 'From Tradition to Print: Ballads on Broadsides', in Flemming G. Andersen, Otto Holzapfel, and Thomas Pettitt, *The Ballad as Narrative: Studies in the Ballad Traditions of England, Scotland, Germany and Denmark* (Odense: Odense University Press, 1982), pp. 39–58.
21 Chappell, *Ballad Literature and Popular Music of the Olden Time*, pp. 144–45; Claude M. Simpson, *The British Broadside Ballad and its Music* (New Brunswick, NJ: Rutgers University Press, 1966), pp. 773–75.
22 William Sandys, *Christmas Carols, Ancient and Modern* (London: Richard Beckley, 1833), tune no. 18.
23 Simpson, *The British Broadside Ballad*, p. 100.
24 Bertrand Harris Bronson, *The Traditional Tunes of the Child Ballads*, 4 vols (Princeton: Princeton University Press, 1959–72), II, 88.

really were a 'new' tune, and therefore presumably not the same as 'Who list to lead a soldier's life', then what was it? The scope for speculation is almost endless, but the fact remains that exactly when the ballad was matched with the tune that was later collected from singers is not known.

This, then, is the nature of the evidence for a hypothesis that this particular ballad text enjoyed a diachronic continuity over a span of some two and a half centuries. It depends on oral tradition scarcely at all; and if further evidence of oral transmission were to come to light, it would neither negate nor bolster this existing evidence. It is not watertight, however, and if it could be shown that there was a real gap in the printed record, when the ballad was simply out of print and forgotten – to be rediscovered among the Ballad Warehouse stock, perhaps – then that would falsify the claim to continuity. Quite how such a thing could be demonstrated in practice is difficult to imagine, but as a thought experiment it is possible. In other words, the hypothesis is theoretically falsifiable.

Unfortunately, it is really very rare to have such a full record. 'Fair Margaret and Sweet William' (Child 74) has a comparably good record in broadside and chapbook print from *c*.1720 through to the 1820s.[25] It, too, appears in the Dicey firm's catalogues, and in Percy's *Reliques* and David Herd's *Ancient and Modern Scottish Songs*. Percy provides the conduit, too, for a few copies that derive from memory rather than directly from print, around the 1760s/70s.[26] Thomas Macqueen collected a text in Scotland in 1827.[27] At the beginning of the nineteenth century, the extant chapbook copies are all from Scotland. Then, however, there is a lacuna of the best part of a century before the ballad was collected in England and especially in North America, but not, apparently, in Scotland. The musical record, too, is almost exclusively for the ballad as collected in the twentieth century.[28]

As if that were not enough, at the other end of the chronological scale, more than a century before the first survival of the ballad in print, lines that echo 'Fair Margaret and Sweet William' appear in the Beaumont and Fletcher play *The Knight of the Burning Pestle* (*c*.1607):

---

25 Note that 'Fair Margaret and Sweet William' (Child 74) needs to be distinguished from what is usually referred to as David Mallet's 'William and Margaret'.
26 Child 74 B, C; and see [Thomas Percy], *Reliques of Ancient English Poetry*, 2nd edn, 3 vols (London: J. Dodsley, 1767), III, 119.
27 E. B. Lyle, ed., *Andrew Crawfurd's Collection of Ballads and Songs*, 2 vols (Edinburgh: Scottish Text Society, 1975, 1996), II, xxv, 22–24.
28 Bronson, *Traditional Tunes*, II, 155.

> When it was growne to darke midnight,
> And all were fast asleepe,
> In came Margarets grimely Ghost,
> And stood at Williams feete.

The presence of these lines in the drama (like other snatches of song scattered throughout it) makes much more sense if they reference something familiar to its audience. So it has often been stated, or at least implied, that they provide evidence for the existence of 'Fair Margaret and Sweet William' right at the beginning of the seventeenth century.[29]

Thus there are problems with the evidence as it relates to 'Fair Margaret and Sweet William'. The folk song specialist might well want to advance oral tradition as a hypothesis to bridge the gaps at either end of the ballad's presumed life. But this time it is difficult to imagine how such a hypothesis could be falsified, even as a thought experiment. For every conceivable hiatus in the line of oral transmission, one could simply posit another route. Unlike the hypothesis for continuity built on the printed record, the oral tradition hypothesis is inherently non-falsifiable. That is why the placing of evidence for oral transmission alongside evidence for printed transmission would really make no difference. The two things are different in kind, not necessarily in relation to ballad practice, but simply in terms of their nature as evidence.

This discussion of the falsifiability of a hypothesis necessarily alludes to the philosophy of science of Karl Popper's *The Logic of Scientific Discovery*.[30] It might well be objected that Popper's method is inappropriate to the ballad material or, indeed, to the humanities at all. Certainly, ballad research should not be confused with scientific investigation. Nevertheless, even without direct reference to his work, Popper's epistemology has found wider acceptance as a means of drawing a general distinction between explanatory hypotheses that are capable of refutation, and systems that have to be accepted as something like articles of faith. There may be supporting evidence in either case, and general conclusions may well usefully be derived by induction from that evidence; but if those conclusions cannot be tested, then in Popper's terms they would be no more than pseudo-explanations. Lightly applied, the criterion of falsifiability can therefore be

---

29 *ESPB*, II, 199. The argument is complicated in that these lines also echo the David Mallet 'William and Margaret', but that, too, is unknown in print before c.1724. See David Atkinson, '"William and Margaret": An Eighteenth-Century Ballad', *Folk Music Journal*, 10.4 (2014), 478–511.

30 Karl Popper, *The Logic of Scientific Discovery* (London: Routledge, 2002 [1959]).

useful in distinguishing explanations of different kinds, even within the humanities. A concern about the nature of evidence and the possibility of falsification is, for instance, important to the development of D. F. McKenzie's approach to bibliography and the sociology of texts, which in turn has potentially much to offer in charting the still largely unknown territory of ballads and street literature in the eighteenth century.[31] On more familiar literary ground, Richard Levin invokes the criterion of falsifiability in a highly polemical (and in places quite amusing) article about 'negative evidence' in the interpretation of early modern drama (though without mention of either Popper or even the term 'falsifiability').[32]

While the oral tradition hypothesis can apparently never be falsified, that does not mean that it is necessarily incorrect; but it does mean that the most we can say is that the hypothesis is correct for those particular occasions on which a ballad was collected from someone who had learned it from someone else just by listening to it. Moving on from the argument over falsifiability, then, the oral tradition hypothesis still presents problems, albeit of a rather more self-evident kind. Thus the mere fact that someone sang or recited a ballad from memory means little in itself, especially in relation to a performance genre such as folk song. Henry Burstow of Horsham, Sussex, had a list of 420 songs that he knew and left a good account of how he had learned them:

> In learning and retaining all my songs my memory has seemed to work quite spontaneously, in much the same way as the faculties of seeing and hearing: many of the songs I learnt at first time of hearing; others, longer ones, I have learnt upon hearing them twice through; none, not even 'Tom Cladpole's trip to London', nor 'Jan Cladpole's trip to 'Merricur', each of which has 155 verses, has ever given me any trouble to acquire. Besides those I learnt from my father, I also learnt several from my mother, and a great many more from various other people; my brother-in-law, Joe Hopkins, one of the old Horsham stone diggers; Harry Vaughan, bootmaker, who lived in the Causeway; Gaff Batchelor, tailor, Bishopric; Bob Boxall, labourer, Bishopric; Bill Strudwick, sailor, Bishopric; Jim Shoubridge, ex-soldier, Bishopric; Hoggy Mitchell, labourer, Bishopric; Richard Collins, the parish clerk, The Causeway; Michael Turner, bootmaker, Warnham; Tim Shoubridge, labourer, Bishopric; Jim Manvell, bricklayer, Queen Street. Jim could compose songs on any subject. 'Now Jim, sing us a song about so and

---

31 D. F. McKenzie, *Making Meaning: 'Printers of the Mind' and Other Essays*, ed. Peter D. McDonald and Michael F. Suarez (Amherst and Boston: University of Massachusetts Press, 2002), esp. pp. 14–18.
32 Richard Levin, 'Negative Evidence', *Studies in Philology*, 92 (1995), 383–410.

so,' some one would ask, and perhaps in 20 minutes, or half-an-hour, Jim would have his new song ready, to which all were eager listeners. Besides these, many of the shoemakers, bellringers, and other workers with whom I came into contact, each and all of them knew several songs, and those to which I took a fancy I committed to memory: others again I learnt of 'Country Wills' in the taprooms and parlours of public houses in the Towns and Villages round, where song singing was always regularly indulged in during the evenings all the year round, and where the words of many songs have been taught and learnt, exchanged or sold, for perhaps a pint of beer. The remainder I learnt from ballad sheets I bought as they were being hawked about at the fairs, and at other times from other printed matter.[33]

The quotation is rather lengthy, but is worth giving in full because Burstow describes here a good mixture of oral and written sources, apparently without much distinction between them. Most of the oral sources he mentions were at just a single remove. Of course, there are elsewhere instances where songs are said to have been in a family for several generations – the Copper family of Rottingdean, Sussex, being a prime example. It is true, too, that there are virtually no known instances of singers who learned their tunes from music notation, meaning that an oral tradition for the transmission of melodies is an absolutely necessary hypothesis, falsifiable or not.

Raymond Williams observes that while it takes only two generations to make anything 'traditional', the description tends nonetheless to move towards the 'age-old'.[34] It is not difficult to identify items passed from father to son, mother to daughter, even grandmother/father to mother/father to daughter/son, and so forth, among the established folk song collections. Nor do the pathways need to be intrafamilial. It is, however, difficult in most instances to go far beyond, say, three generations – and certainly not into the 'mists of time'. Thus there is no evidence for the oral transmission of 'Fair Margaret and Sweet William' between c.1607 (*The Knight of the Burning Pestle*) and c.1720 (a *Fair Margaret's Misfortune* broadside issued by the London bookseller Sarah Bates). Neither is there any evidence for further broadside printings that are no longer extant but that would, in theory, help bridge the chronological gap. In general, it is the case both that there were broadsides entered in the Stationers' Register that no longer survive, and that not every ballad that was printed was entered in the

---

33 Henry Burstow, *Reminiscences of Horsham, being Recollections of Henry Burstow, the Celebrated Bellringer & Songsinger*, [ed. William Albery] (Horsham: Free Christian Church Book Society, 1911), pp. 107–08.
34 Williams, *Keywords*, p. 319.

Register.³⁵ But in the absence of actual evidence, neither unrecorded oral transmission nor unrecorded printing provides a satisfactory explanation for the early history of 'Fair Margaret and Sweet William'.

There is a conceptual difference, though. If one imagines that there were an oral tradition, it is still likely – even probable – that it would *never* be possible to find the evidence for it. Conversely, it is not really possible to imagine a previously unknown broadside printing, or other written record, without imagining precisely the sort of evidence that would reveal its existence. The prime reason for this conceptual distinction is that, outside of the realm of theology, oral tradition itself was an eighteenth-century construct, linked (to simplify greatly) to such things as overseas discoveries of native cultures, the *Ossian* controversy, and reconsiderations of Homeric verse.³⁶ It is no accident that oral tradition emerged as the theoretical basis for balladry in the Romantic period: it could not have done so any earlier. That collectors tend to find what they are looking for should occasion no surprise. Samuel Pepys found in the ballads he acquired after the Restoration a record of the manners of his own and earlier times, and of the development of the print trade. William Motherwell found in the ballads he collected at the beginning of the nineteenth century a record of the poetic practices of the 'unlettered'. If there is no evidence for ballads in oral tradition before the late eighteenth century, that is most likely to be because the idea had no real meaning before that time.

That is not, of course, the same as saying that ballads were not passed on by word of mouth in the seventeenth century. Historians of early modern Britain have for some time now been documenting oral culture – meaning transmission, memorization, and recall – and its complementary existence alongside written culture.³⁷ Intuitively, there is every reason to believe

---

35 St Clair, *Reading Nation*, pp. 27, 499; Tessa Watt, *Cheap Print and Popular Piety, 1550–1640* (Cambridge: Cambridge University Press, 1991), p. 42.

36 Nicholas Hudson, '"Oral Tradition": The Evolution of an Eighteenth-Century Concept', in *Tradition in Transition: Women Writers, Marginal Texts, and the Eighteenth-Century Canon*, ed. Alvaro Ribeiro and James G. Basker (Oxford: Clarendon Press, 1996), pp. 161–76; Nicholas Hudson, 'Constructing Oral Tradition: The Origins of the Concept in Enlightenment Intellectual Culture', in *The Spoken Word: Oral Culture in Britain, 1500–1850*, ed. Adam Fox and Daniel Woolf (Manchester: Manchester University Press, 2002), pp. 240–55. There is an interesting precursor, however, in John Aubrey's seventeenth-century enthusiasm for supposedly oral ballads. See Henk Dragstra, '"Before woomen were Readers": How John Aubrey Wrote Female Oral History', in *Oral Traditions and Gender in Early Modern Literary Texts*, ed. Mary Ellen Lamb and Karen Bamford (Aldershot and Burlington, VT: Ashgate, 2008), pp. 41–53.

37 For example, Jonathan Barry, 'Literacy and Literature in Popular Culture: Reading and

that singing was widespread, and while we know that there were uses for broadside ballads other than singing them, there is also plenty of evidence for ballad singers.[38] Still, that is a long way from saying that the ballad was 'originally an oral genre', or that it dates back to 'medieval times'.

Nevertheless, Emily Lyle has put forward a cogent argument for a position of what she calls 'parity of ignorance' in relation to the ballads: 'The lack of known precedent for an item is not evidence in itself for the absence of that item earlier on the diachronic scale.'[39] Lyle's discussion stems from Child's treatment of 'Sir Colin' (Child 61). Child's primary copy of this ballad is from the Percy folio manuscript of c.1650, and he relegated a couple of later, nineteenth-century, Scottish copies to an appendix. In brief, he thought these were re-creations based on the text Percy had published in *Reliques of Ancient English Poetry*. Much more recently, however, an earlier copy was discovered in a sixteenth-century manuscript in the Scottish Record Office, with the date 1583 at the end of the ballad, which 'offers proof that the nineteenth-century Scottish versions could have been descendants of a deeply rooted Scottish tradition'.[40] More generally, the discovery of the manuscript reinforces the general conclusion: 'There is nothing safe or objective about taking first known occurrence as directly indicative of first occurrence.'[41]

The force of all this is slightly undercut by a couple of considerations. Firstly, the best assessment of the Percy folio manuscript (London, British Library, Additional MS 27879) is that it is an antiquarian anthology compiled during the 1640s, up to c.1650 (the date usually assigned to it), from written and printed sources ranging in period from late medieval to more or less contemporary (some examples of Cavalier poetry).[42] It is not,

---

Writing in Historical Perspective', in *Popular Culture in England, c.1500–1850*, ed. Tim Harris (Basingstoke: Macmillan, 1995), pp. 69–94; Adam Fox, *Oral and Literate Culture in England, 1500–1700* (Oxford: Clarendon Press, 2000); R. A. Houston, *Scottish Literacy and the Scottish Identity: Illiteracy and Society in Scotland and Northern England, 1600–1800* (Cambridge: Cambridge University Press, 1985); Barry Reay, *Popular Cultures in England, 1550–1750* (London: Longman, 1998), pp. 36–70.

38 Christopher Marsh, *Music and Society in Early Modern England* (Cambridge: Cambridge University Press, 2010), pp. 238–50.

39 Emily Lyle, 'Parity of Ignorance: Child's Judgment on "Sir Colin" and the Scottish Verdict "Not Proven"', in *The Ballad and Oral Literature*, ed. Joseph Harris (Cambridge, MA: Harvard University Press, 1991), pp. 109–15 (p. 114).

40 Lyle, 'Parity of Ignorance', p. 112.

41 Lyle, 'Parity of Ignorance', p. 114.

42 Joseph Donatelli, 'The Percy Folio Manuscript: A Seventeenth-Century Context for Medieval Poetry', *English Manuscript Studies, 1100–1700*, 4 (1993), 114–33.

therefore, to be expected that there would be anything in the manuscript that did not exist prior to its compilation, even though there are ballads in it for which precursors have not (to date) been identified. Secondly, in relation to 'Sir Colin', Lyle concedes that 'any degree of memorization or of recreation could have been involved in the transmission';[43] and while she is evidently thinking here of the ballad's supposed Scottish transmission from 1583 down to the nineteenth century, the concession actually also means that Child's scenario could still be valid. The trouble is that 'proof that . . . could have . . .' is not really proof of anything at all.

For all that the argument for parity of ignorance is important, it does not really take us any further forward, but instead gives credence to the 'mists of time' scenario for ballad continuity. Even when earlier manuscript evidence does turn up, it does not provide a date, but only evidence that the ballad did indeed pre-exist the source in question, since ballad manuscripts are rarely (if ever) taken to be authorial holographs. In fact, it is possible to argue that, theoretically, any text must necessarily pre-exist its initial appearance in writing or print. Directly, there always has to be some sort of mental conception of a work prior to its taking form as a written text. Less directly, there also has to be some kind of source material(s) that feed(s) into that work. The latter point is true for all music and literature (no one now believes in the autonomous genius as writer or composer), but it is especially pertinent to the ballads.

Child, like Percy before him, very much wanted his ballads to be old and imagined them descending by a devolutionary sort of oral tradition, probably from something like an early medieval *ur*-text.[44] In practice, however, he was much more committed to tangible evidence. As Mary Ellen Brown describes it, although logic dictated that there had to have been an original conception somewhere, Child himself resisted the temptation to try to pin down the origins of individual ballads, and instead sought to connect them with a body of materials that were old and widely distributed and perhaps came from the 'general stock of mediæval fiction', which might comprise whole ballads or merely elements (plot devices, motifs, names, and so forth), and which could be found across literature in

---

43 Lyle, 'Parity of Ignorance', p. 112.
44 Mary Ellen Brown, *Child's Unfinished Masterpiece: The English and Scottish Popular Ballads* (Urbana, Chicago, and Springfield: University of Illinois Press, 2011), pp. 237–38. See also F. J. Child, 'Ballad Poetry', in *Johnson's New Universal Cyclopædia*, eds-in-chief Frederick A. P. Barnard and Arnold Guyot, 4 vols (New York: A. J. Johnson, 1881 [1874]), I, 365–68.

different languages.[45] Noting the general resemblance between 'Sir Colin' and the Danish ballad 'Liden Grimmer og Hjelmer Kamp', for example, Child writes of 'the points of agreement permitting the supposition of a far-off connection, or of no connection at all'.[46] He then compounded these heterogeneous comparative relationships into the headnotes to individual items in *The English and Scottish Popular Ballads*.

These headnotes delineate not so much a path of descent as a site of intertextuality. Among the most elaborate of them is the headnote relating to 'Sir Aldingar' (Child 59), one of the ballads in the Percy folio for which there is no known earlier copy.[47] However, a Scandinavian ballad, 'Ravengaard og Memering', with sufficient resemblances both in outline and in detail to be described as an analogue of 'Sir Aldingar', can be dated a hundred years before the Percy folio.[48] 'Sir Aldingar' is an 'accused queen' story, a narrative device regularly exploited in medieval literature, both pseudo-historical and overtly fictional.[49] 'Sir Aldingar', moreover, incorporates several other literary and historical motifs that give it a medieval feel, such as trial by combat (probably obsolete in law, if not in fiction, by the end of the thirteenth century), leprosy (beginning to die out in Britain in the fifteenth century), and the dream-vision (readily paralleled in medieval chronicle and romance), as well as various instances of seemingly archaic language.

In particular, the evidence of names, combined with the outline of the narrative, supposedly links the ballad back to pseudo-historical events of the eleventh century, first recounted in William of Malmesbury's *Gesta regum Anglorum* (c.1125–35).[50] William tells how Gunhild, daughter of King Cnut and Queen Emma, was married in 1036 to Henry III, king of the Germans and later Holy Roman Emperor, and after a period of marital fidelity was accused of adultery, her name eventually being

---

45 Brown, *Child's Unfinished Masterpiece*, pp. 237–38, citing *ESPB*, III, 50.
46 *ESPB*, II, 57, cited in Brown, *Child's Unfinished Masterpiece*, p. 238.
47 *ESPB*, II, 33–44.
48 *ESPB*, II, 34.
49 Margaret Schlauch, *Chaucer's Constance and Accused Queens* (New York: New York University Press, 1927).
50 This summary is based on Paul Christophersen, *The Ballad of Sir Aldingar: Its Origin and Analogues* (Oxford: Clarendon Press, 1952), esp. pp. 17–32, with some modifications drawn from the entries for the various chroniclers in the *Oxford Dictionary of National Biography*. The relationships between the chronicles are complicated and the dates uncertain, but a (very) condensed summary should suffice here. The connection between 'Sir Aldingar' and the Queen Gunhild story was first mooted in Percy, *Reliques* (1767), II, 49.

cleared through trial by combat, where her champion, a small page-boy, overcame her accuser, who was a man of giant stature. William of Malmesbury's account is then repeated in subsequent chronicles with various additions, the most important of which for the present purpose is that the dwarf who fights as the queen's champion is named as *Mimecan*. In the *Abbreviationes chronicorum* of Ralph de Diceto, a marginal note names the queen's champion as *Mimekin* and her accuser as *Rodingar* (c.1200). The *Estoire de Seint Aedward le rei*, the French metrical Life of Edward the Confessor attributed to Matthew Paris, has the name *Mimecan* in the text, but this is accompanied by an illustration of the combat with a descriptive verse that names both *Mimecan* and his opponent *Rodegan* (1236–45). The *Chronica majora* of Matthew Paris likewise has a sketch of the fight, with the antagonists identified as *Mimekan* and *Rodogan* (c.1235–59). Later, the chronicle ascribed to John Brompton names the antagonists as *Municon* (or *Mimicon*) and *Roddyngar* (14th century).

In the Scandinavian ballad, the antagonists are named *Ravengaard* (or similar) and *Memering* (or similar). There is sufficient plot resemblance to connect 'Sir Aldingar' with 'Ravengaard og Memering' on the one hand, and perhaps enough to connect it with William of Malmesbury's account of Queen Gunhild on the other – provided the exact nature of the connections is not specified. Once the connection is made, though, it is just too tempting to claim that *Rodingar* (*Rodegan*) is the forerunner of *Aldingar*.[51] Then, Paul Christophersen's study of 'Sir Aldingar' concludes, 'If we insist on a connexion between the various occurrences of the names Mimecan and Rodingar (and a connexion, surely, there must be, however remote or involved), the simplest way is to assume an oral tradition.'[52] In a footnote, he adds, 'By oral tradition I mean first of all ballads.'[53]

Add to this, William of Malmesbury states that in his own day people still sang in the streets about the splendour of Gunhild's wedding and, according to a note in a manuscript connected with the abbey of Bury St Edmunds, its fame persisted as late as the fourteenth century.[54] This has been enough, then, for scholars to assert the existence in the first half of

---

51 *ESPB*, II, 36.
52 Christophersen, *Ballad of Sir Aldingar*, p. 29.
53 Christophersen, *Ballad of Sir Aldingar*, p. 29 n. 2.
54 Christophersen, *Ballad of Sir Aldingar*, pp. 19, 30. William's text reads: *Celebris illa pompa nuptialis fuit, et nostro adhuch seculo etiam in triviis cantitata, dum tanti nominis virgo ad navem duceretur.*

the twelfth century of a ballad that recounted Gunhild's accusation and trial.[55] Child writes: 'Nor can we well doubt that William of Malmesbury was citing a ballad, for the queen's wonderful deliverance in so desperate an extremity would be even more likely to be celebrated in popular song than her magnificent wedding'.[56] But the fact is, William of Malmesbury wrote that Gunhild's wedding was remembered in popular song; he did *not* say that the accusation and trial were recorded in song. Yet even those who have been careful to acknowledge this objection have nonetheless still located the accusation and trial story in a hypothetical oral tradition – either probably a ballad;[57] or else a ballad, romance, or folktale, or all three.[58] The reason for all this hypothesizing is clear enough from Entwistle's account, where he claims 'Sir Aldingar' is both 'the most important of our ballads' and 'the oldest English ballad'.[59] 'With the date of *Sir Aldingar*', he asserts, 'goes the dating of the ballad *genre* in southern England.'[60]

This is not the place to attempt a wholesale refutation of the argument as it relates to 'Sir Aldingar', but a statement by E. K. Chambers can stand for more detailed objections: 'surely there could be no more gratuitous hypothesis than an assumption that a poem which, like *Sir Aldingar*, comes to us from the Percy MS. of about 1650 can be identical in style with one known to William of Malmesbury in the twelfth century'.[61] Just as the argument for ballad continuity has frequently depended on

---

55 Svend Grundtvig, et al., eds, *Danmarks gamle Folkeviser*, 12 vols (København: Samfundet til den danske Literaturs Fremme, Universitets-Jubilæets danske Samfund, et al., 1853–1976), I, 183, cited in translation in Christophersen, *Ballad of Sir Aldingar*, p. 30; William J. Entwistle, *European Balladry* (Oxford: Clarendon Press, 1939), pp. 66–67, 195, 233–34; W. J. Entwistle, '"Sir Aldingar" and the Date of English Ballads', *Saga-Book of the Viking Society*, 13 (1946–53), 97–112.

56 *ESPB*, II, 37. Child continues, 'and a ballad is known to have been made upon a similar and equally fabulous adventure which is alleged in chronicle to have occurred to Gunhild's mother'. The reference is to an account in the annals of Winchester which tells how Queen Emma was accused of having a bishop for her lover and to vindicate herself submitted to the ordeal of walking over red-hot ploughshares (end of 12th century). The register of St Swithin's priory then records a musical entertainment of 1338, where: *cantabat joculator quidam Herebertus nomine canticum Colbrondi, necnon Gestum Emme regine a judicio ignis liberate, in aula prioris*. See *ESPB*, II, 38; Christophersen, *Ballad of Sir Aldingar*, pp. 33–36. Christophersen points out that there is no evidence whatsoever that this was a ballad (a romance, probably in French, seems more likely).

57 Christophersen, *Ballad of Sir Aldingar*, pp. 29–31.

58 Donald S. Taylor, 'The Lineage and Birth of Sir Aldingar', *Journal of American Folklore*, 65 (1952), 139–47.

59 Entwistle, *European Balladry*, pp. 233, 234.

60 Entwistle, '"Sir Aldingar" and the Date of English Ballads', p. 112.

61 E. K. Chambers, *English Literature at the Close of the Middle Ages* (Oxford: Clarendon Press, 1945), p. 154.

non-falsifiable hypotheses of oral tradition, so, it seems, does that for an early origin of the English-language ballads.[62] Chambers offers a balanced view of the early history of stories that found their way into ballads: 'We must not [. . .] forget that there were other channels, besides songs, for the transmission and perversion of historical and legendary themes, through oral tradition, easily long-lived in monasteries, and still more through chronicles in prose and verse.'[63]

As already noted, the presence of an item in, say, the Percy folio manuscript can be taken as evidence for its pre-existence. Yet parity of ignorance does not justify an indefinite backward projection of ballads in time. As we think back in time, considerations such as prevailing styles of language, versification, and melody will eventually come to militate against the ballad as we know it. Sooner or later in the early post-Conquest period, the English language itself will no longer be a vehicle that can readily accommodate the ballad as we know it. Although no one would claim the ballad (either verse or melody) is a fixed or easily defined genre, as with any other artistic form (the novel, say, or late Tudor drama) there is a point – albeit a 'point' that might very well be extremely imprecise and extended over time – at which it emerged out of something else. At that point, the weight of evidence concerning the beginnings of the ballad genre starts to outweigh the parity of ignorance principle, to prevent the ballad being pushed back indefinitely.

Thomas Garbáty describes a range of overlapping genre terms, some of them contemporary and some of more modern introduction, that can be attached to vernacular poetry of the thirteenth, fourteenth, and fifteenth centuries – including 'ballad', 'carol', 'geste', 'lyric', 'ryme', 'romance' – and concludes that what was taking place in late medieval English verse was a 'confluence of form'.[64] At the later end of his period, for example, he shows that the preference in both romance and ballad – taking as examples the romance *The Weddynge of Sir Gawen and Dame Ragnell* and

---

62 For a further example, see David Buchan, 'History and Harlaw', in *Ballad Studies*, ed. E. B. Lyle (Cambridge: D. S. Brewer; Totowa, NJ: Rowman and Littlefield, for the Folklore Society, 1976), pp. 29–40 (esp. p. 38).
63 Chambers, *English Literature at the Close of the Middle Ages*, p. 156.
64 Thomas J. Garbáty, 'Rhyme, Romance, Ballad, Burlesque, and the Confluence of Form', in *Fifteenth-Century Studies: Recent Essays*, ed. Robert F. Yeager (Hamden, CT: Archon Books, 1984), pp. 283–301. See also Peter Dronke, "Learned Lyric and the Popular Ballad in the Early Middle Ages," *Studi Medievali*, 3rd ser., 17 (1976), 1–40; Holger Olof Nygard, 'Popular Ballad and Medieval Romance', in *Ballad Studies*, ed. E. B. Lyle (Cambridge: D. S. Brewer; Totowa, NJ: Rowman and Littlefield, for the Folklore Society, 1976), pp. 1–19.

the ballad 'The Marriage of Sir Gawain' (Child 31) – is for such things as a fast-moving, single narrative focus, an ironic tone, and a matter-of-fact world view expressed through an un-heroic protagonist, all of which can be identified with the heritage of Chaucer and the *Gawain*-poet from the fourteenth century.

At the earlier end of the period, the thirteenth-century 'Judas' (Child 23) is quite ballad-like in its narrative, although rather less so in its versification, and John Hirsh has argued that it was more amenable to popular performance than the probable monastic provenance of the written text might initially suggest.[65] The scepticism sometimes expressed as to whether 'Judas' really deserves its place in *The English and Scottish Popular Ballads* illustrates Garbáty's point about the medieval 'confluence of form' rather well. 'Twelfth Day', from the same manuscript and in the same hand as 'Judas', actually looks rather more like a ballad (especially if printed in quatrains) but is lacking in dramatic narrative style.[66] The *pastourelle* beginning 'As I me rode this endre dai' (c.1300), formally a carol (a poem with a 'burden' – that is, a line or group of lines that precedes the first stanza and is then repeated after the first and all other stanzas) and not at all ballad-like in versification, nevertheless invites comparison with later ballads in terms of plot situation, character, and tone or point of view – yet it, too, is ultimately lacking in narrative development.[67]

(Some) further examples could be added, but the point is that, without straying beyond the evidence of extant texts, these generic considerations introduce an important element of probability into the parity of ignorance principle. Thus, to return to 'Sir Aldingar', at *c*.1650, the date of the Percy folio, we can say with a high degree of confidence that the ballad was already in existence. At *c*.1550, the date of the Karen Brahe manuscript which includes the earliest extant copy of the Danish 'Ravengaard og Memering', we can say with some confidence that the English ballad *could* have been in existence – and it might or might not have actually been so.[68]

---

[65] John C. Hirsh, 'The Earliest Known English Ballad: A New Reading of "Judas"', *Modern Language Review*, 103 (2008), 931–39.

[66] Carleton Brown, ed., *English Lyrics of the XIIIth Century* (Oxford: Clarendon Press, 1932), pp. 39–41; W. W. Greg, 'A Ballad of Twelfth Day', *Modern Language Review*, 8 (1913), 64–67; 9 (1914), 235–36.

[67] Brown, ed., *English Lyrics of the XIIIth Century*, pp. 119–20; Thomas G. Duncan, ed., *Medieval English Lyrics and Carols* (Cambridge: D. S. Brewer, 2013), p. 70 (and see introduction, pp. 3–4).

[68] Not considered any further here is the inherently problematic nature of invoking European analogues as evidence for international ballad relations. See W. F. H. Nicolaisen, 'On the

But at c.1250 (Matthew Paris), or before c.1150 (William of Malmesbury), it is very much less probable that the ballad 'Sir Aldingar' *could* have been in existence, and even something recognizable as the basic story is much more likely to have been recorded, in verse, in the language and metres of Latin or Anglo-Norman French.

Superficially, the argument from proper names (summarized above) gains some additional support from the much later version in Walter Scott's *Minstrelsy of the Scottish Border*, in which the queen's accuser is named *Rodingham* and her champion *Sir Hugh le Blond*. Scott gave his source as (indirectly) 'the recitation of an old woman, long in the service of the Arbuthnot family' and claimed the ballad as the original of 'Sir Aldingar'. This was not, however, taken seriously by Child.[69] T. F. Henderson, editor of the *Minstrelsy of the Scottish Border*, adds: 'It may even be nothing more than a mere vamp of that ballad ["Sir Aldingar"] after its publication in the *Reliques*.'[70] The truth of the matter is for Scott specialists to determine; but if oral tradition is one scenario that the parity of ignorance principle keeps open, then the deliberate reinvention of ballads must, as Chambers suspected, be another.[71]

An example of ballad rewriting that has been generally accepted is the recasting of *The Berkshire Tragedy; or, The Wittam Miller* ('Young men and maidens all give ear') as *The Cruel Miller* ('My parents educated me'), probably around the beginning of the nineteenth century (both ballads listed as Roud 263). In twenty-two eight-line stanzas, *The Berkshire Tragedy* tells the story of a miller who kills a young woman he has made pregnant and throws her body into the river, but he falls under suspicion nonetheless, and when the corpse is found he is apprehended and brought to trial, the ballad ending with his plea for God's mercy. *The Berkshire Tragedy* has a good record in chapbook and broadside print from 1744 up until around the second decade of the nineteenth century. Then, at much the same time in the early nineteenth century, there appeared the ballad variously titled *The Cruel Miller*, *Bloody Miller*, or *False Hearted Miller*, which tells the same story in nine stanzas of four long lines, ending more or less with the discovery

---

Internationality of Ballads', in *Gender and Print Culture: New Perspectives on International Ballad Studies*, ed. Maria Herrera-Sobek ([n.p.]: Kommission für Volksdichtung, 1991), pp. 99–104.

69 *ESPB*, II, 34.

70 Sir Walter Scott, *Minstrelsy of the Scottish Border*, ed. T. F. Henderson, 4 vols (Edinburgh: Oliver and Boyd, 1902), III, 66.

71 Chambers, *English Literature at the Close of the Middle Ages*, p. 180.

of the body, the trial verdict and sentence being merely summarized in the last two lines. *The Cruel Miller* is well represented in broadside print from before 1820 until the latter part of the nineteenth century.

'Murdered-sweetheart' ballads represent a common and frequently highly formulaic sub-genre of balladry,[72] but in view of a great deal of agreement in narrative detail, as well as numerous very close verbal parallels, there has been a general consensus that *The Cruel Miller* is directly based upon *The Berkshire Tragedy*.[73] It is difficult to convey the parallels without giving the two texts side by side in their entirety, but a few examples will have to suffice (Table 2.1).[74] The setting for *The Cruel Miller* is often named on broadsides as Wexford, although the copy cited in Table 2.1, which is probably one of the earliest, leaves a blank. In *The Berkshire Tragedy* the action takes place in the vicinity of Oxford. Of course, if we do accept the textual evidence that the ballad was recast, it is still not possible to identify precisely when that would have been done, or by whom, or how (whether this was simply an act of rewriting, or whether oral reception and memory played a part), or why. These are all legitimate matters for scholarly debate, drawing largely on textual and print trade evidence, since the ballad does not seem to have been collected much before the early twentieth century and there is no pertinent melodic evidence.

The Berkshire Tragedy	*The Cruel Miller*
And promis'd I would marry her, If she would with me lie	I told her I would marry her if she would with me lie
Then took a stick out of the hedge, And struck her in the face	I took a stick out of the hedge, and struck her to the ground

---

72 See Thomas Pettitt, 'Journalism vs. Tradition in the English Ballads of the Murdered Sweetheart', in *Ballads and Broadsides in Britain, 1500–1800*, ed. Patricia Fumerton and Anita Guerrini (Farnham and Burlington, VT: Ashgate, 2010), pp. 75–89.

73 See G. Malcolm Laws, Jr., *American Balladry from British Broadsides: A Guide for Students and Collectors of Traditional Song* (Philadelphia: American Folklore Society, 1957), pp. 104–22 (where American variants are also considered). Laws observed that the rewriting of ballads, which he attributes primarily to the broadside trade (pp. 121–22), had received little attention from scholars (p. 104) – and the situation has not changed much over the intervening years.

74 Cited from *The Berkshire Tragedy; or, The Wittam Miller* (London: Sympson's Printing Office, [1765?]) [ESTC T21545; Roxburghe Ballads 3.802–803]; *The Cruel Miller; or, Love and Murder* ([London]: J. Catnach, [1813–38]) [London, British Library, L.R.271.a.2., vol. 4, no. 384].

But she fell on her bended knee, And did for mercy cry	She fell upon her bended knees, and did aloud for mercy cry
Thus in the blood of innocence, My hands were deeply dy'd	Now with the blood of innocence, my hands & clothes were dy'd
How came you by that blood upon, Your trembling hands and cloaths? I presently to him reply'd, By bleeding at the nose.	He asked me and questioned me, what stained my hands and clothes! I made him answer as I thought fit, by the bleeding of my nose.
Her sister did against me swear, She reason had no doubt	Her sister persecuted was, for reason and for doubt
Floating before her Father's door, At Henly Ferry Town	A floating by her brother's door, who lives in — town

Table 2.1 Parallels in *The Berkshire Tragedy* and *The Cruel Miller*

To give just one example of the direction that research might take, it is sometimes said that the appearance after the beginning of the nineteenth century of ballads that are shorter, less prolix, and less explicitly moralistic (but does the textual evidence actually bear out this last point, or is the difference rather just one of language?) is evidence of a change in popular taste and sensibility. However, these later ballads are also smaller in format (frequently so-called 'slip songs', printed on a narrow piece of paper and often formed by cutting a larger broadside into two or more strips), and the explanation may lie instead in aspects of the print trade that have yet to be fully researched – in particular, improvements in paper and printing that James Catnach is said to have introduced after he moved to London in 1813/14, which were subsequently also adopted by John Pitts.[75] Pitts printed both *The Berkshire Tragedy* (in more than one issue) and *The Cruel Miller*.[76] It does appear that the ballad genre was changing around the early

---

[75] Charles Hindley, *The Life and Times of James Catnach, (Late of Seven Dials), Ballad Monger* (London: Reeves and Turner, 1878), p. 44; Leslie Shepard, *John Pitts: Ballad Printer of Seven Dials, London, 1765–1844* (London: Private Libraries Association, 1969), p. 58; W. Weir, 'St. Giles's, Past and Present', in *London*, ed. Charles Knight, 6 vols (London: Charles Knight, 1841–44), III, 257–72 (p. 264).

[76] *The Berkshire Tragedy; or, The Wittam Miller* ([London]: J. Pitts, [1802–19]) [Oxford, Bodleian Library, Harding B 6(101)]; *The Berkshire Tragedy; or, The Wittam Miller* ([London]: Pitts, [1819–44]) [Oxford, Bodleian Library, Harding B 6(102)]; *The Cruel Miller* ([London]: Pitts, [1819–44]) [Oxford, Bodleian Library, Harding B 11(755)].

decades of the nineteenth century, even while it would be difficult to argue that *The Berkshire Tragedy* and *The Cruel Miller* are not still the 'same' thing.

At least it ought in principle to be possible to assign to ballad accounts of murder cases a *terminus post quem*.[77] The earliest known text of *The Berkshire Tragedy* is in a chapbook of 1744, where it is followed by (in prose) 'The last dying Words and Confession of John Mauge, a Miller; who was Executed at Reading in Berkshire, on Saturday the 20th of last Month, for the barbarous Murder of Anne Knite, his Sweet-heart'.[78] Although the information given here is not comprehensive, the printing of the confession along with the ballad does seem to imply that publication was more or less contemporaneous with the crime and execution, and the proper names and date (1744) certainly look as if they relate to an actual event. Yet no one (to the best of my knowledge) has been able to identify the crime in question.[79] And there is something odd about the chapbook itself – which actually exists in two editions, printed, according to the title page, for the same bookseller, John Keed, at Edinburgh and at York, both dated 1744. The two editions are different settings of type, with some textual variants and different title-page woodcuts. No other trace has been found of a bookseller named John Keed;[80] and why would an account of what was presumably a topical event in the Reading area have been printed at either Edinburgh or York (rather than, say, London)?

Among the elements of the ballad story that lend an appearance of historicity is the perpetrator's claim that he posted a notice in a newspaper offering a reward for information about his victim's whereabouts. The Edinburgh chapbook names the publication as the *Post Boy*, which was published 1695–1728 (or perhaps the *Daily Post Boy*, 1728–36?) – which

---

77 See, for example, Tom Pettitt, 'Mediating Maria Marten: Comparative and Contextual Studies of the Red Barn Ballads', in *Street Ballads in Nineteenth-Century Britain, Ireland, and North America: The Interface between Print and Oral Traditions*, ed. David Atkinson and Steve Roud (Farnham and Burlington, VT: Ashgate, 2014), forthcoming.

78 *The Berkshire Tragedy; or, The Whittam Miller* (Edinburgh: John Keed, 1744) [ESTC T60621]; *The Berkshire Tragedy; or, The Whittham* [sic] *Miller* (York: John Keed, 1744) [ESTC N49176] (quotation from the Edinburgh printing).

79 There is, for example, no trace in reports of either Berkshire or Oxford assizes in the *Daily Post*, 10 March 1743, 21 July 1743, 8 March 1744, 12 July 1744, 14 March 1745, 1 August 1745. My thanks to Richard Clark of the http://www.capitalpunishmentuk.org website who confirms that he has likewise found no trace of this case, its victim, or perpetrator (personal communication, 15 June 2013), and to Tom Pettitt for sharing his own notes on the historicity (or not) of the ballad.

80 No other entries in ESTC and no relevant listings in either the British Book Trade Index, currently available at http://www.bbti.bham.ac.uk or the Scottish Book Trade Index, available at http://www.nls.uk/catalogues/scottish-book-trade-index.

immediately poses a problem of dating vis-à-vis the chapbook, compounded by the fact that nothing relevant has been identified in the newspaper itself. The title, moreover, is the site of a textual variant, with the York chapbook naming it as the *Gazett[e]*, which is harder to pin down and is perhaps just a generic title, although the variously titled *Reading Mercury/Oxford Gazette and Reading Mercury/Reading Mercury and Oxford Gazette*, which began in 1723, might fit. It is true that fictitious or misleading imprints are not altogether unknown; and likewise that the *raison d'être* for early modern murder ballads was less reportage of real events than revelation of the working out of divine providence.[81] Yet the deception, if that is really what it is (and, of course, something might turn up in a newspaper or other source), seems exceptionally elaborate for a fairly run-of-the-mill murdered-sweetheart ballad.

The Berkshire Tragedy/The Cruel Miller provides evidence of ballad rewriting, apparently for the purpose of print and, even more importantly, of ballad rewriting as a factor in continuity and variation – in relation not just to the particular ballad text (and perhaps tune) but to the genre as a whole. How that might then interact with oral transmission is a question that largely remains still to be researched.[82] Ballad research has frequently resorted to filling in the gaps around extant items and points of historical reference (actual or supposed) – but while parity of ignorance demands that absence of evidence is not taken as evidence of absence, neither is it an open invitation to invoke a favoured mechanism to fill in the gaps. Rather, an informed scepticism is more likely to allow the ballad genre to unfold at its own pace.

---

81 Pettitt, 'Journalism vs. Tradition', esp. pp. 76–77; Malcolm Gaskill, 'Reporting Murder: Fiction in the Archives in Early Modern England', *Social History*, 23 (1998), 1–30. The latter is also in Malcolm Gaskill, *Crime and Mentalities in Early Modern England* (Cambridge: Cambridge University Press, 2000), pp. 203–41. In the nineteenth century, a species of street literature known as 'cocks' related sensational but fictitious narratives of murders and the like. See Hindley, *Life and Times of James Catnach*, pp. 355–56. While 'news' is a useful generic description for broadside ballads from different periods, it should not be assumed that this amounts to factual reportage.

82 See David Atkinson and Steve Roud, eds, *Street Ballads in Nineteenth-Century Britain, Ireland, and North America: The Interface between Print and Oral Traditions* (Farnham and Burlington, VT: Ashgate, 2014).

3. Textual Authority and the Sources of Variance

The previous chapter touched on the iconic status accorded to oral tradition in ballad studies, the corollary of which is the denigration of print. Philip Bohlman writes: 'So strong is the correlation of oral tradition with folk music that most definitions treat oral tradition as fundamental to folk music, if not its most salient feature.'[1] Loosely applied, 'oral tradition' might indicate nothing more precise than that ballads in general are amenable to singing or recitation, and/or that a particular item was collected from a singer who had memorized it. However, the implication of non-literacy is frequently there in the qualifier 'oral', and that of transmission from person to person over time and/or place in the substantive 'tradition'. Accordingly – seductively – oral tradition comes to be equated with the very engine of ballad variation, that complex of processes involving remembering and forgetting, addition, subtraction, and rearrangement, substitution, borrowing, and consolidation (to name just a few) that scholars have codified to account for textual and melodic stability and change.[2] After all, the argument implicitly runs, it is much harder to reproduce a text learned by word of mouth than one learned from a printed source. Tunes are even more prone to variation than words.[3] It is generally understood that the

---

1 Philip V. Bohlman, *The Study of Folk Music in the Modern World* (Bloomington and Indianapolis: Indiana University Press, 1988), p. 14.
2 Bohlman, *Study of Folk Music*, pp. 17–24. See also Roger D. Abrahams and George Foss, *Anglo-American Folklsong Style* (Englewood Cliffs, NJ: Prentice-Hall, 1968), pp. 12–36; Tom Burns, 'A Model for Textual Variation in Folksong', *Folklore Forum*, 3 (1970), 49–56; Eleanor R. Long, 'Ballad Singers, Ballad Makers, and Ballad Etiology', *Western Folklore*, 32 (1973), 225–36.
3 Ian Russell, 'Stability and Change in a Sheffield Singing Tradition', *Folk Music Journal*, 5.3 (1987), 317–58.

http://dx.doi.org/10.11647/OBP.0041.03

melodies have nearly always been learned by ear; although musical literacy was not that rare in the past, ballad tunes were not so frequently printed and, given their relatively simple, strophic nature, seem unlikely to have required recourse to notation.

The oral argument finds its apotheosis, in the wake of the publication of Albert Lord's *The Singer of Tales* in 1960,[4] in the attempt to apply the theory of oral-formulaic improvisation directly to the Anglo-Scottish ballads, most notably in David Buchan's *The Ballad and the Folk*.[5] It is fair to say that this particular application of the oral-formulaic theory has been effectively refuted;[6] but it is equally fair to say that the presence of ballads in printed form – in particular, the cheap printed formats of broadsides and chapbooks – is still widely regarded as, at best, a conundrum. Bohlman calls it a 'blatant paradox'.[7] Print is acknowledged as a means of ballad transmission and a source of new material, but there is a general urgency to hurry the song along into oral tradition.[8] The distrust of print goes all the way back to early folk song collectors such as Sabine Baring-Gould and Cecil Sharp.[9] Likewise, Francis James Child's work on ballads was marked by an uneasy relationship with broadside print.[10]

---

4   Albert B. Lord, *The Singer of Tales*, 2nd edn, ed. Stephen Mitchell and Gregory Nagy (Cambridge, MA: Harvard University Press, 2000).
5   David Buchan, *The Ballad and the Folk* (London: Routledge & Kegan Paul, 1972). See also James H. Jones, 'Commonplace and Memorization in the Oral Tradition of the English and Scottish Popular Ballads', *Journal of American Folklore*, 74 (1961), 97–112. Lord himself wrote briefly and inconclusively about ballads in an incomplete article, 'The Ballad: Textual Stability, Variation, and Memorization', published in Albert Bates Lord, *The Singer Resumes the Tale*, ed. Mary Louise Lord (Ithaca, NY: Cornell University Press, 1995), pp. 167–86.
6   Albert B. Friedman, 'The Oral-Formulaic Theory of Balladry – A Re-rebuttal', in *The Ballad Image: Essays Presented to Bertrand Harris Bronson*, ed. James Porter (Los Angeles: Center for the Study of Comparative Folklore & Mythology, University of California, Los Angeles, 1983), pp. 215–40. See also Flemming G. Andersen and Thomas Pettitt, 'Mrs. Brown of Falkland: A Singer of Tales?', *Journal of American Folklore*, 92 (1979), 1–24; Holger Olof Nygard, 'Mrs. Brown's Recollected Ballads', in *Ballads and Ballad Research*, ed. Patricia Conroy (Seattle: University of Washington, 1978), pp. 68–87; Kenneth A. Thigpen, Jr., 'A Reconsideration of the Commonplace Phrase and Commonplace Theme in the Child Ballads', *Southern Folklore Quarterly*, 37 (1973), 385–408.
7   Bohlman, *Study of Folk Music*, p. 28.
8   Bohlman, *Study of Folk Music*, pp. 28–30.
9   S. Baring Gould and H. Fleetwood Sheppard, *Songs and Ballads of the West* (London: Methuen, [1891–95]), p. viii; Cecil J. Sharp, *English Folk-Song: Some Conclusions* (London: Simpkin; Novello, 1907), p. 101. See also Cambridge, MA, Harvard University, Houghton Library, MS Eng 863, Appendix no. 5, Sabine Baring-Gould to Francis James Child, 23 August 1890, available at http://pds.lib.harvard.edu/pds/view/22250626.
10 Mary Ellen Brown, 'Child's Ballads and the Broadside Conundrum', in *Ballads and Broadsides in Britain, 1500–1800*, ed. Patricia Fumerton and Anita Guerrini (Farnham and Burlington, VT: Ashgate, 2010), pp. 57–72.

All of this is problematic, now that the true depth and breadth of the print culture that lies behind the English and Scottish ballads is becoming apparent, thanks on the one hand to the painstaking efforts of researchers in libraries and archives, and on the other to the increasing availability of digitized images of broadside and chapbook collections and related materials. It is thought that as many as 90 per cent of the English and Scottish ballads and folk songs collected during the Romantic period and in the late nineteenth/early twentieth century could also be found in cheap print.[11] Moreover, while it is widely (and quite reasonably) assumed that printers copied from one another, it is not the case that printed ballads are devoid of variation. In fact, as Dianne Dugaw was perhaps the first to demonstrate in depth, it is possible to identify just the same sorts of textual stability and change among printed ballads as are found among those collected from singers.[12] Variants in printed ballads frequently take the form of lexical omissions and additions, rearrangements, substitutions, and the like, and (usually over a broader chronological and/or geographical span) it is also possible to identify instances of wholesale revision and rewriting, such as the recasting of *The Berkshire Tragedy* as *The Cruel Miller* considered in the previous chapter.

Rarely is it possible to be certain whence these printed variants originated. While some may be the result of lax typesetting, faulty copy, constraints of the printed format, and the like, others could just as easily represent more deliberate 'authorial' interventions, and it is quite likely that some of them may have been influenced by the ballad in its orally circulating form. Where something like a date or a proper name is substantially different as between one broadside ballad and another, it is difficult to imagine that the substitution was not in some way deliberate.[13] Different printings of 'The Mountains High' (Roud 397), for example, name the main character variously as Reynardine, Rinordine, or Ryner Dyne. Similarly, in 'The Bold Princess Royal' (Roud 528), the date of the encounter with the pirate ship

---

11 Figures in this region were first advanced by Robert S. Thomson, 'The Development of the Broadside Ballad Trade and its Influence upon the Transmission of English Folksongs' (unpublished doctoral thesis, University of Cambridge, 1974), p. 274; Rainer Wehse, 'Broadside Ballad and Folksong: Oral Tradition versus Literary Tradition', *Folklore Forum*, 8 (1975), 324–34 [2–12] (p. 333 [11]). They are confirmed by researchers currently working on the material (personal communication).
12 Dianne M. Dugaw, 'Anglo-American Folksong Reconsidered: The Interface of Oral and Written Forms', *Western Folklore*, 43 (1984), 83–103.
13 See Steve Roud, 'Introduction', in *Street Ballads in Nineteenth-Century Britain, Ireland, and North America: The Interface between Print and Oral Traditions*, ed. David Atkinson and Steve Roud (Farnham and Burlington, VT: Ashgate, 2014), forthcoming.

is usually given on broadsides as the 14th of February, but other dates are found among copies collected from singers, and at least one broadside has the 6th of January. In 'The Fatal Ramillies' (Roud 1266), the complement of the battleship appears on broadsides as seven hundred and seventy or seven hundred and twenty, which is close to the historical figure, but also as the much exaggerated seventeen hundred and seventy. If these various broadside texts were indeed copied from one another, then it would seem that the printers must have had some other model in mind when introducing such variant details – that is to say, either some consciously creative input, or some extraneous knowledge of how they thought the ballad 'ought to go'. This whole area demands further investigation and systematization – and it also demands a theoretical model of variation capable of integrating both the printed and the oral ballad.

Just to set out the ground quite clearly: there is no question here of denying that English-language ballads can be, and certainly have been, learned and passed on without the aid of written or printed copies, over the five centuries or so during which the genre has been in existence, and that this may have been a source of textual and melodic variation. Oral transmission has perhaps had a particular importance in remote regions such as Appalachia, or among social groups such as the Scottish Travellers.[14] Ballad melodies, as noted above, were rarely written down as music notation, meaning that a degree of transmission by word of mouth and learning by ear must have been more or less essential. A number of ballads stand out as not having any known record in cheap print, and therefore presumably must have been passed on by oral means. Among them are widely collected items such as 'Lord Randal' (Child 12) and 'The Maid Freed from the Gallows' (Child 95), which are strongly repetitive and incremental in nature, suggesting that they would have been particularly easy to learn and remember. Indeed, one of the most cogent reasons for rejecting the theory of oral-formulaic improvisation in relation to the English-language ballads is that it is simply not necessary: they are just not that difficult to learn by heart. A further reason is that the historical context and literary culture out of which the English-language ballads emerged

---

14 But see, respectively, David E. Whisnant, *All That Is Native & Fine: The Politics of Culture in an American Region* (Chapel Hill: University of North Carolina Press, 1983); Chris Wright, 'Forgotten Broadsides and the Song Tradition of the Scots Travellers', in *Street Ballads in Nineteenth-Century Britain, Ireland, and North America: The Interface between Print and Oral Traditions*, ed. David Atkinson and Steve Roud (Farnham and Burlington, VT: Ashgate, 2014), forthcoming.

was entirely different from that surrounding the South Slavic epic songs that provided the material evidence for *The Singer of Tales*.

In post-Conquest England, oral and literate strands of culture were intertwined from the beginning, with a gradual shifting of emphasis away from the oral and towards the literate – given a tremendous boost, of course, by the invention of printing – being more or less complete by the end of the nineteenth century.[15] The evidence for this is necessarily very diverse in form and chronology. A small selection of the key loci that witnessed the interface of oral and literate culture would include the gradual replacement of oral testimony by written documents in legal proceedings; the ubiquity of preaching as a means of conveying the written word of the Bible to the non-lettered in vernacular languages; the repetition in print from the sixteenth century onwards of classic popular fictional narratives; the pasting up in public and reading aloud of written and printed matter, ranging from official proclamations to libellous verses; the reading aloud of newspapers in coffee houses, facilitating the dissemination of news and the growth of a political culture; the symbiosis of private study and rote learning in the advancement of education and self-improvement, with or without the assistance of the church and/or state, in the industrial era.

It is extremely difficult to cite meaningful figures for the growth of literacy.[16] Using the measurable criterion of people's ability to sign

---

15 See, for example, Jonathan Barry, 'Literacy and Literature in Popular Culture: Reading and Writing in Historical Perspective', in *Popular Culture in England, c.1500–1850*, ed. Tim Harris (Basingstoke: Macmillan, 1995), pp. 69–94; M. T. Clanchy, *From Memory to Written Record: England 1066–1307*, 3rd edn (Oxford and Malden, MA: Wiley-Blackwell, 2013); Adam Fox, *Oral and Literate Culture in England, 1500–1700* (Oxford: Clarendon Press, 2000); Barry Reay, *Popular Cultures in England, 1550–1750* (London: Longman, 1998), pp. 36–70; David Vincent, *Literacy and Popular Culture: England 1750–1914* (Cambridge: Cambridge University Press, 1989). For Scotland, see R. A. Houston, *Scottish Literacy and the Scottish Identity: Illiteracy and Society in Scotland and Northern England, 1600–1800* (Cambridge: Cambridge University Press, 1985).

16 For the earlier period, see, for example, David Cressy, *Literacy and the Social Order: Reading and Writing in Tudor and Stuart England* (Cambridge: Cambridge University Press, 1980); Thomas Laqueur, 'The Cultural Origins of Popular Literacy in England, 1500–1850', *Oxford Review of Education*, 2 (1976), 255–75; R. S. Schofield, 'The Measurement of Literacy in Pre-Industrial England', in *Literacy in Traditional Societies*, ed. Jack Goody (Cambridge: Cambridge University Press, 1968), pp. 311–25; Lawrence Stone, 'Literacy and Education in England, 1640–1900', *Past and Present*, no. 42 (1969), 69–139; Keith Thomas, 'The Meaning of Literacy in Early Modern England', in *The Written Word: Literacy in Transition*, ed. Gerd Baumann (Oxford: Clarendon Press, 1986), pp. 97–131. For the later period, see Barry Reay, 'The Context and Meaning of Popular Literacy: Some Evidence from Nineteenth-Century Rural England', *Past and Present*, no. 131 (1991), 89–129; Vincent, *Literacy and Popular Culture*, pp. 22–32. For Scotland and northern England, see Houston, *Scottish Literacy*, pp. 20–109. There is an excellent overview of the subject in Adam Fox

their names to a document, by the 1640s perhaps 30 per cent of men and 10 per cent of women could do so, rising to 45 per cent and 25 per cent, respectively, by the mid-eighteenth century. On the same measure, England had achieved universal literacy by the outbreak of the First World War. However, writing and reading were entirely separate skills, and it is widely believed that such figures spectacularly underestimate the numbers who could read. By the mid-eighteenth century – and perhaps much earlier – probably a majority of the adult population had attained a degree of functional, pragmatic literacy, enabling them to read print to some extent. Nevertheless, literacy rates were extremely variable, being generally lower among the poorer sections of society, among women than among men, and in rural as opposed to urban areas – with rates in London, the epicentre of ballad printing, being consistently well above the national average. Throughout much of the period in question, those who encountered ballads in cheap printed form might have been just as likely to be able to read them as not – but that is a very general statement indeed.

Moreover, it is no more than a small part of the story. Access to written material was never confined to the literate alone but was made much more widely available through what Roger Chartier terms 'communities of readers'.[17] Through the agency of a literate interpreter, reading could be turned into a collective experience. That might be in the context of the church, the family, the marketplace, the school, the workplace, the coffee house, the trade organization. Right up until the early years of the twentieth century, the experience of reading most characteristically meant reading out loud, and reading was most frequently not a solitary activity at all but one rooted in human interaction and sociability.[18] Some historians of literacy are now inclined to view the dichotomy of literacy *vs.* illiteracy, or literacy *vs.* orality, as little more than a nineteenth-century (or maybe eighteenth-century) ideological construct, tied to a modern construction of interiority, personality, and subjectivity.[19] Perpetuated by influential theorists such as Walter Ong and Marshall McLuhan, the so-called 'great

---

and Daniel Woolf, eds, *The Spoken Word: Oral Culture in Britain, 1500–1850* (Manchester: Manchester University Press, 2002), pp. 21–33.

17 Roger Chartier, *The Order of Books: Readers, Authors, and Libraries in Europe between the Fourteenth and Eighteenth Centuries*, trans. Lydia G. Cochrane (Stanford: Stanford University Press, 1994), pp. 1–23.

18 Vincent, *Literacy and Popular Culture*, p. 275.

19 Patricia Crain, 'New Histories of Literacy', in *A Companion to the History of the Book*, ed. Simon Eliot and Jonathan Rose (Oxford and Malden, MA: Wiley-Blackwell, 2007), pp. 467–79.

divide' theory of literacy *vs.* orality actually reveals rather little about the communal reception of texts in England and Scotland, or even in western Europe at large, at an earlier time.

Instead, for virtually the whole time for which there is anything in the English language that might reasonably be termed a ballad, the picture is one of mutual interdependence of oral and written forms, and of a shared experience of texts regardless of the ability to read. Keith Thomas provides a succinct statement of the matter as it stands in early modern England: 'Literates and illiterates need not necessarily have different mental habits; and the illiterates of early modern England were in quite a different position from the non-literate inhabitants of purely oral societies. They lived in a world which was to a great extent governed by texts, even though they could not read themselves.'[20] Even in post-Roman Britain, the development of a written Old English vernacular, manifest through utilitarian documents such as charters and laws, as well as the more celebrated works of poetry and heroic literature, along with the residual influence of Latin writing, testifies to the continuity of the idea of literacy.[21] Early medieval England did not approach anything like what Ong would consider a state of 'primary orality'.[22] (The world of *Beowulf* is probably something of a literary fiction – mentioned here largely because it seems to correspond in some degree with the putative condition of society, 'in which the people are not divided by political organization and book-culture into markedly distinct classes, in which consequently there is such community of ideas and feelings that the whole people form an individual', that Child envisaged as necessary for the genesis of ballads.[23]) By the thirteenth century, for example, the replacement of oral testimony by writing in legal contexts was well established and its impact was experienced even among the peasantry.[24] Across Europe, too, the growth of markets, towns, and commerce from the eleventh to the thirteenth centuries was associated with the spread of new forms of documentary record-keeping.[25] The assimilation

---

20 Thomas, 'Meaning of Literacy', p. 107.
21 Clanchy, *From Memory to Written Record*, pp. 30–35.
22 Walter J. Ong, *Orality and Literacy: The Technologizing of the Word* (London: Routledge, 1988 [1982]), pp. 6, 11.
23 F. J. Child, 'Ballad Poetry', in *Johnson's New Universal Cyclopædia*, eds-in-chief Frederick A. P. Barnard and Arnold Guyot, 4 vols (New York: A. J. Johnson, 1881 [1874]), I, 365–68 (p. 365).
24 Clanchy, *From Memory to Written Record*, esp. pp. 48–53.
25 Brian Stock, *Listening for the Text: On the Uses of the Past* (Philadelphia: University of Pennsylvania Press, 1996 [1990]), pp. 126–27. A remarkable example of everyday written

of the ideas of spoken and written language as means of communicating, preserving, and transmitting texts that these developments represent was in train well before the era of print, and must have taken place even while overall levels of actual, measurable literacy were quite low.[26]

Here, Brian Stock's notion of 'textual communities' is pertinent.[27] Textual communities can be defined as 'microsocieties organized around the common understanding of a script'.[28] Like Chartier's communities of readers, such microsocieties need not necessarily be composed of literate people, the minimal requirement being just one interpreter with some sort of access to a set of texts and the ability to pass them on to others. The physical presence of a written text was not essential: oral record, memory, and re-performance would suffice.[29] Hence 'textual' rather than 'reading' communities, and the charting of a rise of 'textuality' rather than merely an increase in literacy.[30] Stock envisages the process thus: as the written word gained ground in western Europe, existing oral practices realigned themselves to function in a reference system based on texts; a culture emerged that was both oral *and* written; texts were not always written down, *but they were understood as if they were* (my italics).[31]

This, then, is the environment in which even the earliest of the English-language ballad-like songs, such as 'Judas' (Child 23) and 'Twelfth Day', need to be situated. The presence of these two pieces within a manuscript miscellany containing items in English, French, and Latin, of probable Franciscan provenance, is indicative of the ballads' potential to function within reading/textual communities.[32] Subsequently, there is nothing in *The English and Scottish Popular Ballads* for another couple of centuries, until c.1450, right at the beginning of the era of print and well into an age that was, in Keith Thomas's phrase, 'to a great extent governed by texts'.

---

documentation is provided by the Ely Farming Memoranda, early eleventh-century farming records noted down in Old English. See Clanchy, *From Memory to Written Record*, pp. 32, 67.

26 On the further complication of the coexistence in post-Conquest England of three languages – English, Latin, and French – with distinct spoken and written functions, see Clanchy, *From Memory to Written Record*, pp. 199–225.

27 Stock, *Listening for the Text*, pp. 22–24, 150; Brian Stock, *The Implications of Literacy: Written Language and Models of Interpretation in the Eleventh and Twelfth Centuries* (Princeton: Princeton University Press, 1983), esp. pp. 90–92.

28 Stock, *Listening for the Text*, p. 23.

29 Stock, *Listening for the Text*, p. 37.

30 Stock, *Listening for the Text*, pp. 20, 140, 146; Stock, *Implications of Literacy*, p. 7.

31 Stock, *Listening for the Text*, pp. 19–20.

32 See John C. Hirsh, 'The Earliest Known English Ballad: A New Reading of "Judas"', *Modern Language Review*, 103 (2008), 931–39.

Even today, relatively little is known for certain about ballad singing, reading, and/or recitation during the early modern period, although there are enough contemporary references to merit the assumption that ballads were ubiquitous, or at least were perceived as being so.[33] There are thousands of broadsides which could be – and perhaps were intended to be – sung to named tunes, and at least some of them are the 'same' as ballads collected from singers during the folk song revivals of much later date. There are also plentiful literary references to semi-professional ballad singers (Autolycus and his kind) and ballad writers.[34] There are also Addison's *Spectator* papers of the early eighteenth century, and the beginnings of the appearance of ballads in printed miscellanies. In the eighteenth century, ballads are found among anthologies that can be associated with the growth of musical entertainments in the theatres and metropolitan pleasure gardens. A string of references indicate that it was not uncommon to find broadsides pasted on walls in alehouses and domestic dwellings. Vic Gammon makes the very reasonable point that singing was the most readily available form of artistic expression for much of the population.[35]

Stock's specific examples of textual communities are mostly based around ideological movements, such as the Waldensians, where a group of people would coalesce around vernacular texts of the scriptures and their exposition through (unlicensed) public preaching, establishing an agreed meaning for those scriptural texts which came to comprise, for the group in question, the 'real text'.[36] An example from much closer to home would be the religious revival of 1742 at Cambuslang, Lanarkshire, which culminated in outdoor meetings where tens of thousands gathered from miles around to hear the evangelist George Whitefield.[37] Like the earlier movements studied by Stock, the revival at Cambuslang was focused on the experience of hearing texts expounded through preaching. The most notable difference was that while the earlier episodes were not generally founded on an immediate continuity with a literate tradition (Peter Waldo's

---

33 Christopher Marsh, *Music and Society in Early Modern England* (Cambridge: Cambridge University Press, 2010), p. 225.
34 Marsh, *Music and Society in Early Modern England*, pp. 238–50. See also extracts reprinted in Natascha Würzbach, *The Rise of the English Street Ballad, 1550–1650*, trans. Gayna Walls (Cambridge: Cambridge University Press, 1990), pp. 253–84.
35 Vic Gammon, *Desire, Drink and Death in English Folk and Vernacular Song, 1600–1900* (Aldershot and Burlington, VT: Ashgate, 2008), pp. 10–11.
36 Stock, *Listening for the Text*, pp. 24–29, 146.
37 T. C. Smout, 'Born Again at Cambuslang: New Evidence on Popular Religion and Literacy in Eighteenth-Century Scotland', *Past and Present*, no. 97 (1982), 114–27.

initial contact with the scriptures was essentially an oral experience), virtually all of the converts at Cambuslang were well able to read the Bible for themselves. At least one girl is recorded as saying, 'I used to read the Bible at my parents desire tho' I had more delight in reading story books and ballads.'[38] But in so far as the shared experience can be understood in terms of the (admittedly temporary) emergence of a textual community focused around the revivalist preaching of the scriptures, the ability to read or otherwise is largely irrelevant.

While textual communities established around religious ideological movements provide a particularly potent instance for the shared engagement of a group of people with a text, it is clear that the general principle can apply to a much broader range of groups united by a general agreement over the meaning(s) of a text, or set of texts. These might embody aspects of everyday civic and cultural life – the requirements for commercial activity, for example, or the ethical values arising from a body of literature – in which similar social origins could be expected to comprise a sufficient (though not a necessary) condition for participation.[39] A number of essays in *The Cambridge History of Medieval English Literature* make reference to the idea of textual communities when discussing the readership and reception of Middle English literature (testimony to the far-reaching influence of Stock's concept on medieval studies), including Lollard textual networks in London and Essex; an East Anglian readers' circle centred on regional collections of saints' lives; the vernacular 'self-help' afforded by early Middle English guides to spiritual well-being; monastic communities responsible for sponsoring literary genres such as hagiography, exegesis, or biblical redactions; women's textual communities, both as they may have existed in real life and as imagined through literature; implied readerships for *Piers Plowman*, ranging from the vernacular to the university-trained; and the importance of lowland Scots in the development of a national consciousness, exemplified by Gavin Douglas's translation of the *Aeneid* shortly before the Scottish defeat at Flodden (1513).[40]

Then there are the several audiences for the Middle English romance, which have been characterized at different times as courtly and aristocratic,

---

38 Smout, 'Born Again at Cambuslang', p. 124.
39 Stock, *Listening for the Text*, p. 37.
40 David Wallace, ed., *The Cambridge History of Medieval English Literature* (Cambridge: Cambridge University Press, 1999), pp. 677–78, 686–87 (Lollards), 626–27 (saints' lives), 90–91 (spiritual well-being), 349–50 (religious communities), 109–21, 307, 350 (women's reading), 527–30 (*Piers Plowman*), 247 (vernacular Scots).

gentry and middle-class, popular, male or female.[41] This variety arises not least because the genre was an exceptionally heterogeneous one, extending over a very long period of time, well into the age of print. Indeed, the continuing popularity of romance stories in chapbooks into the eighteenth and nineteenth centuries should not be overlooked.[42] Clearly, different audience groups would have their own ideological interests, which would inform their shared understanding of romance stories. Regardless of social composition, the audience for romance is commonly characterized as being a 'listening' audience, and while the romances were literate compositions, they lent themselves to the whole spectrum of receptive experience from listening to singing, recitation, or reading aloud, right through to private reading.

It is accordingly not difficult to envisage textual communities united around a shared understanding and appreciation of certain ballad texts. Angela McShane, for example, argues that political ballads of the period from the beginning of the civil wars to the Glorious Revolution 'not only supplied a commentary on the upheavals of the period but provided too a political frame of reference for their often unsophisticated, but not uninformed readers'.[43] There is a risk, however, of imparting too much weight to the (presumably) shared experience of ballad singing/recitation/reading. The notion of textual community involves a significant degree of the fashioning of a group identity out of the shared experience of interpreting a text, and Richard Green has given voice to a certain scepticism about the blanket application of the idea to groups of medieval English texts and their readers/audiences.[44] Instead, he suggests, the later

---

41 Derek Pearsall, 'Middle English Romance and its Audiences', in *Historical & Editorial Studies in Medieval & Early Modern English for Johan Gerritsen*, ed. Mary-Jo Arn and Hanneke Wirtjes, with Hans Jansen (Groningen: Wolters-Noordhoff, 1985), pp. 37–47; Ad Putter and Jane Gilbert, eds, *The Spirit of Medieval English Popular Romance* (Harlow: Longman, 2000), pp. 20–26; Andrew Taylor, 'Fragmentation, Corruption, and Minstrel Narration: The Question of the Middle English Romances', *Yearbook of English Studies*, 22 (1992), 38–62; Wallace, ed., *Cambridge History of Medieval English Literature*, pp. 152–76, 690–719.
42 See John Simons, 'Romance in the Eighteenth-Century Chapbook', in *From Medieval to Medievalism*, ed. John Simons (Basingstoke: Macmillan, 1992), pp. 122–43.
43 Angela McShane Jones, '"Rime and Reason": The Political World of the English Broadside Ballad, 1640–1689' (unpublished doctoral thesis, University of Warwick, 2004), pp. 1–2. See also Angela McShane, 'Typography Matters: Branding Ballads and Gelding Curates in Stuart England', in *Book Trade Connections from the Seventeenth to the Twentieth Centuries*, ed. John Hinks and Catherine Armstrong (New Castle, DE: Oak Knoll Press; London: British Library, 2008), pp. 19–44.
44 Richard Firth Green, 'Textual Production and Textual Communities', in *The Cambridge Companion to Medieval English Literature, 1100–1500*, ed. Larry Scanlon (Cambridge: Cambridge University Press, 2009), pp. 25–36.

medieval period witnessed the emergence of something more like the 'interpretive communities' of reader-response theory, the term originated by Stanley Fish to describe groups of readers who bring a shared 'horizon of expectations' to the interpretation of a text.[45] That would certainly fit the potentially differing purposes in authoring and presenting medieval romances to courtly and/or gentry audiences, and the corresponding differences in the way they might be received and understood. It would fit, too, with the production and reception of political ballads. Later on, it is sometimes claimed that certain ballads could be expected to have special meaning for particular social groups. The bothy ballads sung by the farm servants of north-east Scotland, the texts of some of which relate directly to their personal and professional circumstances, provide a good example.[46] The idea, sometimes expressed, that 'The Gypsy Laddie' (Child 200) should be especially dear to the hearts of Gypsy/Traveller singers might fall into the same category. Equally, ballads are as open to variety of interpretation as any other kind of verse or music.[47]

What this exploration of the textual environment into which the genre emerged does indicate is that, quite regardless of questions of literacy *vs.* non-literacy and written *vs.* oral transmission, ballads would be conceived and understood as texts. They were not always written down, but they were understood as if they were. It is reasonable to speak of ballad 'textuality' without reference to a specific means of transmission. Although it is even conceivable that a text learned by ear might be memorized in a manner qualitatively different from one learned by eye, these still amount only to different routes to access the same thing – like viewing an object without touching it, or handling it in the dark.

The ballad text, on this model, has an autonomy of its own – not an essentialist, New Critical, signification of its own, but an imaginary, abstract existence, separable from any intended meaning that might accompany its production (singing/recitation/printing) or its reception (listening/reading).

---

45 Stanley Fish, *Is There a Text in This Class? The Authority of Interpretive Communities* (Cambridge, MA: Harvard University Press, 1980).

46 Peter A. Hall, 'Farm Life and the Farm Songs', in *The Greig–Duncan Folk Song Collection*, ed. Patrick Shuldham-Shaw, Emily B. Lyle, et al., 8 vols (Aberdeen: Aberdeen University Press; Edinburgh: Mercat Press, for the University of Aberdeen in association with the School of Scottish Studies, University of Edinburgh, 1981–2002), III, xxi–xxxiv.

47 New research into the history of reading, directing attention to the sheer variety of experience, potentially has much to contribute to ballad studies. See, for example, James Raven, 'New Reading Histories, Print Culture and the Identification of Change: The Case of Eighteenth-Century England', *Social History*, 23 (1998), 268–87.

A simple illustration of this can be found in the deictic or 'orientational' features of ballad language. Deictics are linguistic markers that ostensibly relate to the immediate situation of utterance and hearing (to use terms that deliberately invoke an oral situation, while considering properties that belong to written and oral texts alike), but which in actual fact relate only to imagined constructs in the mind of speaker and listener. A moment's thought will reveal that, far from introducing immediacy and presence, their effect is to distance and depersonalize the content from both speaker and listener alike.[48] Examples of deictics in poetic usage include personal pronouns, anaphoric articles and demonstratives, adverbs of place and time, and the use of the historic present tense.

Thus the poetic 'I' and the activity mentioned in the common folk song incipit 'As I walked out on a midsummer morning' references neither singer nor listener but a construct – or, rather, separate constructs – in the mind of each, which may or may not largely overlap with one another and/or with a common understanding among a putative 'balladic' (ballad-singing, ballad-listening, ballad-reading, ballad-inscribing) textual community. This may be difficult to appreciate because at first blush, 'midsummer' might seem temporally objective; but it can still refer either to a specific day or to a less precisely defined season, personally experienced in many different ways. Midsummer has been associated historically, for instance, with bonfires and processions, and practices for love divination – but these customs are strictly localized (temporally as well as geographically).[49] The extent to which any of these, or other, associations might actually be relevant is highly dependent on the (real and imagined) identity/ies of the 'I' of the incipit.

Consider further the opening stanza of 'The Outlandish Knight' (Child 4), one of the most widely collected of English-language ballads, as it appears on a number of printed broadsides of the nineteenth century:

An outlandish knight came from the north lands
And he came a wooing to me
He told me he'd take me to the north lands
And there he would marry me.

---

[48] Jonathan Culler, *Structuralist Poetics: Structuralism, Linguistics and the Study of Literature* (London: Routledge, 2002 [1975]), pp. 192–99. For a different perspective, see Würzbach, *Rise of the English Street Ballad* (but see the review in *Folk Music Journal*, 6.2 (1991), 238–39).

[49] Jacqueline Simpson and Steve Roud, *A Dictionary of English Folklore* (Oxford: Oxford University Press, 2000), pp. 238–39.

Connotations for *outlandish* listed in the *Oxford English Dictionary* range from 'Of or belonging to a foreign country; foreign, alien; not native or indigenous', through 'Looking or sounding foreign; unfamiliar, strange. Hence, in extended use: odd, bizarre; going beyond what is considered normal or acceptable; outrageous, extravagant', to 'Out-of-the-way, remote; far removed from civilization'.[50] The English singer Shirley Collins recalled of her neighbours in Etchingham, Sussex, in the 1970s: 'Talking one day to Fanny, who was then in her eighties, about her early life, she told me she'd been courted by another man before she married Will, but couldn't marry him "because he was too outlandish". "What was so outlandish about him?" I asked, intrigued. "Oh, he came from a village about three miles away," she replied!'[51] Conversely, the analogous character who gave rise to Child's standard title for the ballad type, 'Lady Isabel and the Elf-Knight', is seemingly a supernatural being (Child 4 A) – and there are sufficiently diverse characters in romances alone for a knight to be associated with chivalry and courtly love on the one hand and violence, seduction, and betrayal on the other. Outlandish strangers like the one in *Sir Gawain and the Green Knight* bring the idea of supernatural shape-shifting, as well as an element of moral examination, into such tales.[52]

The imagined geographical location of the 'north lands', and the sort of inhabitants who might be expected to reside there, are likewise very dependent on pre-existing spatial and social horizons. For someone living in England, the north lands might suggest Scotland; but for a native of southern England the suggestion might just be of a generic 'north of Watford', to borrow the modern idiom. Conversely, for a ballad collected in the north-east of Scotland, the north lands might have to be equated with the Highlands; even while an English reader might envisage precisely the Scottish north-east. Not to mention the possible perspectives on 'wooing' and 'marry[ing] me' which requires an act of imaginative identification on the listener's part, dependent perhaps on their own gender. But no one believes any of it literally happened to the singer.

Interpretive ideas like these have little to do with the physical presence or absence of a speaker/singer and everything to do with the horizon of

---

50 *OED* outlandish, *adj.* and *n.*
51 Shirley and Dolly Collins, *Love, Death & the Lady*, CD (EMI Harvest 7243 8 29860 2 7, 1994), insert notes.
52 Raymond H. Thompson, "'Muse on þi mirrour . . .': The Challenge of the Outlandish Stranger in the English Arthurian Verse Romances," *Folklore*, 87 (1976), 201–08.

expectations of the reader/listener, or of the textual or interpretive community. The physical presence of a speaker would be most unlikely to resolve any of the inherent uncertainties. It is mistaken to conceive of the ballad, whether conveyed orally or in writing, in terms of a transmission or 'informational' model of communication, whereby a sender conveys a message of their own devising through a particular channel to a receiver (with, in later modifications of the model, the possibility of a feedback loop from receiver to sender, enabling modifications of the message).[53] Now essentially discarded by communication theorists in favour of a diversity of 'constructivist' approaches which recognize that in virtually all communicative situations meaning is actively constructed by both sender and receiver, the transmission model is particularly inappropriate in relation to works of imaginative literature, which exploit the potentials of linguistic excess and redundancy, which conversely constitute 'noise' in the transmission model.[54] Yet the transmission model has a seductive appearance of conformity with 'common sense', and (at the risk of setting up a man of straw) it seems that it might also embody something of the immediacy and subjectivity that are sometimes thought to characterize sound or speech – and hence the iconic oral tradition – as opposed to writing.

Yet, so far as we know, oral performance and transmission of ballad texts has always taken place alongside written and printed 'performance' and transmission. Indeed, it still does, as a couple of examples – exceptional only in terms of their quality – will illustrate. The Copper family of Rottingdean, Sussex, sing songs some of which have probably been in the family for a couple of centuries and which were written down in songbooks in the 1920s and 1930s, and they still make use of a family songbook in performance even though they must surely know all the items by heart.[55] The Traveller culture of north-east Scotland is to a great extent an oral one, even while many of their ballads can be identified with items printed in the eighteenth and nineteenth centuries, and members of one of the celebrated families

---

53 Claude E. Shannon and Warren Weaver, *The Mathematical Theory of Communication* (Urbana: University of Illinois Press, 1949). For a useful introduction, see Daniel Chandler, 'The Transmission Model of Communication' (1994), available at http://www.aber.ac.uk/media/Documents/short/trans.html.
54 Jerome J. McGann, *The Textual Condition* (Princeton: Princeton University Press, 1991), p. 14; Peter L. Shillingsburg, *Resisting Texts: Authority and Submission in Constructions of Meaning* (Ann Arbor: University of Michigan Press, 1997), pp. 108–09.
55 [The Copper Family], *The Copper Family Song Book: A Living Tradition* (Peacehaven: Coppersongs, 1995).

of Traveller singers, the Stewarts of Fetterangus, have written down their songs in order to enrich their culture and to ensure its continuity.[56] In neither of these cases is writing a 'substitute' for oral performance and transmission: the two paths exist in parallel, providing complementary routes of access to the respective song traditions.

The idea that, in the sort of textual environment sketched in over the course of this chapter, those who learned texts by ear should find it more difficult to commit them accurately to memory than those who learn them by eye, would seem to be the product of a modern, almost exclusively literate, sensibility. Conversely, there is good historical evidence that, without the visual support of writing, people's mnemonic powers were often highly developed.[57] The clergyman and writer Nicholas Bownd (d.1613) could complain that there were too many people who showed no interest in singing psalms, 'though they can sing some other vain songs very perfectly; and though they cannot reade themselues, nor any of theirs, yet will haue many Ballades set vp in their houses, that so they might learne them, as they shall haue occasion'.[58] In Izaak Walton's *Compleat Angler* (1653) a proud mother promises the anglers her (admittedly fictional) daughter, 'shal sit by and sing you the good old Song of the *Hunting in Chevy Chase*, or some other good Ballad, for she hath good store of them: Maudlin hath a notable memory'.[59] The eponymous hero of an eighteenth-century broadside ballad, *The Proud Pedlar*, claims: 'I never sung a Song in all my whole Life, / But I could sing it again.'[60] Ballads were composed using familiar linguistic patterns, refrains, and so forth, all of which could serve as mnemonic devices, as well as endeavouring to engage a prospective audience through the choice of narrative material.[61] And there is reason to think that melody and words generally have a mutually reinforcing mnemonic effect.

---

56 Thomas A. McKean, 'The Stewarts of Fetterangus and Literate Oral Tradition', in *The Singer and the Scribe: European Ballad Traditions and European Ballad Cultures*, ed. Philip E. Bennett and Richard Firth Green (Amsterdam: Rodopi, 2004), pp. 181–207.
57 Fox, *Oral and Literate Culture*, pp. 22–23, 135; Marsh, *Music and Society in Early Modern England*, pp. 255–56; Thomas, 'Meaning of Literacy', pp. 107–10; Vincent, *Literacy and Popular Culture*, pp. 60–62, 182–84, 194–95.
58 Nicholas Bownde [sic], *The Doctrine of the Sabbath* (London: printed by the Widdow Orwin, for Iohn Porter, and Thomas Man, 1595), p. 241 [ESTC S113231].
59 [Izaak Walton], *The Compleat Angler; or, The Contemplative Man's Recreation* (London: printed by T. Maxey, for Rich. Marriot, 1653), p. 203 [ESTC R202374].
60 *The Proud Pedlar* ([London?, 1740?]) [ESTC T46054; Roxburghe Ballads 3.656].
61 Marsh, *Music and Society in Early Modern England*, pp. 284–86.

Knowledge of the Bible, in particular, was often excellent among people who could not actually read it for themselves.[62] This is a particularly good instance, because it can be presumed that at least some of the imperative towards accurate memory and recall derives from the authority vested in that particular text, considered as the Word of God. With the best will in the world, ballads do not aspire to be considered the word of God, and in most instances not even the word of any particular author. Thus far, the idea of ballad textuality has been used in Stock's sense of a reference system based on access to a corpus of texts, not always written down but understood as if they were. Ballad textuality, however, must embrace not just the reference system and its routes of access, but the authority that resides in the system of texts. So, while verbatim recall of the Bible might be assumed to be a desideratum, clearly that is not necessarily the case for the ballad.

Variation is frequently stated to be the key, defining, characteristic of ballads and folk songs, and of folk literature at large. Yet the actual level of variation from one instance to another is not necessarily any greater than, say, the different published texts of modernist poets such as W. B. Yeats and Marianne Moore, to name just a couple of examples from mainstream, canonical literature.[63] The bulk of collected texts of a single ballad type such as 'The Outlandish Knight' (Child 4), or 'The Cruel Mother' (Child 20), or 'Barbara Allan' (Child 84), or 'The Maid Freed from the Gallows' (Child 95), or 'The Battle of Harlaw' (Child 163), or 'The Golden Vanity' (Child 286), actually vary rather little, although certainly some are more complete than others. Substantial change is usually apparent only with equally substantial chronological and geographical spread. The difference, of course, is that the authority for variation in modernist poetry is generally assumed to lie with the individual, named author,[64] whereas in the case of the ballad it is often ascribed to a process, namely oral tradition. Yet if oral tradition is seen to be actually rather beside the point in relation to the transmission and reception of the English-language ballads, and if oral transmission is also perfectly capable of ensuring verbatim reproduction, then the motor for ballad variation must be located elsewhere. What is

---

62 Fox, *Oral and Literate Culture*, p. 22.
63 George Bornstein, *Material Modernism: The Politics of the Page* (Cambridge: Cambridge University Press, 2001).
64 Although the gist of Bornstein's argument, and of much recent materialist criticism, is that the shape of the text is often driven by factors beyond the author's immediate control – place and format of publication, presumed readership/audience, external political developments, and so on.

being posited here is that this motor lies in just the opposite direction from the apparent situation of modernist poetry: it lies in the *absence* of the sort of authority over the text that is deemed to belong to the individual author.

What can be envisaged for ballads – oral and written alike – is a condition very much akin to what Bernard Cerquiglini has posited to account for variation in medieval vernacular literature that cannot be readily ascribed to an individual author, under the term *variance*.[65] Cerquiglini argues that in the Middle Ages the literary work was 'a variable', usually anonymous, to which the fact of an originating authorship was less important than the continual rewriting of the work, which then 'belonged' to whoever prepared it and gave it form again.[66] A state of purposeful variation – *variance* – was intrinsic not only to the transmission but to the very aesthetic of medieval vernacular literature. The varying written realizations of a medieval vernacular work represent not 'errors', scribal departures from a single text authenticated by the persona of the author, but a state of 'generalized authenticity'.[67] What Cerquiglini seems to envisage is a dispersed textual authority shared across all of the renderings, and perhaps all of the possible renderings, of what can be loosely identified as the 'same' literary work.

Middle English literature is indeed generally lacking in a sense of stable textual authority, with many works being either actually or effectively anonymous, becoming varied and expanded in the course of textual transmission, and being realized in manuscripts of varying content and layout.[68] Variation characterizes some of the romance texts, where it might be the consequence of scribal activity or more directly of vocal performance, in each case rerouted back into the extant written manuscripts.[69] But these are all models founded in the study of written texts, notwithstanding the undoubted importance for medieval literature of oral expression and transmission, and of an oral dimension to scribal copying – scribes are thought sometimes to have worked by reading aloud,

---

65 Bernard Cerquiglini, *In Praise of the Variant: A Critical History of Philology*, trans. Betsy Wing (Baltimore: Johns Hopkins University Press, 1999).
66 Cerquiglini, *In Praise of the Variant*, p. 33.
67 Cerquiglini, *In Praise of the Variant*, pp. 34, 51.
68 Tim William Machan, *Textual Criticism and Middle English Texts* (Charlottesville: University Press of Virginia, 1994).
69 Albert C. Baugh, 'Improvisation in the Middle English Romance', *Proceedings of the American Philosophical Society*, 103 (1959), 418–54 (esp. pp. 434–40); Nancy Mason Bradbury, *Writing Aloud: Storytelling in Late Medieval England* (Urbana and Chicago: University of Illinois Press, 1998), pp. 1–21; Taylor, 'Fragmentation, Corruption, and Minstrel Narration', esp. pp. 43–46.

or at least sub-vocalizing, and therefore 'hearing' at least a part of their texts.[70] Cerquiglini's *variance* is thus specifically distinguished from Paul Zumthor's probably rather better-known concept of *mouvance*, which is tied specifically to the precedence of the voice over writing.[71]

Cerquiglini, moreover, is prepared to extrapolate his conception of dispersed textual authority: 'When our literary presuppositions have become sufficiently unhinged that Shakespeare is affected, it is not hard to conceive of the disturbance gradually spreading to most of premodern writings.'[72] Here he is alluding to the now widely acknowledged instability that pervades Shakespearian texts – the variant *Hamlet*s, *King Lear*s, *Macbeth*s, and so on, which mean that it is impossible to pin the play down to a single authoritative version, and instead the work we call *Hamlet*, or *King Lear*, or *Macbeth* exists only as an abstract compounded of all its instances. 'Shakespearian writing is no longer presented as a closed, original, and seminal utterance; it is constant and multiple production.'[73]

Certainly, this 'medieval' model for textual authority – or, rather, the absence thereof – is particularly well suited to the ballads in English. In this manner the circle can be squared: ballads can be understood as texts in Stock's sense of being not always written down but being understood as if they were, but also as texts that can accommodate variation which may be variously accidental or deliberate. Variation, in turn, though not evidently bounded by an identifiable authority such as the name of an author, is nonetheless in practice constrained by, it would seem, a mutual sense of textual community. That is to say, a shared set of understandings and expectations ensures that in practice a ballad does remain recognizable from one instance to another, one rendition to the next, and that ballad transmission is actually fairly conservative. Empirically, this means that ballad types demonstrate relative stability across time and space, even while their versions can be distinguished one from another – and that variation is present between texts transmitted orally and/or in print, without distinction.

---

70 H. J. Chaytor, *From Script to Print: An Introduction to Medieval Literature* (Cambridge: Cambridge University Press, 1945), pp. 13–21.

71 Cerquiglini, *In Praise of the Variant*, pp. 84–85 n. 10. See Paul Zumthor, *Essai de poétique médiévale* (Paris: Éditions du Seuil, 1972), p. 507; Paul Zumthor, *La lettre et la voix: De la 'littérature' médiévale* (Paris: Éditions du Seuil, 1987), p. 160.

72 Cerquiglini, *In Praise of the Variant*, p. 39.

73 Cerquiglini, *In Praise of the Variant*, p. 39. See further John Jowett, *Shakespeare and Text* (Oxford: Oxford University Press, 2007).

Some ballads have remained quite recognizable, in some cases even down to verbal details, over a period of as much as half a millennium. Either end of that time span might be marked by a record in the form of writing (and at the latter end recorded sound), but frequently there is rather little evidence as to precisely what went on in between. Such ballads may have been written down and/or printed, or they may have been recalled from memory, or more probably there is a largely unknown history of interaction of these processes through time. That is to say, they were not always written down, but they could have been – the converse of which is that they were not always memorized, but they could have been. Both processes permit access to the text, and both can be expected to leave deliberate or accidental textual traces on it – formulaic language, recurrent structural patterns, deictic markers, moralizing conclusions, purposeful variants, as well as the arguably more casual effects of 'faulty' memory and typesetting, and so on and so forth. Cerquiglini asserts, 'in the Middle Ages the literary work was a variable', and his chapter title celebrates the condition as one of 'joyful excess'.[74] We now know that in one sense or another *Hamlet* and *King Lear* and *Ulysses* are variables, too. The textuality of the English-language ballads was characterized by *variance* well before the idea began to adhere to such literary icons.

---

74 Cerquiglini, *In Praise of the Variant*, p. 33.

4. The Material Ballad

In a piece titled 'Of the obseruation, and vse of things', the courtier, diplomat, and essayist Sir William Cornwallis (*c*.1579–1614) wrote:

> Pamphlets and lying Stories and News and twoo penny Poets, I would know them but beware of beeing familiar with them. My custome is to read these and presently to make vse of them. For they lie in my priuy; and when I come thither and haue occasion to imploy it, I read them (halfe a side at once is my ordinary), which when I haue read it, I vse in that kind that waste paper is most subiect too but to a cleanlier profit.[1]

There is little doubt that the early modern broadside ballads fall into Cornwallis's category, and his observations are a salutary reminder that paper itself was for a long time a physical commodity the value of which could easily outweigh the aesthetic value of whatever was printed on it.[2] Still, although the need for paper for hygienic purposes remained, we might imagine that lower down the social scale a greater intrinsic value could have attached to the broadside or chapbook as physical object, a prized possession to be preserved rather than used in the privy.[3]

---

1   Don Cameron Allen, ed., *Essayes by Sir William Cornwallis, the Younger* (Baltimore: Johns Hopkins Press, 1946), p. 50. As an aside, at a later date, when the Cheap Repository Tracts were introduced at the end of the eighteenth century, the chapmen who distributed them insisted from the beginning that they be printed on soft paper, so that they would find takers even if they were never read. See William St Clair, *The Reading Nation in the Romantic Period* (Cambridge: Cambridge University Press, 2004), p. 354. Since the Cheap Repository Tracts were intended to price out the long-standing ballads and chapbooks and replace them with their own moral tales, this is a rather gratifying observation.

2   St Clair, *Reading Nation*, pp. 26–27; Margaret Spufford, *Small Books and Pleasant Histories: Popular Fiction and its Readership in Seventeenth-Century England* (Cambridge: Cambridge University Press, 1981), pp. 48–50.

3   It is a little difficult to cite evidence on precisely this point (due to the absence of items of such small value from wills and inventories), but ownership of ballads and chapbooks among the common people of early modern England is nonetheless quite well documented. See Spufford, *Small Books and Pleasant Histories*, pp. 45–82. For a later period, see David Vincent, *Literacy and Popular Culture: England 1750–1914* (Cambridge: Cambridge University Press, 1989), pp. 61–62.

http://dx.doi.org/10.11647/OBP.0041.04

Another kind of value to the physical ballad lies in the fact that broadsides were normally illustrated with woodcut images, and could thus be used to provide a cheap form of decoration.[4] The practice of pasting ballads on to the walls of alehouses and domestic dwellings is well attested. Izaak Walton, for example, writes in *The Compleat Angler* (1653), 'I'll now lead you to an honest Ale-house, where we shall find a cleanly room, Lavender in the windowes, and twenty Ballads stuck about the wall'.[5] Decoration did not, of course, preclude reading. In *The Spectator*, no. 85 (7 June 1711), the paper in which he goes on to discuss the ballad of 'The Children in the Wood' (Roud 288), Addison observes:

> This my inquisitive Temper, or rather impertinent Humour of prying into all sorts of Writing, with my natural Aversion to Loquacity, give me a good deal of Employment when I enter any House in the Country; for I can't, for my Heart, leave a Room before I have thoroughly studied the Walls of it, and examined the several printed Papers which are usually pasted upon them.[6]

At a later date, the memoirs of the writer Thomas Holcroft (1745–1809) recall how such ballads formed an integral part of his early education:

> Even the walls of cottages and little alehouses would do something; for many of them had old English ballads, such as Death and the Lady, and Margaret's Ghost, with lamentable tragedies, or King Charles's golden rules, occasionally pasted on them. These were at that time the learning, and often, no doubt, the delight of the vulgar.[7]

Educated gentlemen like Addison and Cornwallis (but probably not the young Holcroft) might have read ballads silently to themselves, but throughout the period covered by these quotations and beyond, reading would have generally meant reading out loud.

The physical presence of the ballad, it seems safe to assume, must have been both unavoidable and unremarkable for virtually the whole of the time during which printed broadsides and chapbooks were in common circulation, say from the sixteenth to the nineteenth century. Certainly, for the booksellers and printers, and for the pedlars and chapmen who

---

4 Hyder E. Rollins, 'The Black-Letter Broadside Ballad', *PMLA*, 34 (1919), 258–339 (pp. 336–38); Tessa Watt, *Cheap Print and Popular Piety, 1550–1640* (Cambridge: Cambridge University Press, 1991), pp. 148–49, 194.
5 [Izaak Walton], *The Compleat Angler; or, The Contemplative Man's Recreation* (London: printed by T. Maxey, for Rich. Marriot, 1653), p. 49 [ESTC R202374].
6 Angus Ross, ed., *Selections from The Tatler and The Spectator of Steele and Addison* (Harmondsworth: Penguin, 1982), p, 362.
7 Thomas Holcroft, *Memoirs of the Late Thomas Holcroft*, 3 vols (London: Longman, Hurst, Rees, Orme, and Brown, 1816), I, 135–36.

were responsible for their dissemination during much of their history, ballads were first and foremost material objects to be carried and sold around the country.[8] The materiality of texts has become the concern of literary scholars engaged in the now well-established discipline that is sometimes termed *l'histoire du livre*, or materialist criticism, or analytical bibliography. In practice, this embraces a continuum of concerns, from the cultural and economic history of book production, distribution, and preservation, through the sociology of texts, to the signifying functions of physical characteristics such as typography, layout, design, and illustration, paper and binding, iterations of editions, and so forth.[9] These last are sometimes termed 'bibliographic codes' – that is, 'the symbolic and signifying dimensions of the physical medium through which (or rather *as* which) the linguistic text is embodied'.[10] The application of this approach to the ballad poses certain special problems, because in principle a single ballad text, both words and music, can simultaneously inhabit a number of material formats. Thus sound can exist in performance and in various recording media and digital files, while writing can exist as manuscript, as print, and again as digital files. This sort of multiplicity requires careful differentiation if signifying characteristics are to be elucidated from such a range of physical forms.

In the first instance, a 'text' can be defined as a unique sequence of words and pauses, or of musical notes and pauses.[11] Generally, such definitions go

---

8   With respect to the ballad, the 'middlemen of literature' (in Robert Darnton's phrase), and in particular the chapman distribution network, would benefit from much further research. See, for example, Margaret Spufford, 'The Pedlar, the Historian and the Folklorist: Seventeenth Century Communications', *Folklore*, 105 (1994), 13–24; St Clair, *Reading Nation*, pp. 37–39; Andrew Taylor, *The Songs and Travels of a Tudor Minstrel: Richard Sheale of Tamworth* (York: York Medieval Press, 2012), pp. 1–2, 19–28.

9   See, for example, Thomas R. Adams and Nicolas Barker, 'A New Model for the Study of the Book', in *A Potencie of Life: Books in Society*, ed. Nicolas Barker (London: British Library; New Castle, DE: Oak Knoll Press, 1993), pp. 5–43; Robert Darnton, 'What Is the History of Books?', *Daedalus*, 111.3 (1982), 65–83; D. F. McKenzie, *Bibliography and the Sociology of Texts* (Cambridge: Cambridge University Press, 1999); D. F. McKenzie, *Making Meaning: 'Printers of the Mind' and Other Essays*, ed. Peter D. McDonald and Michael F. Suarez (Amherst and Boston: University of Massachusetts Press, 2002). The economic approach developed in St Clair, *Reading Nation*, also belongs here.

10 Jerome J. McGann, *The Textual Condition* (Princeton: Princeton University Press, 1991), p. 56. See also Peter L. Shillingsburg, *From Gutenberg to Google: Electronic Representations of Literary Texts* (Cambridge: Cambridge University Press, 2006), pp. 16–18.

11 This definition is pared down and adapted from Peter L. Shillingsburg, *Scholarly Editing in the Computer Age: Theory and Practice*, 3rd edn (Ann Arbor: University of Michigan Press, 1996), p. 46: 'A text is the actual order of words and punctuation as contained in any one physical form, such as manuscript, proof, or book.'

on to specify that this sequence must be contained within a single physical form – that is to say, an individual item comprising a discrete physical medium, such as a manuscript, a printed book, a phonograph cylinder, LP record, or CD. This 'vessel', as it were, that contains the text is termed a 'document'. This is very important: because it is often difficult to conceive of a text in isolation from its physical form, the 'vessel' or document that it inhabits, it is all too easy to conflate the two separate concepts of text and document. The distinction, however, is not impossible to maintain, if only because exactly the same sequence of words, or musical notes, can inhabit such different physical entities as a collector's notebook and a phonograph cylinder.[12] Ideally, a collector's accurate transcription of a ballad and a sound recording of the same rendition would contain exactly the same text, but within a quite distinct physical container or document. So it is possible to abstract the text from its physical container, even if it requires some considerable exercise of the imagination in order to do so. But it is certainly very difficult then to do anything with it that does not involve either simply placing it back into the same container, or transferring it into a different one. To consider a text is in practice almost necessarily to allude also to the document within which it is contained – the 'packaging' that necessarily surrounds it – so that the unit of discussion is commonly what might be termed the 'documentary text'.[13]

In the case of a ballad that is simply sung or recited out loud, the physical document is comprised, not of sequential written or printed marks on paper, the contoured grooves on a phonograph cylinder, or etched pits and lands on a CD, but of sequential vibrations in air – the invisible, gaseous, but nonetheless physical substance that surrounds us. To be sure, the document that is a ballad performance is ephemeral.[14] Its transience as a document, however, is nonetheless exactly comparable with that of the grooves of a phonograph cylinder, the wax substrate of which might be shaved in order

---

12 Shillingsburg, *Scholarly Editing*, p. 47, likewise allows that the same text can be stored in more than one place, using more than one set of signs (such as written words, impulses on magnetic tape, or digital 1s and 0s).

13 Peter L. Shillingsburg, *Resisting Texts: Authority and Submission in Constructions of Meaning* (Ann Arbor: University of Michigan Press, 1997), pp. 73–74, uses the term 'material text' to refer to the union of text with document, reaffirming the necessity of the physical medium. For the present purpose, it is desirable to maintain at least a conceptual separation of text from document.

14 Towards the end of his life, Guglielmo Marconi is said to have become convinced that sounds once generated never die, but simply become fainter and fainter until they can no longer be detected.

that the cylinder could be reused.[15] Likewise, the pattern of impulses on magnetic recording tape can be destroyed by demagnetizing the tape, and pencil marks on a sheet of paper are always susceptible to being erased. Perhaps it is worth drawing a distinction between these sorts of situations and that of the broadsides that, if Cornwallis is to be believed, ended up as toilet paper. All of these instances witness the destruction of a document, but in the case of those broadsides that would involve the despoilment not just of the writing but of the physical medium, the paper, itself. It is a nice distinction, between what we might call the 'textual carrier' – writing, contoured grooves, etched pits and lands – and the 'substrate' – paper, wax cylinder, magnetic tape, CD.[16] The attenuation of the vibrations in air that carry a sung ballad is not quite to be equated with the degradation of the earth's atmosphere itself.

Early ethnographic collectors using the phonograph habitually treated their recordings as transient documents, the value of which was simply that they would enable the collector to derive an accurate written transcription, which, presumably, was thought of as having greater permanence (and probably precision).[17] Pragmatically, Percy Grainger recommended writing down the words and melodies independently of the phonograph recordings, partly because of the danger of damage to the cylinders, partly because it is not always easy to distinguish unfamiliar words.[18] The texts the cylinders contained were carefully (sometimes not so carefully) transferred from one document to another, and from one form of textual carrier to another, and the cylinders, it seems, were often subsequently discarded – a practice that neatly, albeit incidentally, illustrates the point that it is extremely difficult to dissociate text from an awareness of its physical packaging. It is possible to read at the heart of the Latin tag *littera scripta manet*, 'the written word remains', a simple preference for the stability of some physical substrates

---

15 This was the early practice of the American collector James Madison Carpenter, who began collecting and recording in Britain in 1928 (Washington, DC, Library of Congress, American Folklife Center, Archive of Folk Culture, AFC1972/001, James Madison Carpenter Collection, MS p. 09637).
16 Shillingsburg, *Scholarly Editing*, p. 47, uses the term 'storage medium', which effectively combines textual carrier and substrate.
17 Erika Brady, *A Spiral Way: How the Phonograph Changed Ethnography* (Jackson: University Press of Mississippi, 1999), p. 62; D. K. Wilgus, *Anglo-American Folksong Scholarship since 1898* (New Brunswick, NJ: Rutgers University Press, 1959), p. 232.
18 Percy Grainger, 'Collecting with the Phonograph', *Journal of the Folk-Song Society*, 3.3 (no. 12) (1908), 147–242 (p. 148).

(papyrus, parchment, paper) over the fragility of others (air, wax, magnetic tape, the flimsy metal coatings of CDs).

Conversely, modern approaches to folk literature tend to embody a preference for the more vulnerable substrates associated with sound rather than writing. There are a number of interrelated reasons for this. They include, from a historical perspective, the Enlightenment 'discovery' of oral tradition and the opening up of a perceived dichotomy between orality and literacy, which has enabled oral tradition to continue to enjoy iconic status. From a more theoretical perspective, the preference for sound over writing in the study of the ballad can be considered as a (rather minor) subset of 'phonocentrism', the general precedence that, Derrida argues, has been afforded to speech over writing in Western metaphysics.[19] The study of folklore, in some manifestations at least, has seen a shift away from the study of texts of any sort and towards context, performance, and ethnography.[20] Finally, there is the mere fact that ballads, folktales, and the like are susceptible to vocal performance, which is the source of much aesthetic pleasure – and which in the ballad case gives access to the melody, which in its written form is frequently inaccessible to the non-specialist. Nevertheless, these are simply not very good arguments for the primacy of the substrates associated with sound over those associated with writing.

An acknowledgement of the significance of documentary media is scarcely a new idea. Marshall McLuhan's famous (if not unproblematic) dictum 'the medium is the message' provides the classic expression of this insight.[21] Nevertheless, the physical packaging of ballad texts remains worthy of further consideration. Here, the work of Harold Innis, a notable influence on McLuhan, who considered the 'bias' towards either time or space that is inherent in different systems of communication, provides a useful starting point.[22] Thus stone tablets bearing hieroglyphs exhibit a strong temporal bias, in that they can endure for millennia, but they cannot readily be transported from one place to another. Conversely, texts written on paper, being light and easily transportable, can be disseminated in space, but their very lightness renders them vulnerable to degradation and loss with time.

---

19 Jacques Derrida, *Of Grammatology*, corrected edn, trans. Gayatri Chakravorty Spivak (Baltimore: Johns Hopkins University Press, 1997).
20 Jeff Todd Titon, 'Text', in *Eight Words for the Study of Expressive Culture*, ed. Burt Feintuch (Urbana and Chicago: University of Illinois Press, 2003), pp. 69–98.
21 Marshall McLuhan, *Understanding Media: The Extensions of Man* (London: Routledge & Kegan Paul, 1964).
22 Harold A. Innis, *The Bias of Communication* ([Toronto]: University of Toronto Press, 1951).

Now, this observed inverse relationship between time and space is not directly transferable to the ballad field. For example, while printed materials disseminated by chapmen and pedlars from early modern times provide one of the readiest explanations for the presence of recognizably similar sets of ballad words in widely separated places, they also provide some of the oldest records of ballads. On the other hand, broadsides rarely carry music notation, although earlier examples do mostly include the name of a tune, and the dissemination of ballad melodies through both space and time is assumed to be largely dependent on an oral/aural communication system. Paradoxically, such a system is the most ephemeral imaginable, in terms of both space and time. Communicative biases certainly are present in ballads when they occur as different kinds of physical documents, but to trace these it is necessary to consider a range of the signifying qualities that are presented by ballads as documents.

Even supposing an ideal situation where the text of a ballad (the sequence of words and pauses, and of musical notes and pauses) is identical whether carried by a written transcription or by a sound recording, and therefore what that text actually 'says' should in principle be unvarying, the documentary signals will be quite different. Most obviously, of course, the textual carriers within the two documents belong to two different semiotic systems. One employs physical marks on paper to be decoded by the human eye and brain; the other, physical arrangements (contoured grooves, patterns of magnetic impulses, etched pits and lands) to be decoded first by a mechanical apparatus and subsequently by the human ear and brain. 'Biases of the ear and eye', in Daniel Chandler's phrase,[23] will therefore operate in the apprehending of even a single ballad text through different semiotic systems.

Even prior to that stage, the moment one is presented with a broadside or a CD, one is faced with a distinct set of requirements and expectations. These are instantly signalled by the packaging, even before any direct reference is made to the respective semiotic system – that is, before the broadside is read, or the CD inserted into the player. It is difficult to compile a systematic list of the ways in which different physical formats give out different signals, but one means of suggesting something of the range is to draw a few ready comparisons between some different documentary formats – in particular, phonograph recordings and printed broadsides,

---

23 Daniel Chandler, 'Biases of the Ear and Eye: "Great Divide" Theories, Phonocentrism, Graphocentrism & Logocentrism' (1994), available at http://www.aber.ac.uk/media/Documents/litoral/litoral.html.

with some mention of modern digital recordings and 'pencil and paper' collecting, along with the ephemeral materiality of performance. Among the properties of documents that suggest themselves for comparison are those of (*i*) permanence, (*ii*) accessibility, (*iii*) precision, and (*iv*) information capacity.

(*i*) Unlike performance, both broadsides and phonograph cylinders constitute documents that signal a degree of permanence, although the broadsides – which, of course, have a much longer history – can more easily be seen to have stood the test of time. Yet it is likely that their cheapness and portability were initially valued more than their potential permanence. Besides their use in the privy, broadsides and all sorts of printed sheets could also be employed as wrapping paper, for book bindings, for lighting fires, and for writing on the verso and in the blank spaces, and it is generally thought that numbers of printed ballads have not survived in so much as a single copy.[24] Nevertheless, time has in some degree vindicated the format. The pasting of broadsides on walls testifies to the fact that at least some contemporary consumers were aware of their potential longevity. And treated with moderate care, especially in libraries and private collections, some broadsides have readily survived four centuries or more.

A phonograph cylinder kept in a suitable conservation environment can equally be expected to last for a long time – that is, so long as it is not often played, for frequent listening to a cylinder can cause damage to both the substrate and the textual carrier. Stylus wear results in loss of signal as well as the acquisition of quantities of extraneous noise. Much the same can, in fact, be said about the effects of playing wear on acetate or vinyl records and on recording tape. Although in the domestic context the textual carrier of a CD is pretty well immune to damage from repeated playing, the protective plastic covering and lacquer film which constitute part of the substrate *in toto* are very vulnerable to scratching, which can on occasion render the whole document unreadable. From an archival point of view, moreover, substrate decay over time, as well as format obsolescence, pose real threats to the longevity of recordable optical media.[25] Wax cylinders

---

24 St Clair, *Reading Nation*, pp. 26–28. Even now, there is no clear answer to the question of what proportion of the ballads printed in any particular historical period have survived or, conversely, been lost.

25 Kevin Bradley, *Risks Associated with the Use of Recordable CDs and DVDs as Reliable Storage Media in Archival Collections – Strategies and Alternatives*, Memory of the World Programme, Sub-Committee on Technology (Paris: UNESCO, 2006), available at http://unesdoc.unesco.org/images/0014/001477/147782E.pdf.

are fragile, easily broken if accidentally dropped, and subject to ageing effects and especially to mould, which can produce auditory artefacts and ultimately render the cylinder unplayable.[26]

In contrast, while reading a broadside necessarily entails some handling, which over a long period of time will cause damage to the substrate, short of it becoming so torn or grimy that the words cannot be read (which can happen), or its being deliberately sabotaged by overwriting, just so long as the substrate remains intact then the textual carrier is likely to remain essentially unimpaired. But the real permanence of the printed broadside lies not just in its relative durability, but in its multiplicity. Print runs for broadsides numbered at least in the thousands,[27] multiplying the chances of survival of the texts inscribed thereon. The wax cylinder and its text, while quite probably treated with much greater care, might also be unique. Elizabeth Eisenstein describes the preservation of texts as perhaps the most important contribution of the printing revolution, and is at pains to point out that this derives not so much from quality as from quantity.[28]

(*ii*) Broadside ballads were readily accessible. They were available at low cost, usually priced at a halfpenny or a penny, and though the relative value of that sum varied over time, the price generally remained low and can be taken as an indicator of access.[29] Ballads were widely distributed by pedlars and hawkers, and by the later eighteenth century they were being issued by booksellers/printers across England and Scotland (and Wales). Ballads, as noted above, were also frequently displayed in public. Broadly, accessibility was a consequence of a comparatively cheap paper substrate and the development of a printing process that permitted the multiple imposition of a textual carrier at low cost, although pricing structures within the book trade at large could be complicated by factors beyond the manufacturing costs alone.[30]

In contrast, phonograph recordings (of ethnographic items such as ballads – we are not concerned here with the wider, commercial phonograph and gramophone market) were relatively expensive manufactured objects, and

---

26 Jonathan Sterne, *The Audible Past: Cultural Origins of Sound Reproduction* (Durham, NC: Duke University Press, 2003), pp. 325–27.
27 Watt, *Cheap Print and Popular Piety*, pp. 11, 52; St Clair, *Reading Nation*, p. 340.
28 Elizabeth L. Eisenstein, *The Printing Revolution in Early Modern Europe*, 2nd edn (Cambridge: Cambridge University Press, 2005), pp. 87–88.
29 Watt, *Cheap Print and Popular Piety*, pp. 11–12 (and see pp. 260–64); St Clair, *Reading Nation*, pp. 40, 343–44.
30 St Clair, *Reading Nation*, pp. 28–29. Some of the variety in format among ballads and chapbooks over time might be related to pricing strategies.

they required mechanical coding and decoding on a suitable, and again relatively expensive, machine.³¹ Several of the early folk song collectors (in fact, probably most of them) at least experimented with phonograph recording, and they shared access to the machines.³² The practicalities of transporting the heavy machine and the controlled conditions required for recording imposed spatial limitations on its use, although at various times recordings were made, for example, on the Isle of Skye and in rural Wales, as well as in various places in England. Phonograph cylinders are essentially unique items. The machines themselves were never exactly common and have now become quite rare, imposing a further limitation on the pragmatic longevity of the texts they were used to create. Although digitization has facilitated the (still relatively limited) redistribution of the recordings, it has done so only by transferring the texts to another substrate and carrier – another kind of packaging which, as already suggested, poses problems of its own in relation to the issue of permanence, even if it helps address that of accessibility. Unlike the wide geographical distribution of broadsides and chapbooks, that of phonograph recordings was strictly limited.

Recording technologies at large have accorded to sound the quality of reproducibility, which was long regarded as the particular characteristic of written words and musical notations. This has been a gradual process, however, reaching its fruition well after the close of the period of phonograph recording. On the other hand, once set up to play, in principle anyone could access phonographic sound, whereas access to a printed broadside requires that at least someone possess the basic ability to read it. To some extent, in the past this potential obstacle was bypassed by virtue of the ballads being sung or recited by their vendors, as well as through the existence of the 'reading communities' discussed in chapter three. Right up to the twentieth century, the presence of cheap print of the broadside kind – and also such things as newspapers, magazines, hand-bills, and

---

31 Phonographic recording machines were eventually manufactured in substantial numbers for the office dictation market (where 'dictaphone' was used as a generic term), and it was such a machine that J. M. Carpenter used for his collecting in Britain in the late 1920s/1930s.

32 C. J. Bearman, 'Percy Grainger, the Phonograph, and the Folk Song Society', *Music & Letters*, 84 (2003), 434–55; C. J. Bearman, 'The Folk-Song Society and the Phonograph', *Folk Music Journal*, 10.3 (2013), 370–74. For an interesting account of phonographic recording by collectors in Slovenia before the First World War, see Drago Kunej, '"We have plenty of words written down; we need melodies!": The Purchase of the First Recording Device for Ethnomusicological Research in Slovenia', *Traditiones* [Ljubljana], 34.1 (2005), 125–40.

so forth – signalled not so much the activity of private, silent reading, as that of communal, oral, reading aloud, recitation, or even singing. The phonograph, in contrast, remained a more socially privileged technology.

(*iii*) Phonograph recording required particular environmental conditions in order to be successful. The wax, for instance, needed to be reasonably warm in order to retain its plasticity. Cecil Sharp expressed reservations about the tendency of the phonograph to blur words and to emphasize certain consonants more than others; Anne Gilchrist made similar observations and criticized the machine's limited dynamic range.[33] Modern authorities have endorsed such reservations, additionally pointing out such things as the frequency limitations of the machine.[34] Even Percy Grainger, often portrayed as the champion of the phonograph, was prepared to concede some of these points.[35] Thus the precision of wax cylinder recordings is strictly limited.[36] On the other hand, they can certainly preserve elements of musical style, vocal ornamentation, and so forth, which are extremely difficult to represent graphically in stave notation. Grainger's phonograph recordings of Joseph Taylor and other Lincolnshire singers provide a prime illustration of this capability.[37] His own complex notations of some of the same songs offer a direct point of comparison and invite debate as to whether notation on paper really is capable of attaining the same degree of precision.[38]

Conversely, printed broadsides generally attain a high degree of precision in the representation of ballad words. Of course, such faults as typographical errors, as well as broken or turned letters, can occur, type can fall out, or a printer can set nonsense.[39] By and large, though, the verbal infidelities that do arise are not sufficient to inhibit comprehension, and

---

33 London, EFDSS Archives, Cecil Sharp Collection, Correspondence, Cecil Sharp to Percy Grainger, 23 May 1908 (photocopy); Anne Gilchrist Collection, AGG/8/142, Anne Gilchrist to Lucy Broadwood, 1 and 2 June 1908.

34 Bearman, 'Percy Grainger, the Phonograph, and the Folk Song Society', pp. 441–42. See further Drago Kunej, 'Digitised Early Sound Recordings as Scholarly Resources', in *Trapped in Folklore? Studies in Music and Dance Tradition and their Contemporary Transformations*, ed. Drago Kunej and Urša Šivic (Wien: Lit Verlag, 2013), pp. 181–96.

35 Grainger, 'Collecting with the Phonograph', pp. 148–49.

36 On the pursuit of fidelity in sound recording at large, see Sterne, *Audible Past*, pp. 215–86.

37 Some of these can be heard on *Unto Brigg Fair: Joseph Taylor and Other Traditional Lincolnshire Singers Recorded in 1908 by Percy Grainger*, 12-inch LP (London: Leader LEA 4050, 1972).

38 See Grainger, 'Collecting with the Phonograph'.

39 Rollins, 'Black-Letter Broadside Ballad', p. 263, observes (with perhaps a degree of licence): 'the [earlier, black-letter] broadsides abound in typographical errors hardly less grotesque and absurd than the amazing woodcuts that embellished the sheets'.

while they undeniably fall short of the aim of complete precision, they are often much less serious than the shortcomings of phonograph recordings. Broadsides do not generally carry music notation, but many of the earlier examples do carry a tune direction, 'To the tune of . . .'. This can be taken as a sufficient shorthand representation, at least for anyone familiar with the melody under the title given. A number of late seventeenth- and eighteenth-century broadsides do carry notation, although there is some reason to think that this is sometimes (though certainly not always) decorative in purpose and musically either nonsensical or misleading. Later broadsides mostly do not carry even an indication of the tune, which has to be counted as a loss. A number of popular tunes would have been accessible from other published sources, such as Playford's dance and music books, and anthologies like Johnson's *Scots Musical Museum*. Presumably, though, the general assumption was that the tune would either be known or else learned from the ballad seller.[40]

At that point, print and performance are closely connected. Performance, however, remains crucially dependent on individual skill, in both the handling of melody and the pronunciation of words, to transmit a ballad text with precision. A garbled word can be much harder to make out than a poorly printed one, a badly rendered tune more difficult to interpret than a scribbled notation. It is not a matter of chance that written or printed words and music have proven to be the favoured tools for scholarly analysis (well beyond the field of ballad studies). The precision of performance is also constrained by environmental factors such as extraneous noise, acoustic properties of the location, physical distance or barriers that might otherwise interfere with transmission of a transient, once-only signal. These are considerations that can impact upon sound recordings, too – even the most sophisticated of modern digital recordings.[41]

(*iv*) Both sound recordings and printed documents carry large quantities of information both integral to and supplementary or complementary to the verbal and musical text. Vocal inflections and marks of punctuation, for example, can impart elements of interpretation, such as a lift in the voice or the presence of a question mark at the end of a sentence. These things can

---

40 See Anthony Bennett, 'Sources of Popular Song in Early Nineteenth-Century Britain: Problems and Methods of Research', *Popular Music*, 2 (1982), 69–89 (pp. 77–78).
41 The fact that the digital signal is only ever an approximation to its analogue original, and the subsequent reconversion to analogue form involves a further approximation, may not impact discernibly upon the issue of textual precision, but should presumably trouble anyone overly concerned with 'authenticity' in the abstract.

reasonably be regarded as integral to the text. Written or printed texts often provide substantial punctuation, indicating such things as a change of speaker through the presence of quotation marks (which just occasionally can prove more ambiguous than otherwise). Conversely, the absence of audible punctuation from sound recordings might invite uncertainty or confusion, but might also preserve a fluidity that can be thought of as integral to ballad texts.

Typographic layout organizes ballad narratives into blocks of lines and stanzas which correspond (most of the time) to syntactic units – a kind of punctuation by spatial layout. At the level of the stanza, though less so at that of the line, this effect is paralleled in sound by the strophic nature of ballad tunes. Just occasionally, too, such patterns may prove disconcerting. Most ballad lines are in some degree end-stopped, with sense and metre coinciding in a pause at the line end, so that the rare case of enjambement, where the sense requires the eye to run on beyond the end of the line without a pause, can come as something of a jolt (and even more so where the syntax actually runs across a stanza break). This sort of occasion prompts a readjustment of expectations on the part of the reader, which may be either inhibited or facilitated by typography – inhibited by the stanza break, or facilitated by the absence of the expected full point. Layout, spelling, and punctuation all enable the closer interrogation of texts, and in very much the same way the details of musical notation enable the analysis of melodies.

While the symbols of musical notation and of writing or print are readily considered as integral to the texts they represent, this is not the case with all the kinds of information that can be carried by a document. The gothic typeface of a black-letter broadside, for example, which can be considered as merely ancillary to the physical nature of the textual carrier, nonetheless also signifies something about the historicity of both the document and the text it contains.[42] Indeed, the entire *mise en page*, or *mise en livre*, of the broadside situates the document within the economic and ideological history of cheap print, just as the scratchiness of the sound from a phonograph recording situates the document within the early history of recording technology. Similarly, the handwriting in a manuscript or collector's notebook can signify care taken in transcription, perhaps distinguishing a fair copy from a rough copy, thus signalling the

---

42 See Charles C. Mish, 'Black Letter as a Social Discriminant in the Seventeenth Century', *PMLA*, 68 (1953), 627–30; St Clair, *Reading Nation*, p. 341.

relative authority of the text. Information of this kind largely takes on its significance with a historical perspective, which is akin to saying that its signification is in some sense accidental. The information capacity of documents need not necessarily be reflective of 'intention'.

Characteristics such as the vocal quality or timbre of a performance or on a recording might also be compared with the choice of typeface on a broadside. The presence of woodcuts and other decorations might be considered roughly equivalent to some of the other kinds of information that can accompany sound, such as movement, gesture, and body language. (Broadside woodcuts, it is perhaps worth observing, are entirely separable from the accompanying words and, it seems, were sometimes used as wall decorations in their own right.[43]) Fieldworkers often value video recording for its capacity to capture a wide range of extratextual information generated during a performance and to facilitate its analysis. These are all further examples of the capacity for documents to carry supplementary signifying information that is, strictly speaking, outside of the domain of text as it has been defined here.

Clearly, many or all of the aspects touched on in the foregoing comparative remarks could be elaborated in much more detail, but the purpose of this admittedly rather impressionistic account of permanence, accessibility, precision, and information capacity in documents is simply to point to some of the ways in which performance, print, and sound recordings bring with them their own sets of expectations. They do not conform in a straightforward manner with Innis's model of communication systems and its inverse biases towards time and space, although there is perhaps a trade-off to be discerned between time and space on the one hand, and information capacity on the other. This is especially apparent when the extratextual capacity of live performance is considered against its ephemeral nature. Conversely (from the present historical standpoint), although printed broadsides appear biased towards the dimensions of accessibility and permanence, an awareness of the importance of the broadside bibliographic code(s) expands greatly the range of information that can be read from the document.

A consequence of these sorts of comparisons, then, is to pose a challenge to the idea that primacy can necessarily be ascribed to any particular documentary format, to any one or other substrate. Scholars of an

---

43 Barry Reay, 'The Context and Meaning of Popular Literacy: Some Evidence from Nineteenth-Century Rural England', *Past and Present*, no. 131 (1991), 89–129 (p. 116).

ethnographic persuasion, for instance, are perhaps likely to hold that the primary manifestation of the ballad is in performance. Failing that, a sound recording might represent the primary document for the realization and preservation of the ballad text (as opposed, say, to a collector's notation). That position no doubt embodies an underlying deference to phonocentrism, but more immediately it reflects the ethnographic interest in aspects of performance (style, expression, vocal quality) that, strictly speaking, lie outside the ballad text per se. Yet, as has already been noted, written or printed words and music are the favoured tools for the critical analysis of words and melody. Other researchers might be equally interested in the physical characteristics of a collector's notation or, more likely, the typeface and illustrations of a broadside print. These are all things that are preserved in documents, and all make a substantial contribution to the historical, aesthetic, and intellectual import of the various kinds of whole. It is incomplete to consider the ballad in isolation from its 'packaging'.

The pursuit of a single ballad text through all of its potential documentary formats further demonstrates just how misleading it would be to ascribe 'intention' to it. The ballad text in this scenario is simply an intangible object that can migrate from one documentary format to another. History, it is worth observing, has quite undermined the charge that Margaret Laidlaw, James Hogg's mother, is supposed to have laid against Walter Scott: 'there war never ane o' my sangs prentit till ye prentit them yoursel', an' ye hae spoilt them awthegither. They war made for singing an' no for reading; but ye hae broken the charm now, an' they'll never be sung mair. An' the worst thing of a', they're nouther right spell'd nor right setten down.'[44] The text of this famous anecdote exists in another version which omits the claim that 'ye hae broken the charm now, an' they'll never be sung mair'.[45] But perhaps even more curious is the paradox it embodies (in both versions): the ballads were 'intended' only to be sung, and yet there was nonetheless a 'correct' way to transfer them into print ('right spell'd' and 'right setten down'), of which Scott was accused of having fallen short.[46] The question of sound versus writing is considered in chapter five. Meanwhile, a broadside can equally serve to decorate a wall as to preserve for future generations a

---

[44] James Hogg, *Memoir of the Author's Life* and *Familiar Anecdotes of Sir Walter Scott*, ed. Douglas S. Mack (Edinburgh: Scottish Academic Press, 1972), p. 137.

[45] Hogg, *Memoir* and *Familiar Anecdotes*, p. 62.

[46] See further Valentina Bold, '"Nouther right spelled nor right setten down": Scott, Child and the Hogg Family Ballads', in *The Ballad in Scottish History*, ed. Edward J. Cowan (East Linton: Tuckwell Press, 2000), pp. 116–41.

set of ballad words and at least the name of a tune. A collector's notebook may be used to analyse narrative and melody or it may simply be put away indefinitely in an archive. And while either of those paper-based documents could enable someone to sing the ballad again, either could just as easily be used to make a shopping list or to wrap a parcel – while the vibrations in the air that constituted a performance have long since attenuated beyond the possibility of detection.

One of the things that this brief consideration of material properties of the ballad is intended to underline is that the text itself – at least in the idealized scenario proposed, where it remains the same from one format to another – is to all intents and purposes intangible. Short of some kind of imaginary telepathic transfer, the text cannot be either expressed or transmitted without the packaging of a physical document, be it a performance, sound recording, printed sheet, or something else. All of those physical documents signify in different ways, so that it becomes extremely difficult to prioritize between forms of ballad 'packaging'. Rather than comprising a hierarchy of documents, then, each contributes to an intangible idea of what *is* the ballad.

Scholarship is familiar with the perspective of 'version' and 'type', and is beginning to awaken to the problems inherent in the notion of 'version' vis-à-vis the particular instance or intellectual item – each rendition by the same singer, or each copy of the same broadside printing, for example – which is by definition materially different and therefore distinguishable from any other. There is a parallel here with Leo Treitler's idea of 'exemplification' to describe the status of the individual, and potentially variant, written score in the ontology (that is to say, the nature and conditions of identity or being) of works in Western art music:

> Obviously we can't read any one of these scores as unique identifier of the work, or denotation of the sound pattern that must be executed to produce a flawless performance of the work. Each score can do no more than exemplify the work. In some traditions exemplification is the main task of scores. In such a tradition identification and instruction are accomplished only indirectly, through exemplification. The score in such a tradition is functionally and ontologically parallel, at the same theoretical level, with the performance. The questions 'what is this piece' and 'how does it go' could both be answered either by writing out a score or by making a performance.[47]

---

[47] Leo Treitler, 'History and the Ontology of the Musical Work', in *With Voice and Pen: Coming to Know Medieval Song and How It Was Made* (Oxford: Oxford University Press, 2003), pp. 298–316 (p. 312).

What Treitler is arguing here is that the individual documentary text, which in this instance comprises a score, merely 'exemplifies' the larger, abstract whole that is the musical work – which might equally be exemplified by another score, a performance, or a recording.

The crucial distinction here is between on the one hand the concrete exemplification, and on the other the work as an imagined whole. But the imaginary entity that is a musical or literary work is itself founded upon whatever exemplification(s) of it happen(s) to be available to any particular individual. This may be, for example, the originator, an editor, a reader, or a listener – whose access to particular exemplifications, and whose perspectives on the whole, can be expected to vary accordingly.[48] Treitler's precise equation of score with performance places two quite different kinds of documentary text on exactly the same theoretical level, each to stand as a concrete and discrete exemplification of the work. His score and performance, in the ideal situation, might contain exactly the same sequence of musical notes and pauses (and, on occasion, words and pauses as well) – that is to say, the same text – in just the same way as, say, the idealized collector's notation and phonograph recording imagined earlier in this chapter. Yet there is little doubt that the respective documents – the score written or printed on paper, and the performance sounded through the air of the concert hall – will continue to signify in very different ways.

In 'History and the Ontology of the Musical Work', Treitler is also seeking to demonstrate that multiplicity does in fact pervade Western art music – to redress the view that works have been 'cast once and for all by a composer in a final form that is represented in a score and presented essentially unchanged in performances'.[49] In fact, the 'work concept', exemplified by the music of Beethoven, is a product of the history of musical practice and aesthetics which only emerged c.1800.[50] Nevertheless, it has become a more or less accepted principle of musical aesthetics (or at least of the aesthetics of Western art music) and it more or less effectively closes off the notion of multiplicity. Treitler maintains, however, that it is not in fact difficult to find exceptions to disprove the assumed rule that the musical work is

---

48 Shillingsburg, *Scholarly Editing*, pp. 42–44.
49 Treitler, 'History and Ontology', p. 301. It is only right to record that Treitler adds, in parentheses, 'Everything depends, of course, on what lies beneath that word, "essentially"' (p. 301), since every performance is necessarily in some way unique.
50 Lydia Goehr, *The Imaginary Museum of Musical Works: An Essay in the Philosophy of Music*, rev. edn (New York: Oxford University Press, 2007).

determinate, fixed once and for all by its composer. He cites examples such as Stockhausen's *Klavierstück XI*, where the order of the sections is determined only by the performer at the moment of performance, or a particular performance of a raga by Ali Akbar Khan – and it is not difficult to imagine further examples from genres such as jazz and blues. Multiplicity, moreover, is to be found not just among items that can be realized only in live performance, that are not cast into a final form represented in a score, and where the text can reasonably be expected to vary from one instance to the next, but also among items from the mainstream of Western art music. Treitler points to pieces by Chopin, such as the *Nocturne in B major*, op. 62, no. 1, which exist (or have existed) in several variant forms, both in writing and in print, as well as in performance. Textual indeterminacy in a work like the Chopin *Nocturne* can be directly compared with that encountered in medieval chant, as well as in more modern, more 'experimental' pieces. Even in rock music, an item as it is performed can vary considerably from a supposedly 'definitive' recording.

As we saw in chapter one, these ideas of textual indeterminacy lend themselves well to the ballad situation, with regard to types and versions, and transmission and reinterpretations. What is being added to the argument here is an emphasis on the material aspect of the items that fall under the umbrella of the work. For Treitler and for Western art music, these are primarily score and performance. The ballads, too, are nothing if not multifarious in the documentary sense. When one reads a collector's manuscript notebook or a printed broadside, places a CD in the player, or attends a performance, the action is accompanied by a set of expectations that are to an important extent dependent on the nature of the substrate and textual carrier that provide the material base for the document in question. Each of these different documents offers a distinct exemplification of the ballad as work, even in the ideal instance where the text remains identical from one document to the next. In that idealized situation, the different documents all provide different access routes to the same thing, but together they render its realization increasingly rich and rounded – permanent and accessible, accurate and detailed, filled out with extratextual information, present to both eye and ear. Indeed, one reason for the resilience of ballad words and music can be posited to lie in their ability to inhabit different material formats – different documents – and to move with apparent ease between them.

Treitler also maintains that the perceived boundaries of the work are historically determined, that they can and do change with time and historical circumstance.⁵¹ Modern performers, he observes, tend not to stray from the published scores of Chopin and are usually unaware of the extent to which their predecessors did so. While the ontology of the ballad is informed by the entire range of its actual and potential documentary exemplifications, the conception is also potentially subject to change over time. Thus recorded sound is a fairly recent phenomenon, while the modern publication of ballad books scarcely matches up to the ubiquity of broadsides in, say, the seventeenth, eighteenth, or nineteenth centuries.⁵² Concerning the extent of actual performances, we are sadly under-informed for the earlier periods, but it is at least worth observing that the elevation of sound to primary status in ballad ontology coincides with the long decline of broadside publication after the middle of the nineteenth century.

Prior to and after a period from, say, the end of the nineteenth century up until the Second World War, as well as being something you (or someone else) might sing, the ballad was something you could pick up and hold in your hand. Earlier, that would have taken the form of a broadside or chapbook; later, it would be a record of some kind, an LP or a CD. During that putative interval in the first part of the twentieth century, there were both publications and recordings, but, for a combination of technological and economic reasons, they were probably rather more thin on the ground. The interval in question happens to coincide with the folk song revival, when large numbers of songs were collected from a supposedly oral tradition, while many (though not all) of the collectors themselves were uneasy about such printed broadside copies as they did encounter. It is a moot point as to whether it would really be possible to draw a causal correlation between the documentary environment and the ideological impulses behind the folk song revival, but it does look as if there was at least something of a temporal correlation.⁵³ It is certainly

---

51 Treitler, 'History and Ontology', p. 316.
52 A proper account of broadside history has yet to be written. For sound recording, Sterne, *Audible Past*, is excellent.
53 Yet broadsides were still in commercial circulation around the end of the nineteenth century in England, and somewhat later in Scotland, and it is quite possible that their presence was deliberately played down. This may well be one of the more accurate insights into the revival provided by the revisionist thesis. See Dave Harker, *Fakesong: The Manufacture of British 'Folksong', 1700 to the Present Day* (Milton Keynes: Open University Press, 1985), esp. pp. 141, 182, 193–94.

easier to overlook the material nature of a singer's performance than of a broadside ballad.[54] If it is correct that the perceived boundaries of the work are historically contingent – and the argument certainly appears both sensible and convincing – then it is at least worth giving some consideration to ways in which the timing of the folk song movement might have impacted on its direction and content.

---

54 And of a digital download than of an LP or CD – encouraging, perhaps, an illusory sense in some quarters of a late return to a pre-Gutenberg heyday.

5. Sound and Writing

As previous chapters have insisted, the ballad has coexisted in different media from early modern times right up to the present day. Although we know comparatively little for certain about the practice of ballad singing prior to the folk song revivals, there is no real reason to doubt that ballads were sung from an early date.[1] So, for four centuries and more, we can take it that the written ballad has happily coexisted with its vocal performance. More recently, however, the assumption has gained hold that the written ballad is, or ought to be, conceptually tied to its vocal performance. This is almost certainly a twentieth-century phenomenon, attributable in no small part to Bertrand Bronson's advocacy of 'the ballad as song' and his definitional challenge: '*Question*: When is a ballad not a ballad? *Answer*: When it has no tune.'[2] Bronson, however, was reacting against a scholarly legacy that had paid little attention to the music of the ballads, and he was perhaps led to overstate his case. In fact, a hierarchy of ballad documentation that seeks to privilege sound is misleading, because the ballad has always been, and remains, accessible through complementary media which fulfil different purposes and follow different conventions – all leading towards the position that different and complementary sets of instructions can quite independently facilitate access to the intangible ballad.

An earlier version of this chapter was published as 'Sound and Writing: Complementary Facets of the Anglo-Scottish Ballad', *Twentieth-Century Music*, 7 (2010), 139–65, and the material is reused with permission.

1   Vic Gammon, *Desire, Drink and Death in English Folk and Vernacular Song, 1600–1900* (Aldershot and Burlington, VT: Ashgate, 2008), pp. 10–11; Christopher Marsh, *Music and Society in Early Modern England* (Cambridge: Cambridge University Press, 2010), chapters 5, 6.
2   Bertrand Harris Bronson, *The Traditional Tunes of the Child Ballads*, 4 vols (Princeton: Princeton University Press, 1959–72), I, ix–xiii (the famous question and answer are on p. ix). See also Bertrand Harris Bronson, *The Ballad as Song* (Berkeley and Los Angeles: University of California Press, 1969).

Landmark figures in the history of ballad scholarship such as Francis James Child, his Scottish predecessor William Motherwell, and even (belatedly) Sir Walter Scott were alert to the potential aesthetic merit of variations on the ballad theme ascribed to individual singers. But Child's *English and Scottish Popular Ballads* still has a place for printed broadsides, as well as manuscripts that were written down for reasons that might have had nothing to do with vocal performance, such as the Percy folio manuscript, described as the 'foundation document of English balladry'.[3] The collectors of the Victorian/Edwardian folk revival published songs from individual contributors in specialist outlets such as the *Journal of the Folk-Song Society*, and also in volumes aimed at a more general audience, often harmonized with piano accompaniments. The sources of the songs might be duly credited, but it is difficult to imagine that the distinction could ever have become blurred between the contributor's ephemeral vocal rendition, more often than not noted down with pencil and paper, and the printed words and music notation. The two were self-evidently different things.

Of course this cannot be proved, because people at the time were not writing in these terms. But some comments of Cecil Sharp's certainly suggest an awareness of the distinction. Writing to Percy Grainger in 1908, Sharp stated that when transcribing a folk song, 'our aim should be to record its artistic effect, not necessarily the exact means by which that effect was produced [. . .] it is not an exact, scientifically accurate memorandum that is wanted, so much as a faithful artistic record of what is actually heard by the ordinary auditor'.[4] These remarks came in the context of an exchange with Grainger concerning the use of the phonograph in recording folk songs and the practice of transcription from phonograph recordings. Grainger, on the other hand, in notations published in the *Journal of the Folk-Song Society*, did seek to reproduce as much information as could possibly be accommodated within a conventional system of stave notation – 'a detailed notation of the more or less slight variations occurring throughout a singer's

---

[3] John W. Hales and Frederick J. Furnivall, eds, *Bishop Percy's Folio Manuscript: Ballads and Romances*, 3 vols (London: Trübner, 1867–68), I, ix. See further Joseph Donatelli, 'The Percy Folio Manuscript: A Seventeenth-Century Context for Medieval Poetry', *English Manuscript Studies, 1100–1700*, 4 (1993), 114–33.

[4] London, EFDSS Archives, Cecil Sharp Collection, Correspondence, Cecil Sharp to Percy Grainger, 23 May 1908 (photocopy).

performances of the song'.⁵ The list of things Grainger considered to be of account includes variations in pitch and relation of intervals, variations of speed, rhythmic irregularities, melodic variations from one stanza to the next, dynamic details, lengths of notes, ornamentation, dialect phonetics and blends of vowel sounds, and meaningless additional syllables. Where Sharp stated that he did not want a 'scientifically accurate memorandum', Grainger, though he did not phrase it in quite those terms, evidently did. Indeed, the obsession with such details can be understood as an important component of Grainger's modernist musical aesthetic.⁶

It is likely that the supposed dispute between Grainger and other members of the Folk-Song Society has been much exaggerated, and that the differences between Grainger's collecting methods and Cecil Sharp's derived as much as anything from their immediate social and personal circumstances.⁷ Nevertheless (and at the risk of misrepresenting Sharp's notations, which do in fact take considerable account of such things as variations in melody between different stanzas), there is still a philosophical difference between the two collectors. It seems reasonable to suppose that this bore some relation to their rather different intentions vis-à-vis folk song collecting: close musicological analysis of folk song practice, style, and structure on Grainger's part; the reinvigoration of English musical practice and the popularizing of folk song, particularly in schools, on Sharp's.

The music writing practices of Sharp and Grainger can be related to the distinction made at a later date between so-called 'prescriptive' and 'descriptive' uses of music writing, which Charles Seeger defines, respectively, as the difference 'between a blue-print of how a specific piece of music shall be made to sound and a report of how a specific performance of it actually did sound'.⁸ Seeger went on to advocate a further, 'scientific',

---

5   Percy Grainger, 'Collecting with the Phonograph', *Journal of the Folk-Song Society*, 3.3 (no. 12) (1908), 147–242 (p. 151).
6   Graham Freeman, '"That chief undercurrent of my mind": Percy Grainger and the Aesthetics of English Folk Song', *Folk Music Journal*, 9.4 (2009), 581–617; Graham Freeman, '"It wants all the creases ironing out": Percy Grainger, the Folk Song Society, and the Ideology of the Archive', *Music & Letters*, 92 (2011), 410–36.
7   C. J. Bearman, 'Percy Grainger, the Phonograph, and the Folk Song Society', *Music & Letters*, 84 (2003), 434–55; C. J. Bearman, 'The Folk-Song Society and the Phonograph', *Folk Music Journal*, 10.3 (2013), 370–74. For a short account of the supposed conflict, see Michael Yates, 'Percy Grainger and the Impact of the Phonograph', *Folk Music Journal*, 4.3 (1982), 265–75.
8   Charles Seeger, 'Prescriptive and Descriptive Music-Writing', *Musical Quarterly*, 44 (1958), 184–95 (p. 184). It is perhaps worth observing that, to the layperson, this terminology can

graphic form of descriptive music writing enabled by electro-mechanical recording using an oscillograph, against which conventional written notations could be compared. This is actually something that Percy Grainger had envisaged, though it was not available at the time he was writing.[9] But Seeger's account never allows the impression that music as sound and music as writing could ever be held as ontological equivalents.

The possibility of automatic graphic music representation can be traced back to the 1850s and the phonautograph invented by the French printer Édouard-Léon Scott de Martinville. This device turned sound into a set of visible tracings on paper blackened by smoke from an oil lamp, by means of a stylus attached to a diaphragm vibrating in response to the sound waves. Scott envisaged a time when 'the musical phrase escaping from the lips of the singer will come to write itself [. . .] on an obedient page and leave an imperishable trace of those fugitive melodies that the memory no longer recalls by the time it searches for them'.[10] In the twenty-first century, scientists at Lawrence Berkeley National Laboratory have realized that possibility, employing optical imaging techniques to enable the replaying of one of Scott's phonautogram tracings, dating from 1860, of an unknown vocalist (possibly Scott himself) singing a line of 'Au claire de la lune'.[11] Unlike Charles Seeger's graphic music writing experiments, however, for Scott the phonautogram tracings were an objective in their own right. When, later in the century, he came to evaluate Edison's phonograph, he considered it a failure because it reproduced merely sound, not writing.[12] In Scott's conception, it seems, music could exist in either medium, sound or writing, simultaneously and interchangeably.

This should not be overly surprising. For some traditions of Western art music, the written score is functionally and ontologically parallel with the

---

seem confusing: 'prescriptive' transcriptions, which sound rigid and constraining, are in fact generally less detailed than 'descriptive' transcriptions.
9 Grainger, 'Collecting with the Phonograph', pp. 152–53.
10 Quoted in Jonathan Sterne, *The Audible Past: Cultural Origins of Sound Reproduction* (Durham, NC: Duke University Press, 2003), p. 45.
11 Jody Rosen, 'Researchers Play Tune Recorded before Edison', *New York Times*, 27 March 2008, available at http://www.nytimes.com/2008/03/27/arts/27soun.html?_r=2&em&ex =1206763200&en=fe155ca1d4c4f90f&ei=5087&oref=slogin&; Ron Cowen, 'Earliest Known Sound Recordings Revealed: Researchers unveil imprints made 20 years before Edison invented phonograph', US News & World Report: Science, 1 June 2009, available at http://www.usnews.com/science/articles/2009/06/01/earliest-known-sound-recordings-revealed.
12 Quoted in Sterne, *Audible Past*, p. 46.

sounded performance: 'The questions "what is this piece" and "how does it go" could both be answered either by writing out a score or by making a performance.'[13] Or, as James Grier has it, 'The piece [. . .] resides equally in the score and in the performing conventions that govern its interpretation at any particular historical moment.'[14] This leads on to a comparison and a distinction that will be critical to what follows here:

> For most of the Western art tradition, the act of creating a musical work consists of two stages, composing (which is usually synonymous with the inscription of the score) and performance. These two intermediary steps place the musical work on the same plane as dance and drama, in which the execution of a work, which could exist in written form (the script in drama and choreographic notation in dance), occurs in performance. At the same time, it marks a distinction between the work, which depends equally on the score and performance for its existence, and a text, either written (a score) or sounding (a performance)[,] that defines a particular state of the work.[15]

In other words, at least in the Western tradition (which may be relatively unusual in this respect), ontologically music can be conceived – interchangeably, simultaneously, and independently – as either sound or writing.

A crucial point, which Grier's brief comparison with dance and drama makes explicit, is that the one – sound or writing – is not, and is not expected to be, an exact mirror of the other. The philosopher C. S. Peirce distinguishes three kinds of signs: *likenesses* (or icons), *indications* (or indices), and *symbols* (or general signs).[16] A *likeness* is a sign that conveys the idea of something simply by imitating it. An *indication* is a sign that conveys information about something by virtue of being physically connected with it. A *symbol*, or general sign, is one that is connected with the object it represents merely by agreed convention. We will be less concerned here with likenesses, but drawings of things, imitative sounds, and onomatopoeic words can all

---

13 Leo Treitler, 'History and the Ontology of the Musical Work', in *With Voice and Pen: Coming to Know Medieval Song and How It Was Made* (Oxford: Oxford University Press, 2003), pp. 298–316 (p. 312).
14 James Grier, *The Critical Editing of Music: History, Method, and Practice* (Cambridge: Cambridge University Press, 1996), p. 22.
15 Grier, *Critical Editing of Music*, pp. 22–23.
16 Charles S. Peirce, 'What Is a Sign?', in *The Essential Peirce: Selected Philosophical Writings*, vol. 2 (1893–1913), ed. the Peirce Edition Project (Bloomington and Indianapolis: Indiana University Press, 1998), pp. 4–10, available at http://www.iupui.edu/~peirce/ep/ep2/ep2book/ch02/ep2ch2.htm.

be considered as likenesses. The whistling of a ballad tune might, under certain circumstances, be considered a likeness of what it is supposed to represent. On the other hand, an oscillogram made electro-mechanically from a pre-existent sound recording would be categorized as an indication. It bears a causal, 'indexical' relationship with the sound that brought it into being, by virtue of a direct physical connection between the two things. Scott de Martinville's phonautogram tracings, and the variable pitch grooves cut or pressed into phonograph cylinders and gramophone records, retain this indexical connection with their source. Rothenbuhler and Peters, however, argue that in the digital environment that physical connection has been severed, and that a sequence of 0s and 1s is no more than a series of symbols or general signs.[17] Ordinary words are symbols, and the same is true of written musical notations. It is also the case that ordinary words remain symbols regardless of whether they are written down or vocalized.

A symbol, moreover, does not indicate a particular thing, rather it indicates a kind of thing. Peirce explains the point thus:

> Any ordinary word, as 'give', 'bird', 'marriage', is an example of a symbol. It is *applicable to whatever may be found to realize the idea connected with the word*; it does not, in itself, identify those things. It does not show us a bird, nor enact before our eyes a giving or a marriage, but supposes that we are able to imagine those things, and have associated the word with them.[18]

So the written word 'bird' refers by convention to a group of things we associate with that sequence of letters, and the spoken word 'bird' likewise refers by convention to a group of things we associate with that sound. But the written word does not necessarily refer to the spoken word at all, or vice versa. A symbol of one kind cannot be assumed automatically to identify a symbol of a different sort just by virtue of the fact that, independently, they both indicate the same kind of thing and therefore enjoy a certain equivalence.

This is comparatively easy to grasp in relation to written and spoken words, not least because it is relatively easy to envisage the sort of real-world referents that they identify. And although it is much harder to describe the things that the individual components that make up a passage of music might identify, it is nonetheless not difficult to apply the analogy of written and spoken words to written and performed music *en masse*.

---

17 Eric W. Rothenbuhler and John Durham Peters, 'Defining Phonography: An Experiment in Theory', *Musical Quarterly*, 81 (1997), 242–64.
18 Peirce, 'What Is a Sign?', p. 9 (§6) (italics in original).

The point is readily illustrated by the consideration that a piece of music written out in stave notation could conceivably be written out using an entirely different semiotic system, such as a hand graph of frequency and amplitude variations, just as there are other systems besides written language for words (sign language, for example). For our purposes, the principle should be clear – that, just like Western art music, the 'same' ballad can happily coexist in two semiotic systems, sound and writing, which are equivalent but which bear neither an indexical nor a symbolic relationship to one another.

Scott de Martinville's experiments proved something of a dead end, as subsequent inventors concentrated on mechanisms capable of reproducing sound, leading to Edison's phonograph and Berliner's gramophone. One can presume that the development of phonography and the ubiquity of recorded sound since the twentieth century have encouraged the idea that, in the context of musical forms, including the ballad, sound and writing exist in a hierarchical relationship, with the former enjoying a position of primacy.

Erika Brady, in her account of the adoption of the phonograph for ethnographic studies, links the popularity of phonography with a wider late Victorian preoccupation with collecting indexical items – items that retain a physical link with the past.[19] In fact, the earliest American ethnographers tended to downplay their reliance on the phonograph, both out of a reluctance to advertise the artificiality it seemingly introduced into the fieldwork situation, and out of a wish to present their results as a clear 'scientific' record untrammelled by the practicalities of their acquisition.[20] The recordings were often valued primarily as a means to acquire written text and music transcriptions.[21] These 'derived texts' became the primary materials for subsequent analysis, textual adjustments were frequently made during their preparation, and in many cases the cylinders themselves were eventually discarded.

As we have noted, most of the leading figures of the English folk song movement experimented with phonograph recording, and such reservations as they had were largely about just how reliable the recordings could be, in comparison with pencil and paper transcriptions made by ear.

---

19 Erika Brady, *A Spiral Way: How the Phonograph Changed Ethnography* (Jackson: University Press of Mississippi, 1999), p. 14.
20 Brady, *A Spiral Way*, pp. 59–60.
21 Brady, *A Spiral Way*, pp. 62–64.

The note inserted by the editing committee of the *Journal of the Folk-Song Society* into the introduction to Grainger's published transcriptions states: 'About the value of the phonograph as an aid to collecting there can be no doubt; whether it is sufficiently perfect as yet to be preferred as a substitute for the human ear is still a disputable point.'[22] Grainger's own remarks indicate that among the perceived advantages of phonograph recording were both the preservation of the singers' performances for posterity, and the ability to play the recordings repeatedly in order that several different musicians could make written notations of the same performance.[23]

From the earliest identifiable dates, however, ballads have coexisted as sound and writing. Historically, the oldest copies are of words in manuscript, while the earliest large corpus is in cheap print of the broadside and chapbook kind. The primary *raison d'être* of printed ballads must have been to provide the words in a readable format (for example, when they were pasted on to walls). Nevertheless, the sellers of ballad sheets are also usually envisaged as singing them out loud at fairs and markets and the like, both to advertise their wares and to pass on the tunes (since it is unlikely that much use was ever made of written music notations for ballad melodies). Even at their earliest appearance, as we have seen, ballads inhabited a social environment that can be characterized as text-based – and arguments over precise levels of literacy, the literacy of individual singers, or instances of demonstrable oral transmission are all beside the point in an environment that could conceive of texts per se, amenable to realization in either writing or speech and to alternation between the two media.

The argument, moreover, is not simply a historical one – though writing must, of course, be known and practised if it is to be brought into the equation at all – but one that derives from the nature of language itself. In Saussurean linguistic terms, language exists in the abstract as *langue* and finds its concrete expression as *parole*, through either speech or writing or any other system one may care to imagine. The words of a ballad actually offer quite a good analogy for the semiotics of language, for they can be envisaged both as being held simultaneously in the minds of numbers of different people, and as being amenable to expression at different times and places through singing, recitation, writing, or print.

The main thrust of Derrida's argument with Saussure (not to mention Plato, Aristotle, and Rousseau) is to counter the notion that writing is

---

22 Grainger, 'Collecting with the Phonograph', p. 159.
23 Grainger, 'Collecting with the Phonograph', p. 150.

subservient or secondary to speech, and that the historical institution of writing somehow 'usurps' speech.[24] The starting point is the Aristotelian definition whereby spoken words are the symbols of mental experience, while written words are but the fallible symbols of spoken words.[25] But Derrida sets out to show that the arbitrariness of linguistic signs characterizes both writing *and* speech, and that this situation precludes any relationship of natural hierarchy and subordination between the two media; and in consequence any unreliability and absence of immediacy that can be charged to writing can also be charged to speech.[26] What is most important here is Derrida's emphasis on the status of both writing and speech as independent, but equally fallible, ways of expressing thought, consciousness, originating ideas. Once speech is acknowledged as being just as unreliable as writing, an incidental consequence is that the special bond that ties the spoken word to its human, intellectual source is broken, and with it the 'metaphysics of presence' that has served to privilege speech since, Derrida would argue, the time of Plato.

This, then, is a point of the greatest significance in relation to the writing down of ballad words. The ballad at large needs to be conceived in terms of something other than written or vocalized words alone, for which 'language' is probably the most appropriate abstract noun, and for ballad tunes the (much less familiar, much more problematic) equivalent would be 'musical language'. Nevertheless, the difficulty of making this imaginative move beyond, or behind, vocalized sound – ballad singing – should not be underestimated. There are numerous different and interrelated reasons for this, not the least of which stems from the metaphysics of presence that is posited by various broadly ethnographic perspectives on folk song. Such approaches ascribe authority to the individual, personalized source – the contributor, informant, or 'bearer of tradition' – and not to the text. For some scholars, authority even resides in the transient moment of performance itself. For some, too, the practice of singing and its social environment are simply of greater interest than the matter of what is sung, which is a perfectly legitimate research preference. More pressingly, the difficulty of conceiving of ballad melodies in written notation as anything but secondary

---

24 Jacques Derrida, *Of Grammatology*, corrected edn, trans. Gayatri Chakravorty Spivak (Baltimore: Johns Hopkins University Press, 1997). For a useful summary of Derrida's argument, see Penelope Deutscher, *How to Read Derrida* (London: Granta, 2005), pp. 7–14, 32–33.

25 Derrida, *Of Grammatology*, pp. 11, 30.

26 Derrida, *Of Grammatology*, pp. 37, 44.

to singing, in a tradition that historically has probably only rarely made reference to written music, must seem to many to be insurmountable; and this in turn reflects back upon the words, even though the historical independence of ballad words in writing and print is incontestable. Again, the authenticity ascribed to 'oral tradition' – to the genuine folk singer as 'unlettered peasant' – maintains a strong hold on the imagination, even while the exclusivity of oral transmission has increasingly come to be challenged. Furthermore, variation can be ascribed, in varying degrees, to the agency of individual performers, elevating the ballad singer in some instances to a position more or less akin to that of the literary author or the composer of art music.

Nevertheless, once the ballad is conceived as rooted in language, then its concrete expression in either sound or writing can be addressed on its own terms. Both speech and writing are systems with their own historically constructed conventions, their own social character, their own strengths and limitations. Sound exists only as it is going out of existence and consequently has to be experienced sequentially.[27] Writing, in contrast, is 'branchable', which is to say that it can be accessed at any point and from there the reader can move backwards or forwards, or jump to another point (hypertexts represent an extension of this capacity of writing). Curiously, while sequential experience matches very well with the inexorable movement of ballad narratives – ballad story-telling – the ability to move backwards and forwards actually matches rather well with the recursive structural patterns that are often particularly evident in the ballad way of presenting narrative, as signalled by formulas and commonplaces. Paradoxically, these are just the elements of ballad structure that have been argued to point towards the essentially oral nature of ballads.[28] Ballads can be thought of as providing an intriguing and instructive, illustrative instance for the respective and mutually supportive strengths of sound and writing.

---

27 Walter J. Ong, *Orality and Literacy: The Technologizing of the Word* (London: Routledge, 1988 [1982]), pp. 31–32; Walter J. Ong, 'Writing Is a Technology that Restructures Thought', in *The Written Word: Literacy in Transition*, ed. Gerd Baumann (Oxford: Clarendon Press, 1986), pp. 23–50 (pp. 24–25).

28 David Buchan, *The Ballad and the Folk* (London: Routledge & Kegan Paul, 1972). For the counter-argument, see Albert B. Friedman, 'The Oral-Formulaic Theory of Balladry – A Re-rebuttal', in *The Ballad Image: Essays Presented to Bertrand Harris Bronson*, ed. James Porter (Los Angeles: Center for the Study of Comparative Folklore & Mythology, University of California, Los Angeles, 1983), pp. 215–40.

Sound is often perceived as communal and participatory, while writing has the capacity to remain individual and detached. Sound is sometimes presented as 'warm' and writing as 'cold', which also reflects this perceived communal-individual opposition, but this probably has more to do with the choice of social situation than with the inherent nature of the semiotic system. The lone reader is no more or less isolated than the individual who sings a ballad entirely for her own pleasure, which may be a much more common scenario than has generally been recognized.[29] Reading aloud, which was an important mechanism for the maintenance of a text-based social environment right up until the early twentieth century, has the capacity to bridge perceived distinctions between the two media. It places the auditor in the presence of the speaker, which is often taken as a characteristic of communication employing sound, while at the same time maintaining the separation of author and reader, which is a common attribute of writing as a communication medium. More or less as reading aloud was beginning to decline as a social practice, recording technologies were beginning to ensure that sound no longer posits the necessary presence of the originating source any more than does writing. Just as one rarely reads a piece of writing in the presence of the author, the listener to recorded music is separated from the performer.

There is, moreover, a theoretical basis for this position. Jonathan Sterne describes how Hermann von Helmholtz's nineteenth-century discoveries in acoustics paved the way not just for the technical advance of sound reproduction technologies, but for the cultural assimilation of recorded sound.[30] Essentially, what Helmholtz demonstrated is that sounds are synthesized not at the point of production but at the point of reception, and that therefore it is the processing of the waveform that is critical, not its source. The cause is, if not irrelevant to, at least separable from the effect – so sound becomes an effect that can be reproduced (heard) in isolation from its ultimate source, just as writing can be reproduced (read) in the absence of its author. Derrida, too, writes about phonography as a technology that enables spoken language to function without the presence of the speaking subject.[31] Between them, Helmholtz and Derrida have successfully divorced the semiotics of sound, as of writing, from the metaphysics of presence.

---

29 Thomas A. McKean, 'Folklore Is Not (Necessarily) about Communication', paper presented at the 2007 Joint Annual Meeting of the American Folklore Society and the Folklore Studies Association of Canada, Québec, 17–21 October 2007.
30 Sterne, *Audible Past*, chapter 1 (esp. pp. 62–67).
31 Derrida, *Of Grammatology*, p. 10.

Another, quite separate, way of addressing the same issue is to distinguish between (*i*) the concrete embodiment of a 'text', and (*ii*) the intangible idea of the literary or musical 'work' – as we saw in chapter one. Texts can be known and studied; works can only be conjectured.[32] Such conjectures are necessarily formed on the basis of the texts that are available, but the extent to which a work can be exemplified by any particular text is equally necessarily limited. This is probably even more apparent in the case of musical than of literary works, for it is self-evident that neither the score nor any single performance can fully represent all the possibilities of a work.[33] Texts can therefore be conceived of as sets of instructions for the reconstruction of works. But any text may nonetheless be a faulty witness to a work, and so any exercise in reading and/or hearing a text is necessarily also an exercise in determining, to the best of one's ability, of what words and punctuation, or of what particular arrangement of musical notes, the work itself is properly comprised.[34] This situation is, of course, most pressing in relation to scholarly editing, but the scholarly editor stands for the general reader or auditor in this regard – attempting to the best of his or her ability to reconstitute a 'correct' set of words and punctuation or arrangement of musical notes that will serve as one particular, and, it is hoped, reasonably reliable, set of instructions for the reconstruction of the work. Just as the inevitably fallible editor may err in doing so, equally he or she may more often be successful in correcting errors in the previously available text(s). (Indeed, it is not inconceivable that an editorial error might fortuitously cancel out a pre-existing error, and so inadvertently recover a more precise rendering of the work.)

Once writing has been liberated from a role that is deemed to be subservient to speech, and once sound itself has been separated from the metaphysics of presence that ties it to a particularized source, then texts comprised either in sound or in writing can be understood as providing independent sets of instructions that permit the reconstruction of works. The intangible work itself, in the case of the ballad, is constituted not out of the vocalized sounds or written words per se, but out of language and

---

[32] See G. Thomas Tanselle, *A Rationale of Textual Criticism* (Philadelphia: University of Pennsylvania Press, 1989); G. Thomas Tanselle, 'The Varieties of Scholarly Editing', in *Scholarly Editing: A Guide to Research*, ed. D. C. Greetham (New York: Modern Language Association of America, 1995), pp. 9–32 (pp. 12–13).
[33] Grier, *Critical Editing of Music*, pp. 20–24; Treitler, 'History and Ontology', p. 312.
[34] Tanselle, *Rationale*, pp. 15–16; Tanselle, 'Varieties of Scholarly Editing', pp. 12–13.

music. The activity of writing down or transcribing the ballad, therefore, can usefully be thought of as very much akin to that of editing, in that it involves the critical establishment of one more set of instructions designed to facilitate access to the intangible work.

But just as there is more than one different kind of editing, there can be more than one kind of ballad writing. Non-historical editing (such as publishing-house copy editing) can be distinguished from historical editing.[35] The latter more evidently involves varying degrees of intervention in a text with a view to bringing it nearer to the work that is conjectured to lie behind it. Different editing activities will more or less inevitably produce somewhat different end results, which will mirror both different perspectives on the relationship of text to work, and different purposes and target audiences for the edited text. It should be apparent now that this account of textual editing is not altogether far removed from the distinction between 'prescriptive' and 'descriptive' levels of music writing, or between Grainger's and Sharp's different intentions for music transcription, where different levels of intervention on the part of the transcriber render different end results, which accord with different goals established at the outset. In the same way, different kinds of textual editing are constrained by different goals, which often impose practical and economic constraints affecting such things as typography and *mise en page*.

What, then, is the purpose of writing down ballads? Why write them down at all if a sound recording is likely to be preserved in any case? Prior to the advent of the phonograph, writing provided the only permanent record of transient sound and, as we have seen, in the early years of phonography writing still provided a more reliable record. Grainger pragmatically acknowledged the wisdom in writing down both words and tune independently of the recording, partly because of the risk of the recording becoming damaged, but also because writing is superior for distinguishing unknown words (especially where the recording is faint), and he also thought it instructive to compare notations made on the spot with those derived from recordings.[36] His observations remain pertinent.

---

35 Peter L. Shillingsburg, *Scholarly Editing in the Computer Age: Theory and Practice*, 3rd edn (Ann Arbor: University of Michigan Press, 1996), pp. 1–2; Tanselle, 'Varieties of Scholarly Editing', p. 11.
36 Grainger, 'Collecting with the Phonograph', p. 148.

In the late 1920s and 1930s, James Madison Carpenter collected ballads and folk songs, sea shanties, folk plays, and instrumental music in Britain and Ireland, using a dictaphone to record on to wax cylinders.[37]

Fig. 5.1 Carpenter Collection, Photo 101, James Madison Carpenter sitting in his Austin Roadster. Courtesy of the American Folklife Center at the Library of Congress, Washington, DC, USA.

His surviving recordings include many of the earliest known sound records of Child ballads from Britain, although many of them are of very poor quality. Besides displaying the effects of age (some of the cylinders are cracked or unplayable due to the effects of mould) and wear (there is considerable extraneous noise in the frequency range of the human voice), the recordings were evidently made at a slow (and variable) speed in order to fit as much recorded sound as possible on to a single cylinder. This was presumably done because of the cost and bulk of the cylinders, and for the same reason the recordings are in most instances not of entire songs but of, say, two to four stanzas of a ballad (though there are some exceptions to this rule of thumb). Subsequent to making the sound recording, his practice was to take down the words in full from dictation, usually on a portable typewriter, asking questions of the contributor when he thought it necessary and making handwritten adjustments to the dictated copy, which was later typed up as a fair copy. He also made his own transcriptions of both music and words from the recordings. This is presumed to have involved

---

37 Julia C. Bishop, '"Dr Carpenter from the Harvard College in America": An Introduction to James Madison Carpenter and his Collection', *Folk Music Journal*, 7.4 (1998), 402–20.

repeated playing of the cylinders, which contributed to their deterioration, and he later made lacquer disc copies, apparently at the suggestion of Alan Lomax.[38] Present-day scholars are able to make their own transcriptions of both music and words from tape and digital copies derived from the cylinder and disc recordings.[39]

Of necessity, the written copies provide a different exemplification of the ballads from the sound recordings. And this is not simply because the sound recordings are not very good in this particular case. While on the one hand the written ballad cannot adequately represent such things as the quality or timbre, or even the local accent, of the recorded voice, on the other hand it can provide lexical, syntactic, and semantic precision that is not available from sound. Writing offers distinctions in matters such as:

- spelling – e.g. the capacity to distinguish between homophones; to distinguish between English and Scots, and between British and American English; to flag up dialect words and *hapax logomena* (that is, words or forms of which only a single instance is found in a corpus)
- capitalization – e.g. to indicate proper names
- word division – e.g. to make visible distinctions between words such as *green wood* and *greenwood*, *holy-day* and *holiday*
- punctuation – e.g. marking the beginning and ending of direct speech, separating repeated words
- verse layout (*mise en page*) – e.g. rendering stanzaic structures immediately evident (an instance of the 'branchability' of writing mentioned above).

All of these possible distinctions are the products of conventions that have evolved historically (and can be expected to continue to evolve) so as to facilitate access to the constitution and the semantics of texts, and thence of

---

38 Washington, DC, Library of Congress, American Folklife Center, Archive of Folk Culture, AFC1972/001, James Madison Carpenter Collection, MS p. 00081.

39 Elaine Bradtke, 'Fiddle Tunes from under the Bed: Extracting Music from Carpenter's Recordings', in *Crossing Over: Fiddle and Dance Studies from around the North Atlantic, 3*, ed. Ian Russell and Anna Kearney Guigné (Aberdeen: Elphinstone Institute, University of Aberdeen, in association with the Department of Folklore, MMaP and the School of Music, Memorial University of Newfoundland, 2010), pp. 35–48; Thomas A. McKean, 'The Dialect Conundrum in Transcribing Early Sound Recordings', in *From 'Wunderhorn' to the Internet: Perspectives on Conceptions of 'Folk Song' and the Editing of Traditional Songs*, ed. Eckhard John and Tobias Widmaier, BASIS, vol. 6 (Trier: WVT Wissenschaftlicher Verlag Trier, 2010), pp. 209–24.

works. This suggests that a prime purpose behind the written ballad lies in the presentation of a 'reading text', which might equate to something closer to the 'prescriptive' than the 'descriptive' end of the spectrum of music writing. This sort of text is particularly suitable for reading for pleasure, for literary and musical analysis and comparison, for social-historical documentation, and for learning the ballad to sing. All of these things would rank among the primary justifications for undertaking a critical edition. The written ballad additionally serves the function of clarification of a text in another system, that of recorded sound, but the two texts still remain quite independent, non-indexically related, entities. Together, they shed their combined light on the nature of the work.

Here, then, it will be worth looking at some examples of exactly what this means. Consider a couple of simple words that crop up in ballads: *castle* as written does not distinguish between southern English pronounced something like 'carsle' and a more northern pronunciation like 'cassel'; *country* does not necessarily indicate when the stress falls on the second syllable, as it does on occasion at the end of a verse line, which can sometimes be found represented by a kind of eye-dialect as *countree*. The latter example is not atypical of a tendency in ballad writing to go some way, though not usually very far, towards representing what might conceivably have been some, though by no means all, of the phonetic aspects of the way a ballad was recited or sung. The spelling *north countree*, for example, is given in a copy of 'The Two Sisters' from Lancashire published in *Notes and Queries* in 1852 (Child 10 R a).[40] Another copy, of similar date, has *West Countree*, this time in a text deliberately written out in a representation of dialect (Child 10 R c).[41] By way of comparison, still in the mid-nineteenth century, a broadside copy of 'The Golden Vanity' (Child 286) printed in London by Such has the conventional spelling *North Country*.[42] So, although the *Oxford English Dictionary* does record both *countree* and *countrie* as archaic spellings,[43] it is most likely that such endings really amount to no more than eye-dialect. But even in a verse context where the stress falls largely on the final syllable, no one actually

---

40 'Ballad of "The Three Sisters"', *Notes and Queries*, 1st ser., 6 (1852), 102.
41 [Thomas Hughes], *The Scouring of the White Horse; or, The Long Vacation Ramble of a London Clerk* (Cambridge: Macmillan, 1859), pp. 158–60. The ballad is titled 'The Barkshire [sic] Tragedy' and begins 'A varmer he lived in the West Countree', so the dialect is presumably meant to be West Country or Berkshire.
42 *The Golden Vanity; or, The Low Lands Low* (London: H. Such, [1849–62]) [Oxford, Bodleian Library, Harding B 11(1086)].
43 *OED* country, *n*.

needs the *–ee* spelling in order to read the word from the page.[44] So when Carpenter took down 'The Golden Vanity' from Richard Warner in Cardiff in 1928 and variously typed *North Country, North Countree, North Countrie* in three different typescript copies, it is not clear that the unorthodox spellings have any particular meaning or authority at all.[45]

In the case of historic copies of ballads that have come down to us in writing alone, there is mostly no way of knowing whether peculiarities of spelling really do reflect aspects of vocal performance. They might, but equally they might not. In some instances, however, sound recordings and music notation can provide clues. Carpenter collected the carol-ballad 'The Holy Well' (Roud 1697) from Samuel Heather in Cornwall in 1934.[46] When he took down the typescript, presumably from dictation rather than singing as such, he initially typed the first stanza thus:

> Sweet Jesus asked of his own dear mother
> Whether he should go to play
> At play thou mightst go,
> And at play thou mightest go
> And at play thou hast now begun
> And let me hear of no complaint
> In the evening when thou come home.[47]

Subsequently, he made a number of handwritten alterations to this initial rough copy typescript, which were incorporated into a later fair copy, where this stanza now reads:

> Sweet Jesus asked of his own dear mother
> Whether he should go to play:
> "A' play thou mightst go, and a' play thou mightest go,
> And a' play thou hast now begon-ne
> And a' play thou hast now begone.
> And let me hear of no complaint
> In the evening when thou come ho-o-o-o-ome,
> In the evening when thou come home."[48]

---

[44] Neither of the *countree* texts was printed with music notation. An idea of the sort of melody that fits this form of 'The Two Sisters' can be gained from the recording of George Fradley on *Down in the Fields: An Anthology of Traditional Folk Music from Rural England*, CD (Veteran VTC4CD, 2001). Fradley's ballad does not actually include the word *country*, but the melody would not seem to demand an especially elongated final syllable for that word.

[45] Carpenter Collection, MS pp. 05092–05094, 05106–05107, 07129.

[46] The full set of references is Carpenter Collection, Cylinder 098 05:21; Disc sides 211 01:32, 212 00:00; MS pp. 05197–05198, 07199–07200, 08356, 11010–11011.

[47] Carpenter Collection, MS p. 05197.

[48] Carpenter Collection, MS p. 07199 (Carpenter uses double quotation marks).

Listening to the recording, there is reason to think that these alterations were probably made in response to the way Samuel Heather sang the carol-ballad. This would account for the repeated lines, the expanded syllables, and the abbreviation of the preposition *at* to *a'*. This particular fair copy thus appears to be something of a hybrid mix of transcription from dictation and from singing.

Carpenter's own transcription of the words and tune, derived from the sound recording, is shown in Fig. 5.2. The words, it will be noted, differ

Fig. 5.2 Carpenter Collection, MS p. 08356. Courtesy of the American Folklife Center at the Library of Congress, Washington, DC, USA.

in some details from those given in the fair copy (and in the rough copy with handwritten alterations). A new transcription, derived from the sound recording as it now survives (in fact taken from a digital surrogate), and attempting to render all of the audible phonemes, might be as follows:

> Sweet Jesus asked of his own dear mother
> Whether he should go to play
> At play thou might'st go, at play thou might'st go
> And a' play thou hast now begu-u-u-un
> And a' play thou hast now begun
> And let me hear of no complaint
> In the evening when thou come ho-o-o-ome
> In the evening when thou come home.

It is possible both to confirm with some confidence that, *pace* Carpenter's fair copy, the sound recording does have *might'st* (twice) and *begun* (not *begone*), and to count the vowel sounds when *begun* and *home* are expanded to fit the melody. It is nonetheless extremely difficult to decide whether the preposition really is *at* or *a'*, and whether or not there might be an *s* sound at the end of *complaint*. (It is worth remarking that these sorts of difficulties cannot be attributed solely to the poor state of cylinder recordings from the 1930s, for it can be just as difficult to make the same kind of decisions when transcribing from – or even just listening to – a modern CD.) The point is that a reader faced with just Carpenter's fair copy might assume that forms such as *mightest* (versus *mightst* in the same line), *begon-ne*, and *ho-o-o-o-ome*, have some real phonological authority, when in fact this is not demonstrably the case.

There are various reasons for presenting ballad music in a written semiotic system – for ease of technical analysis, for example – and such notation also requires that the words be presented in the form of a text underlay. In such a case, the correct number of syllables needs to be presented to fit with the musical notation. So one would indeed want to write *begu-u-u-un* and *ho-o-o-ome*, for example. This is not, however, necessarily the case when presenting the words separately from the music notation. One would wish to distinguish *begun* from *begone* on grounds of semantics, and *might'st* from *mightest* on the ground that –*'st* is a widely recognized contraction. But the argument for preserving *begu-u-u-un* or *ho-o-o-ome* in the absence of the musical notation is a much weaker one, for (while not wishing to exaggerate the difficulty in this particular instance) the regular spellings *begun* and *home* meet the primary demands of lexical familiarity and semantic precision.

Similar difficulties are further compounded in two stanzas (stanzas 3 and 4) of the same carol-ballad collected from Sidney Veal, again in Cornwall in 1934.[49] These might be transcribed from the sound recording, again attempting to render all of the audible phonemes, as follows:

> Sweet Jesus went down to yonder town
> As far as the holy well
> And there did see as fine child-e-ren
> As any tongue could tell
> As any tongue could tell.
>
> He said, God bless you every one
> May Christ your portion be
> Little children, shall I play with you
> And you shall play with me
> And you shall play with me?

This is pretty much what Carpenter's own transcription has. However, both the rough copy and fair copy typescripts have the word *childeren* in both of these stanzas. Of course, there is no way of knowing what Mr Veal said when dictating the words, or what Carpenter thought he said, but as a representation of the sound recording, *childeren* is just as certainly wrong in the second of the stanzas as it is correct in the first. Carpenter's typescripts could almost be thought to have the effect of making Mr Veal look like a speaker of a particular dialect. Although the *English Dialect Dictionary* does not list *childeren* as such, it does record both *childer* and *childern* in dialect use, including in Cornwall.[50] But the issue is a more general one concerning representation. In the first stanza of the same ballad both rough and fair copy typescripts have the word *play-ay-ay*, which has the appearance of representing something closer to singing than to dictated speech, yet the sound recording (and Carpenter's own transcription) quite clearly has the word falling on just a single note – though on the recording it actually sounds rather more like *school* than *play*.

---

49 The full set of references is Carpenter Collection, Cylinder 098 00:00; Disc side 210 01:39; MS pp. 05201–05203, 07211, 08359, 11012–11013, 11014.
50 *EDD* childer, *sb. pl.*, childern, *sb. pl.*

The linguist Dennis Preston has noted how, historically, scholars have been in the habit of transcribing items of verbal folklore in a manner that attempts to convey some details of the original pronunciation.[51] In doing so, he argues, they have been prone to apply non-standard respellings of words, intended to convey the flavour of informants' speech, in a non-systematic fashion. In particular, they have tended mostly to respell 'that which strikes them as nonstandard or unusual',[52] meaning, in effect, that they have more frequently respelled the language of groups of people who are perceived as being 'other'. That is to say, non-standard spellings reflect transcribers' perceptions of their sources; and those perceptions usually, albeit no doubt involuntarily, Preston claims, reflect detrimentally on the status of those sources. In order to avoid such pitfalls, he offers the following pragmatic advice:

> Transcribe differences at the morphological level and above; do not try to show regular phonological differences which may deviate from some preconceived notion of 'standard' unless such differences are important to the discussion of the text or a complete understanding of it. If that is the case, a phonetic transcription, narrow as the point to be made requires, is the appropriate strategy, or, in some cases where the variety differs radically from better-known ones, a new spelling system might be devised.[53]

Preston's detailed prescriptions are quite complex of application, and require some knowledge of linguistic rules governing phonological and morphological changes, but for practical purposes they advise against the respelling of words where a variant pronunciation (or 'phonetic realization') can be considered predictable on the basis of a knowledge of the relevant linguistic and/or interactional environment.[54]

---

51 Dennis R. Preston, "Ritin' Fowklower Daun 'Rong: Folklorists' Failures in Phonology', *Journal of American Folklore*, 95 (1982), 304–26.
52 Preston, "Ritin' Fowklower Daun 'Rong', p. 306.
53 Preston, "Ritin' Fowklower Daun 'Rong', p. 309.
54 Preston's rules are conveniently summarized for the present purpose by Julia C. Bishop, '*Grouping, Grawping* and *Groping* towards a Critical Edition of the James Madison Carpenter Collection of Traditional Song and Drama', Dialect and Folk Life Studies in Britain: The Leeds Archive of Vernacular Culture in its Context, University of Leeds, 19 March 2005, pp. 11–12, available at http://library.leeds.ac.uk/multimedia/imu/2163/JuliaBishop2.pdf. Another set of pragmatic guidelines is provided by Ronald K. S. Macaulay, '"Coz it izny spelt when they say it": Displaying Dialect in Writing', *American Speech*, 66 (1991), 280–91.

Preston's proposal provoked a short but bad-tempered debate with Elizabeth Fine, who mounted a defence of 'literary dialect' spelling as a means of representing performance features in print.[55] She notes, for example, that casual speech can be 'an important contextual indicator of the psychological scene and interpersonal relationships of the participants in a performance. Whether or not casual speech usages indicate a regional dialect, they indicate the conscious or unconscious choices of a performer, which can convey important information about folklore and its social use.'[56] Preston responded in some detail, to the effect that respellings 'make us believe that an accurate transcript has been given when, in fact, no phonetic work has been done at all'.[57] In contrast, what Fine is actually mostly concerned with is the imaginative re-creation or 'translation' of spoken texts into another, written 'language', capable of conveying as much as possible of the characteristics of the 'performance' that lies behind it, in accordance with her rigid conception that folklore equates to 'artistic verbal performance'.[58]

Preston and (to a lesser extent) Fine are primarily concerned with the representation of 'natural' speech and not with the rendering of aesthetic artefacts such as ballads and songs, which employ a different linguistic register from that of everyday conversation. Percy Grainger, for example, remarked on the reduced occurrence of dialect patterns in the folk songs he recorded in Lincolnshire relative to the everyday speech of their singers.[59] Similarly, then, the dropping of the *t* sound from *a' play* in the singing of 'The Holy Well' does not say anything about the everyday linguistic and hence social status of Sam Heather, and the initial typing suggests that when dictating he probably said *at*. Thus Preston's objection to dialect forms on social grounds does not seem especially applicable, but the gist of his objection to a non-systematic, impressionistic respelling remains pertinent, especially if inconsistency is compounded by the introduction of forms that are driven by melodic

---

55 Elizabeth Fine, 'In Defense of Literary Dialect: A Response to Dennis R. Preston', *Journal of American Folklore*, 96 (1983), 323–30; Elizabeth C. Fine, *Folklore Text: From Performance to Print* (Bloomington and Indianapolis: Indiana University Press, 1984), pp. 135–40.
56 Fine, 'In Defense of Literary Dialect', p. 327.
57 Dennis R. Preston, 'Mowr Bayud Spellin': A Reply to Fine', *Journal of American Folklore*, 96 (1983), 330–39 (p. 338).
58 Fine, *Folklore Text*, p. 5. For 'translation' as a central metaphor for the text as the record of a performance, see Fine, *Folklore Text*, pp. 89–112. Preston acknowledges the divergence in their respective purposes in 'Mowr Bayud Spellin'', p. 339.
59 Grainger, 'Collecting with the Phonograph', pp. 160–61.

requirements rather than by genuine linguistic variation. To repeat the point, *child-e-ren* makes perfect sense as the underlay to two quavers and a crotchet, but has little value at all as a rendering of the English word signifying young people, boys and girls.

At the end of the nineteenth century, the Folk-Song Society issued a leaflet called *Hints to Collectors of Folk Music*, which gives some practical advice on the matter: 'The words should be taken down in ordinary English spelling, but with no alterations made for the sake of grammatical correctness.'[60] But on the whole it is folk narrative scholars who seem to have been most alert to the potential pitfalls of writing down words (possibly because expression in prose is less constrained by the requirements of metre and melody, and because folk narratives have less of a printed legacy than do ballads). The different levels at which folk narratives are amenable to transcription range widely, from a loose paraphrase through to the development of elaborate systems for representing such features as pauses of different lengths, asides, self-corrections, interruptions, aspects of stress and intonation, and so on, as well as niceties of regional, dialectal, and idiolectal pronunciation, and the provision of international phonetic alphabet (IPA) and/or other phonetic renderings.[61] Some would wish to go further and incorporate systems for representing proxemic, kinesic, paralinguistic, and interactional information.[62] At least some of these features, we might observe, are beginning to emerge in Grainger's transcriptions. Yet it is immediately evident that such an accumulation of detail will bring with it an accumulation of difficulties, in the areas of precision, consistency, accessibility, and so forth. One solution is to adopt different, simultaneous, levels of transcription, representing, for example, suprasegmental features (stress, intonation, and so on), phonetic or phonemic characteristics, literary dialect (an accessible rendering of unusual phonetic and phonemic forms), and 'translation' into standard English.[63] In fact, what this potential accretion of methods implies more

---

60 *Hints to Collectors of Folk Music* ([London: Folk-Song Society, 1898]). For some more background on this leaflet, see Ian Olson, 'The Folk Song Society's *Hints for Collectors* (1898)', *English Dance & Song*, 57.1 (1995), 2–5; Julian Onderdonk, 'The Revised (1904) Version of the Folk Song Society's *Hints to Collectors*', *English Dance & Song*, 62.3 (2000), 21–23.

61 See Herbert Halpert and J. D. A. Widdowson, *Folktales of Newfoundland: The Resilience of the Oral Tradition*, 2 vols (New York and London: Garland, 1996), pp. liv–lxv.

62 See Fine, *Folklore Text*, and the example of a 'performance-centered text' (chapter 7).

63 Graham Shorrocks, 'Reflections on the Problems of Transcribing Contemporary Legends',

than anything is that different levels of transcription are most suitable for different purposes – the study of performance, linguistic analysis, comparative studies, general reading, and so on.

This accumulating level of potential complexity, discussions of different ways of doing transcriptions, and bad-tempered arguments such as those between Preston and Fine, all stem from what appears to be an orthodox assumption: that 'any published text of a tale should be an *exact* record of the performance'.[64] Other formulations include 'verbatim' texts or transcriptions;[65] 'word for word exactness';[66] and Fine's virtuous asseveration that 'our job is to record the speech we hear as accurately as possible'.[67] Now the reason that lies behind these sorts of expressions of orthodoxy is the long-standing perception that there is no single text of a folktale – or ballad or folk song – either as between its different performers or between its individual performances, but that an equivalent authority rests with each separate iteration of the 'same' thing. To be sure, this insistence on the separation of iterations has to some extent been driven by a reaction against earlier collecting and transcribing practices that involved the conflating or summarizing of texts. It certainly also raises some pressing questions about the exact constitution of 'performances' and their supposedly iconic status. Nevertheless, it is largely unexceptionable as a statement of the unstable nature of folklore items, or 'works', even if it now seems that they share this condition much more closely with works of canonical literature and music than has generally been recognized.

Where the problem arises is with the extrapolation of such a recognition of the integrity of separate iterations into a hierarchy of documentary authority, which descends from 'live' performance, through audio/video recording, to written transcription. Such an assumption of hierarchy brings with it the proposition that a 'verbatim' transcript, made from

---

Contemporary Legend, 2 (1992), 93–117.
64 Herbert Halpert and J. D. A. Widdowson, 'Folk-Narrative Performance and Tape Transcription: Theory versus Practice', *Lore & Language*, 5.1 (1986), 39–50 (p. 39).
65 Bill Ellis, 'Why Are Verbatim Texts of Legends Necessary?', in *Perspectives on Contemporary Legend*, vol. 2, ed. Gillian Bennett, Paul Smith, and J. D. A. Widdowson (Sheffield: Sheffield Academic Press, for the Centre for English Cultural Tradition and Language, 1987), pp. 31–60; Halpert and Widdowson, *Folktales of Newfoundland*, pp. liv–lv.
66 Richard M. Dorson, *Buying the Wind: Regional Folklore in the United States* (Chicago: University of Chicago Press, 1964), p. 1.
67 Fine, *Folklore Text*, p. 140.

either the live performance or an audio recording, is both (theoretically) possible and inherently desirable. Relative to the transcription, the tape recording can be held to be the 'primary document' – even though within the aforementioned hierarchy it patently is not. Arguably, the live performance might be held to constitute the 'primary document', although the effect of the presence of an observer, underwritten by Helmholtz's discoveries in acoustics, would make it difficult to maintain even that position. If not, then maybe the 'primary document' would be something like the contributor's 'mental concept';[68] but even if such a thing could be said to exist, it would surely be a constantly changing abstract, again subject to external influences, including the interest shown by the researcher. So the 'primary document' is a vanishing ideal, in continual retreat from the investigator.

What lies behind this assumption of documentary hierarchy seems to be the metaphysics of presence. The closer to the designated source, both physically and in terms of perceived steps of 'mediation', the more textually authoritative the item is deemed to be. Yet, as the examples given above of *child-e-ren* for *children* or *begon-ne* for the grammatically and semantically requisite *begun* indicate, the apparent authority achieved from representing something in one semiotic system (writing) in a fashion that has the appearance of being that much closer to a rendering of the same thing in another semiotic system (sound) can be quite misleading.

Grainger's phonetic transcriptions provide further instances of the same kind of thing. Fig. 5.3 shows the transcription of Joseph Taylor's 'Lord Bateman' (Child 53).[69] Even granted that many of the hyphens simply indicate where a word is split across two or more musical notes, and that a clear key is provided to the orthographic symbols used in the transcriptions,[70] the difficulty of reading the words is still such that Grainger himself was obliged in some instances to provide a rendering in standard English orthography.

---

68 Compare the idea of 'mental text' in Lauri Honko, *Textualising the Siri Epic*, FF Communications, no. 264 (Helsinki: Suomalainen Tiedeakatemia/Academia Scientiarum Fennica, 1998), pp. 92–99; Lauri Honko, 'Thick Corpus and Organic Variation: An Introduction', in *Thick Corpus, Organic Variation and Textuality in Oral Tradition*, ed. Lauri Honko (Helsinki: Finnish Literature Society, 2000), pp. 3–28 (pp. 18–19). See further chapter 7 below.
69 Grainger, 'Collecting with the Phonograph', pp. 192–93.
70 Grainger, 'Collecting with the Phonograph', pp. 167–68.

Fig. 5.3 Joseph Taylor, 'Lord Bateman', transcribed by Percy Grainger, *Journal of the Folk-Song Society*, 3.3 (no. 12) (1908), 192–93. Courtesy of the English Folk Dance and Song Society.

Sound and Writing   115

At the very least, a standard rendering of the words separately from the music would provide a clear reading text. Grainger's remarks on the phonetic habits of Lincolnshire folk singers, their tendency towards mixed standard and regional pronunciations, and their habit of inserting supplementary syllables into words sung over more than one note, do usefully describe something of the flavour of performances.[71] But given the difficulty of reading and the subjectivity of the renderings, writing *prisun* for *prison*, *greö* for *grew*, *chēned* for *chained*, *Ba/ātemun* for *Bateman*, really takes us no closer to the designated source than does the general direction, 'With even and beautifully sustained tone', that heads the transcription.

While few would want to disagree with that description of Joseph Taylor's singing, there is certainly greater scope for disagreement about the precision of some of the phonetic renderings.[72] But the purpose here is not to argue for any particular standard of verbal or musical transcription: as with the folk narratives mentioned above, different transcription levels are suitable for different purposes, and *none* of them shares an indexical relationship with its source. Rather, the problem lies in equating a documentary hierarchy with the metaphysics of presence at all. As argued above, the semiotics of both sound and writing can be satisfactorily isolated from their putative point of origin. Accordingly, writing and sound enjoy a non-indexical and non-hierarchical relationship.

The ballad as writing and the ballad as sound – live singing and sound recording in various formats, printed broadsides and songbooks, different levels of written transcription – all provide different and complementary sets of instructions to facilitate access to the intangible ballad as 'work'. The notion of 'translation' between media, or from performance to print, is, on this model, simply quite wrong. The problem with the effort, as described by one ballad editor, 'to present the song as it was actually sung',[73] is not so much that it is doomed to failure, as that it represents a confusion of textual categories from the very start.

---

71 Grainger, 'Collecting with the Phonograph', pp. 160–62.
72 Joseph Taylor's recording of 'Lord Bateman' made for the Gramophone Company in 1908 can be heard on *Unto Brigg Fair: Joseph Taylor and Other Traditional Lincolnshire Singers Recorded in 1908 by Percy Grainger*, 12-inch LP (Leader LEA 4050, 1972).
73 Arthur Kyle Davis, Jr., ed., *More Traditional Ballads of Virginia, collected with the cooperation of members of the Virginia Folklore Society* (Chapel Hill: University of North Carolina Press, 1960), p. xvii. (Davis, however, was really expressing a determination to avoid the kind of editorial interventions of which the likes of Thomas Percy and Walter Scott have been accused, and in that light my comment is not entirely fair.)

The equation with the metaphysics of presence of a documentary hierarchy for the ballad that privileges sound is closely paralleled by the demand for 'authenticity' and a concomitant distrust of 'mediation' that came to characterize the folk song revival during the late twentieth century and which is most closely identified with Dave Harker's *Fakesong*.[74] There is also some resonance with what the German critic Walter Benjamin identifies as the 'aura' of the work of art, that quality that supposedly belongs uniquely to the 'original' artefact and its singular presence in time and space, and which is requisite to concepts of 'authenticity' and 'tradition'.[75] The general thrust of Benjamin's famous essay on 'The Work of Art in the Age of its Technological Reproducibility' is that the multiplicity enabled by mechanical reproduction has had the effect of diminishing the 'aura' of artefacts and thus diluting the notions of authenticity, tradition, and authority that can attach to them.

Benjamin's argument, however, is problematic in a number of ways, of which the most important for the present discussion is the scant consideration given to the phenomenon of printing at large, and especially to the early proliferation of popular and ephemeral printed items, of which the broadside ballad sheets are a prime instance. While they vary in quality, together they disclose a remarkable vernacular aesthetic, which is only reinforced by physical aspects of typography, illustration, decoration, and so forth. But their crucial importance for the present discussion is that they embody a functional aesthetic which is complementary to, and yet still quite separate from, vocal expression. They provide the critical historical evidence for the coexistence of the ballad in two separate semiotic systems, sound and writing, each of which can be thought of as conforming to its own conventions and enjoying its own authority. By way of a very brief international comparison, the 'ballad picture show' (*Bänkelsang*) of Germany, current over much the same period, made very deliberate use of complementary media to communicate stories in narrative verse: vocal performance; pictorial display; and the words in print on ballad sheets

---

74 Dave Harker, *Fakesong: The Manufacture of British 'Folksong', 1700 to the Present Day* (Milton Keynes: Open University Press, 1985), p. xiii. On 'mediation', see further Raymond Williams, *Keywords: A Vocabulary of Culture and Society*, rev. edn (London: Fontana, 1988), pp. 204–07.

75 Walter Benjamin, 'The Work of Art in the Age of its Technological Reproducibility', in *Selected Writings*, vol. 3, 1935–1938, trans. Edmund Jephcott, Howard Eiland, et al., ed. Howard Eiland and Michael W. Jennings (Cambridge, MA: The Belknap Press of Harvard University Press, 2002), pp. 101–33.

or in chapbooks, sometimes also including a prose redaction.[76] Similar practices have been noted in Slovenia and Spanish Galicia.[77] A modern English ballad edition, with clear reading text 'in ordinary English spelling' and music notation following established conventions, might lack some of the aesthetic charm of earlier printed ballad sheets or pictorial displays, but it fulfils a similar function.

---

[76] Tom Cheesman, '*Bänkelsang*: Seeing, Hearing, Telling and Singing in the German Ballad Picture Show', *Lore and Language*, 12 (1994), 41–57; Tom Cheesman, *The Shocking Ballad Picture Show: German Popular Literature and Cultural History* (Oxford and Providence, RI: Berg, 1994).

[77] Marija Klobčar, 'Itinerant Singers in Slovenia: Views on a Distinct Phenomenon', in *Songs of People on the Move*, ed. Thomas A. McKean, BASIS, vol. 8 (Trier: WVT Wissenschaftlicher Verlag Trier, 2012), pp. 3–15 (pp. 6–10); Alfonso Franco Vázquez, 'The Galician Fiddle Style', in *Crossing Over: Fiddle and Dance Studies from around the North Atlantic*, 3, ed. Ian Russell and Anna Kearney Guigné (Aberdeen: Elphinstone Institute, University of Aberdeen, in association with the Department of Folklore, MMaP and the School of Music, Memorial University of Newfoundland, 2010), pp. 200–14 (p. 206).

6. Agency, Intention, and the Problem of Version
(with a brief history of ballad editing)

To acknowledge the sources of variance, the material nature of the ballad, the synergy of sound and writing, and the end of the metaphysics of presence does not necessarily undermine the type/version paradigm of ballad studies, but it certainly complicates a matter that, since the dawn of the so-called 'post-Child era of scientific folklore', has appeared relatively unproblematic.[1] One of the reasons for this is that for much of the time the ballad has been represented by a single material instance, in the form of a set of words and a notated melody written down by a collector from a contributor 'in the field'. The editor's task has been conceived as comprising little more than the obligation to reproduce words and music verbatim. Students of the subject have been quick enough to condemn editors who have done anything else – for example, by conflating different texts, or adjusting words to meet the social constraints on publication in Victorian and Edwardian England.[2] Child's *English and Scottish Popular*

An earlier version of this chapter was published as 'Editing the Child Ballads: Agency, Intention, and the Problem of Version', *Variants*, 6 (2007), 123–62, and the material is reused with permission.

1   The phrase apparently comes from Arthur Kyle Davis, Jr., ed., *More Traditional Ballads of Virginia, collected with the cooperation of Members of the Virginia Folklore Society* (Chapel Hill: University of North Carolina Press, 1960), p. xvii.
2   See, for example, Dave Harker, *Fakesong: The Manufacture of British 'Folksong', 1700 to the Present Day* (Milton Keynes: Open University Press, 1985). A more balanced, but nonetheless quite critical, account of ballad editing runs through the work of David Gregory. See E. David Gregory, 'In the Shadow of Child: Other Victorian Perspectives on Ballad Editing', in *Ballad Mediations: Folksongs Recovered, Represented, and Reimagined*, ed. Roger deV. Renwick and Sigrid Rieuwerts, BASIS, vol. 2 (Trier: WVT Wissenschaftlicher

Ballads has been received as definitive particularly because he went back to the manuscripts that lay behind earlier published ballad volumes, such as Thomas Percy's *Reliques of Ancient English Poetry* and Walter Scott's *Minstrelsy of the Scottish Border*, which had tended to conflate sources so as to produce a single representative text. In contrast, Child (ostensibly at least) reproduced discrete ballad versions – individual manifestations of the abstract ballad type.

The type/version paradigm of ballad studies and of Child's edition was outlined in chapter one, but it is worth noting that the Finnish folk narrative scholars Julius and Kaarle Krohn and Antti Aarne had also arrived, apparently quite independently, at the same paradigm of type and version at much the same time.[3] This coincidence is perhaps sufficient to suggest a general indebtedness to the habit of close observation and classification of all kinds of phenomena that came to characterize the intellectual climate of the late nineteenth century. All of the versions of a ballad type or tune family, or a folk narrative type, are considered to be cognate, so that there is no single authoritative text – even though there must have been at some point an 'original' text. This, it is worth observing, means that the ballad or folktale version is, on the face of it, not at all the same as what literary editors mean by a version of a literary work, which usually involves both a degree of authorial intention and the implication of development towards a (more or less well achieved) finality.[4]

Child's editorial approach has left an impression of empiricism, even of scientific method, which has enabled subsequent editors and scholars to envisage the version as the fundamental unit of ballad study. Yet an examination of Child's treatment of versions suggests that there is a sense in which this new method merely poses the same problem as faced Walter Scott, but at one further remove. For the integrity of the version is far from transparent. That much is apparent from the confusion that persists in the

---

Verlag Trier, 2006), pp. 69–77; E. David Gregory, *Victorian Songhunters: The Recovery and Editing of English Vernacular Ballads and Folk Lyrics, 1820–1883* (Lanham, MD: Scarecrow Press, 2006); E. David Gregory, *The Late Victorian Folksong Revival: The Persistence of English Melody, 1878–1903* (Lanham, MD: Scarecrow Press, 2010). One specific target for criticism is the absence of melodies from earlier editions, which is a fair point, but one that, ironically, tends also to emphasize the inherent separability of words and music.

3 Ilana Harlow, 'Tale-Type', in *Encyclopedia of Folklore and Literature*, ed. Mary Ellen Brown and Bruce A. Rosenberg (Santa Barbara: ABC-CLIO, 1998), pp. 641–43.

4 Peter L. Shillingsburg, *Scholarly Editing in the Computer Age: Theory and Practice*, 3rd edn (Ann Arbor: University of Michigan Press, 1996), pp. 44–45.

terminology itself, with differing and often imprecise, but nonetheless frequently interchangeable, usages of the terms 'variant' and 'version' to describe anything from a particular narrative pattern to the single momentary rendering of a song.[5] A little more precisely, a distinction can be drawn between the use of the word 'version' to describe the general way in which a particular individual habitually performs a certain song, and its use to refer to a single, discrete rendition of that song, so that every iteration, even by the same individual, comprises a distinct version. To trace the problem of version back to its roots, it will be useful to consider very briefly the history of ballad editing in English.[6]

Although there are earlier publications that can be considered as ballad editions, the history of ballad editing is often taken to begin with Percy's *Reliques of Ancient English Poetry*, first published in 1765, not least because of the iconic role it played in stimulating the European ballad revival of the Romantic age.[7] The young Walter Scott's account of his discovery of the *Reliques*, which so entranced him as to make him forget his dinner, is well known, but it is perhaps still worth quoting the delight he felt at finding the kind of imaginative literature he had loved since his childhood 'considered as the subject of sober research, grave commentary, and apt illustration, by an editor who showed his poetical genius was capable of emulating the best qualities of what his pious labour preserved'.[8] It is perhaps unfortunate (at least in the view of more recent scholars) that Percy allowed his preface to convey the impression that his work constituted an eighteenth-century edition of a seventeenth-century manuscript, long after

---

5 Scholars who have commented explicitly on this confusion include Ruth Finnegan, *Oral Traditions and the Verbal Arts: A Guide to Research Practices* (London: Routledge, 1992), p. 162; D. K. Wilgus, *Anglo-American Folksong Scholarship since 1898* (New Brunswick, NJ: Rutgers University Press, 1959), pp. 396–97 n. 88.

6 The best critical account of the subject remains Albert B. Friedman, *The Ballad Revival: Studies in the Influence of Popular on Sophisticated Poetry* (Chicago: University of Chicago Press, 1961).

7 One earlier contender in the history of ballad editing is *A Collection of Old Ballads* (1723–25), which shows signs of editing work in terms of the bringing together of items and the provision of headnotes to the ballads. On the other hand, there is no real evidence of textual editing. William St Clair, *The Reading Nation in the Romantic Period* (Cambridge: Cambridge University Press, 2004), pp. 345, 501, maintains that its purpose was to reassert the rights held in the ballads by their current owners. It is still not uncommon to find the poet and playwright Ambrose Philips credited as editor of *A Collection of Old Ballads*, but there is no real evidence for this attribution. See Lillian de la Torre Bueno, 'Was Ambrose Philips a Ballad Editor?', *Anglia*, 59 (1935), 252–70.

8 J. G. Lockhart, *Memoirs of Sir Walter Scott*, 5 vols (London: Macmillan, 1900), i, 29–30.

he had in fact abandoned any such intention: 'The Reader is here presented with select remains of our ancient English Bards and Minstrels . . . The greater part of them are extracted from an ancient folio manuscript, in the Editor's possession, which contains near 200 poems, songs, and metrical romances.'[9] In fact, the *Reliques* constitutes an elaborate bricolage created out of a wide range of sources – among them the Percy folio manuscript; broadside ballads, in particular black-letter broadsides from the Pepys collection and eighteenth-century sheets printed by the Dicey firm; earlier printed collections such as Thomas D'Urfey's *Wit and Mirth; or, Pills to Purge Melancholy*, Allan Ramsay's *Tea-Table Miscellany* and *The Ever Green*, and *A Collection of Old Ballads*; and some verses sent by correspondents, in particular Scottish ballads from David Dalrymple, Lord Hailes, some of which conceivably derive from some sort of field-collecting, though not necessarily without literary 'improvement'.[10] All of Percy's sources were subject to extensive collation and synthesis, alterations of spelling and punctuation, and, in varying degrees, Percy's own 'improvements'. In certain cases – 'The Child of Elle', for example – these last amount to wholesale rewriting. Percy made rather little effort to document his textual sources, and in consequence he has left the impression of having sought to mislead later readers – and for that, as Albert Friedman memorably puts it, 'scholarship has consigned him to the special hell reserved for bad editors'.[11]

The *Reliques of Ancient English Poetry* was a huge literary success, however, with four editions during the editor's lifetime and subsequent reprints throughout the nineteenth and twentieth centuries. Beginning in 1783, the bad-tempered antiquarian Joseph Ritson launched a drawn-out attack on Percy's editorial integrity, accusing him of every kind of forgery and fabrication.[12] Percy's position was not helped by his refusal to produce the folio manuscript in public, though he did have unimpeachable witnesses to attest to its actual existence. He did make some alterations in the fourth edition of the *Reliques* in response to Ritson's criticisms, and introduced a little more clarity into the preface along with a system of marking with asterisks (some of) those instances where 'any considerable liberties' had

---

9 [Thomas Percy], *Reliques of Ancient English Poetry*, 3 vols (London: J. Dodsley, 1765), I, ix.
10 Friedman, *Ballad Revival*, pp. 185–232; Nick Groom, *The Making of Percy's Reliques* (Oxford: Clarendon Press, 1999). A useful brief account is Zinnia Knapman, 'A Reappraisal of Percy's Editing', *Folk Music Journal*, 5.2 (1986), 202–14.
11 Friedman, *Ballad Revival*, pp. 204–05.
12 [Joseph Ritson], *A Select Collection of English Songs*, 3 vols (London: J. Johnson, 1783), I, x.

been taken with the old copies.[13] But, Friedman observes, these adjustments amount to 'admissions of guilt rather than effectual efforts to atone in a substantial way for editorial waywardness'.[14] The eventual publication of a scholarly edition of the folio manuscript tended only to endorse Ritson's criticisms of Percy's editing.[15]

Yet, as Friedman also indicates, there is a certain unfairness about all this criticism, since if Percy had remained more faithful to his sources the ballads would without doubt have been less widely read.[16] It was his literary success that brought the ballads to the attention of the educated elite not just in England but across Europe in the late eighteenth and early nineteenth century. Although Samuel Johnson had been an important influence, encouraging Percy in the direction of an antiquarian edition of the folio manuscript, in the end Johnson's influence was outweighed by that of William Shenstone, whose guiding principle was not antiquarian scholarship but literary 'taste'.[17] Given the eclecticism both of Percy's selection of source materials and of the ways he made use of them, it is evident that, the statement in the preface notwithstanding, the *Reliques* is quite simply *not* intended to represent what modern scholars would call an edition of the folio manuscript, in the sense of being one that vests ultimate textual authority in that document.[18] Bearing in mind that the practice of editing with reference to an identified textual authority was already established with eighteenth-century editions of Shakespeare, in view of Percy's rejection of this principle it might almost be better not really to think of him as an editor at all. Certainly, a tendency among modern scholars to dismiss the *Reliques* as badly edited and consequently 'inauthentic' risks seriously underestimating its impact on the currency of ballad literature over a long period of time and at different social levels.

Walter Scott wrote that in compiling his *Minstrelsy of the Scottish Border*, first published in 1802–03, it had been his intention 'to imitate the plan and style of Bishop Percy, observing only more strict fidelity concerning my

---

13 [Thomas Percy], *Reliques of Ancient English Poetry*, 4th edn, 3 vols (London: F. and C. Rivington, 1794), I, xvi–xvii.
14 Friedman, *Ballad Revival*, p. 205.
15 John W. Hales and Frederick J. Furnivall, eds, *Bishop Percy's Folio Manuscript: Ballads and Romances*, 3 vols (London: N. Trübner, 1867–68); Frederick J. Furnivall, ed., *Bishop Percy's Folio Manuscript: Loose and Humorous Songs* (London: printed by and for the editor, 1868).
16 Friedman, *Ballad Revival*, p. 204.
17 Groom, *Making of Percy's Reliques*, pp. 106–44.
18 Groom, *Making of Percy's Reliques*, esp. p. 227.

originals'.[19] Ritson's attacks appear to have had the effect of compelling subsequent editors at least to begin to take some account of his demands for textual fidelity.[20] Nonetheless, Scott's editorial method was still essentially one of collation and emendation of all the manuscript texts that he happened to have to hand from his various sources, several of which were already subject to a tendency towards 'improvement'. Scott's intention was to offer ballads that were more complete than any of their individual exemplars, even though this inevitably meant the introduction of words, phrases, lines, and occasionally even stanzas of his own making.[21] His key claim as editor was to have taken no further liberties than, where exemplars disagreed, to have preserved 'the best or most poetical reading of the passage', but inevitably he was also obliged to admit to having made rearrangements 'to recover the rhyme' and 'to remove obvious corruptions, and fit the ballads for the press'.[22]

The *Minstrelsy* ballads are thus for the most part composites; but while they are unlikely to resemble any real or imagined 'original' ballad texts, commentators have nonetheless found themselves compelled to acknowledge, with varying degrees of enthusiasm, that Scott's editorial art, if the phrase may be allowed, was, at its best, capable of capturing something of the quintessence of Scottish balladry.[23] And while Scott's method was founded on Percy's, owing to its rather greater regard for textual authority it can, with a little imagination, perhaps be situated within an editorial tradition. That is to say, Scott's collation and emendation of different copies of the same ballad has something in common with stemmatics, or genealogical editing, as a method for recovering the 'original' forms of biblical and classical texts, comprising the analysis of different manuscript witnesses in order to work out their affiliations on the basis of shared

---

19 Sir Walter Scott, *Minstrelsy of the Scottish Border*, ed. T. F. Henderson, 4 vols (Edinburgh: Oliver and Boyd, 1932 [1902]), IV, 52.
20 Friedman, *Ballad Revival*, p. 241.
21 Friedman, *Ballad Revival*, pp. 242–43; Sigurd Bernhard Hustvedt, *Ballad Books and Ballad Men: Raids and Rescues in Britain, America, and the Scandinavian North since 1800* (Cambridge, MA: Harvard University Press, 1930), pp. 28–33; Charles G. Zug, III, 'The Ballad Editor as Antiquary: Scott and the *Minstrelsy*', *Journal of the Folklore Institute*, 13 (1976), 57–73.
22 Scott, *Minstrelsy*, ed. Henderson, I, 167–68 (and see also I, xvii–xxi). A new edition of the *Minstrelsy of the Scottish Border* is in preparation under the general editorship of Sigrid Rieuwerts and can be expected to provide a definitive account of Scott's editing.
23 Friedman, *Ballad Revival*, p. 243; Hustvedt, *Ballad Books and Ballad Men*, p. 33; Scott, *Minstrelsy*, ed. Henderson, I, xxxii–xxxiii.

errors, and the consequent reconstruction of an archetypal text, employing editorial conjecture where correction of the transmitted text is judged necessary in order to restore an original reading.

The practice of stemmatics was not fully established until the mid-nineteenth century, and it would be unwise to exaggerate the extent to which Scott was pursuing any such rigorous method – for one thing, he omitted to provide a record of variants in the form of an editorial collation or apparatus, and he certainly altered far more than any genealogical editor would ever want to justify. All the same, read in T. F. Henderson's edition (which has been the standard reference copy for scholars for more than a century), which records Scott's use of different manuscript sources as well as many of the corrections, emendations, and rewritings, the *Minstrelsy* can take on the outlines of a critical edition of a rather peculiar, 'proto-genealogical', imaginative kind.[24] Years later, James Reeves gave an example of a fully documented instance of this kind of editorial treatment of a folk song, 'O No John' (Roud 146), from the Cecil Sharp manuscripts, which he was the first editor to print and which he wanted to present in the 'completest text compatible with respect for the words of the singers'.[25] It should be added that this was not generally Reeves's editorial policy, and neither did he maintain that it enabled him to restore a lost 'original' – but then, neither did Scott. The important point here is not so much to defend Walter Scott as to emphasize that the pursuit of an archetypal form, by means of textual reconstruction and emendation, is a defensible editorial method.[26]

Scott later came to regret his editorial policy, writing in a letter to William Motherwell of 3 May 1825 that each ballad text, as taken down

---

24 Hustvedt, *Ballad Books and Ballad Men*, p. 32, praises Henderson's edition but considers its merits as an indictment of Scott's editing – these interpretations are essentially opposite sides of the same coin.

25 James Reeves, ed., *The Idiom of the People: English Traditional Verse* [. . .] *from the manuscripts of Cecil J. Sharp* (London: Heinemann, 1958), pp. 33–37 (quotation from p. 34).

26 Scholars of the so-called 'Finnish school' have endeavoured to reconstruct archetypes of folktales and ballads from a collation of extant texts. For some ballad examples, see Eleanor Long, *'The Maid' and 'The Hangman': Myth and Tradition in a Popular Ballad* (Berkeley and Los Angeles: University of California Press, 1971); Holger Olof Nygard, *The Ballad of 'Heer Halewijn', its Forms and Variations in Western Europe: A Study of the History and Nature of a Ballad Tradition* (Knoxville: University of Tennessee Press, 1958); Archer Taylor, *'Edward' and 'Sven i Rosengård': A Study in the Dissemination of a Ballad* (Chicago: University of Chicago Press, 1931); Lajos Vargyas, *Researches into the Mediaeval History of Folk Ballad*, trans. Arthur H. Whitney (Budapest: Akadémiai Kiadó, 1967).

from a particular contributor in a particular part of the country, amounts to an independent literary production:

> I think I did wrong myself in endeavouring to make the best possible set of an ancient ballad out of several copies obtained from different quarters, and that, in many respects, if I improved the poetry, I spoiled the simplicity of the old song. There is no wonder this should be the case when one considers that the singers or reciters by whom these ballads were preserved and handed down, must, in general, have had a facility, from memory at least, if not from genius (which they might often possess), of filling up verses which they had forgotten, or altering such as they might think they could improve. Passing through this process in different parts of the country, the ballads, admitting that they had one common poetical original (which is not to be inferred merely from the similitude of the story), became, in progress of time, totally different productions, so far as the tone and spirit of each is concerned. In such cases, perhaps, it is as well to keep them separate, as giving in their original state a more accurate idea of our ancient poetry, which is the point most important in such collections.[27]

This opinion of Scott's, along with his own accumulating experience of ballad collecting in the field, helped Motherwell formulate the introduction to his *Minstrelsy: Ancient and Modern* of 1827, in which he rejected the practice of editorial collation and emendation – in spite of the fact that he had treated many of his own published ballad texts in just that manner, since the introduction was written after the book had commenced publication (and is therefore probably better considered as an afterword or conclusion).[28] Instead, Motherwell now brought to the matter the zeal – not to mention the rhetoric – of the convert:

> it has become of the first importance to collect these songs with scrupulous and unshrinking fidelity. If they are at all worth preserving [. . .] it assuredly must be in the very garb in which they are remembered and known, and can be proved to exist amongst us. It will not do to indulge in idle speculation as to what they once may have been, and to recast them in what we may fancy were their original moulds.
>
> With many of these ballads, liberties of the most exceptionable and flagrant description have occasionally been taken by their respective editors, liberties

---

27 William Motherwell, *The Poetical Works of William Motherwell*, with memoir by James M'Conechy, Esq., 2nd edn (Glasgow: David Robertson, 1847), p. xxxiii.
28 Mary Ellen Brown, *William Motherwell's Cultural Politics, 1797–1835* (Lexington: University Press of Kentucky, 2001), pp. 78–102. See also Hustvedt, *Ballad Books and Ballad Men*, pp. 75–77; William B. McCarthy, 'William Motherwell as Field Collector', *Folk Music Journal*, 5.3 (1987), 295–316 (esp. pp. 300–04).

as uncalled for as they are unpardonable in the eye of every rigid and honest critick. Some of these offences against truth and correct taste, are of a very deep, others of a lighter shade of criminality, but be they what they may in magnitude, all are alike deserving of unmitigated condemnation.

By selecting the most beautiful and striking passages, which present themselves in the one copy, and making these cohere as they best may, with similar extracts detached from the other copy, the editor of oral poetry succeeds in producing from the conflicting texts of his various authorities, a tirdd [sic] version more perfect and ornate than any individual one as it originally stood. This improved version may contain the quintessence – the poetick elements of each copy consulted, but in this general resemblance to all, it loses its particular affinity to any one. Its individuality entirely disappears, and those features by which each separate copy proved its authenticity, in the collated version, become faint and dubious, confused and undistinguishable.[29]

Each version – which seems, in effect, to mean each copy of the same ballad taken down from a different source – is entitled to be considered of equal 'authenticity' (read 'authority').[30] And where space permits the reproduction of just one text (Motherwell does not quite say this, but it seems to be implied), the editor is still bound to reproduce it with the utmost fidelity:

Under the pressure of such circumstances, then, it surely is the duty of the collector and editor of Traditionary ballads, to avoid the perilous and frequently abortive task, of uniting discordant and essentially incohesive texts, and to content himself with merely selecting that one of his copies which appears the most complete and least vitiated – and to give it purely and simply as he obtained it, without hazarding any emendation whatsoever.[31]

Motherwell's introduction, indebted to Scott's letter, exerted a strong influence on the practice of the Danish ballad editor Svend Grundtvig, who commenced publication of *Danmarks gamle Folkeviser* in 1853 and summarized his own editorial policy as being to print 'all there is . . . as it is', and Grundtvig in turn guided Child.[32] And the rest, as the saying goes, is history.

---

29 William Motherwell, *Minstrelsy: Ancient and Modern* (Glasgow: John Wylie, 1827), pp. iv, v, vi (respectively).
30 Motherwell, *Minstrelsy: Ancient and Modern*, p. vi.
31 Motherwell, *Minstrelsy: Ancient and Modern*, p. vii.
32 Flemming G. Andersen, '"All There Is . . . As It Is": On the Development of Textual Criticism in Ballad Studies', *Jahrbuch für Volksliedforschung*, 39 (1994), 28–40; Mary Ellen Brown, 'Mr. Child's Scottish Mentor: William Motherwell', in *Ballads into Books: The*

Or not quite. For one thing, it would be misleading to exaggerate either (*i*) the extent to which the vesting of authority in a single, discrete text was a novel idea when Child started to publish the volumes of *The English and Scottish Popular Ballads* in 1882; or (*ii*) the impression that there was but a single trajectory in ballad editing extending from *Reliques of Ancient English Poetry* through to Child's edition and beyond. Ritson, for example, edited a number of ballad books which by and large adhere to his insistence on printing texts just as they were found.[33] John Bell, editor of the north-eastern collection *Rhymes of Northern Bards*, which appeared in 1812, has been credited with having treated his sources 'with more respect than any later editor of non-copyright material except Child'.[34] And Child's preface to his own earlier edition of *English and Scottish Ballads*, which began publication in 1857 and which drew its texts from previous printed collections, including Percy's *Reliques*, states: 'With respect to the texts, the Editor, after selecting the most authentic copies, has carefully adhered to the originals as they stand in the printed collections, sometimes restoring a reading which had been changed without reason, and in all cases indicating deviations, whether his own or those of others, in the margin.'[35] Similarly, Hales and Furnivall affirm that their approach to editing the Percy folio is to give the texts just as they stand in the manuscript, with any necessary alterations recorded in the notes.[36] In principle, too, the various volumes published by the Ballad Society in the late nineteenth century adhere to scholarly principles.[37]

Conversely, the practice of editorial collation, synthesis, and imaginative reconstruction continued to be embraced, and defended, by editors after Motherwell and even after Child. The Anglo-Irish poet William Allingham, for example, set out in the *Ballad Book*, which first appeared in 1864, to present a selection of ballads 'in at once the best and the most authentic

---

Legacies of Francis James Child, ed. Tom Cheesman and Sigrid Rieuwerts (Bern: Peter Lang, 1997), pp. 29–39.

33 Friedman, *Ballad Revival*, pp. 237–40; Gregory, *Victorian Songhunters*, pp. 39–42.
34 John Bell, ed., *Rhymes of Northern Bards*, introduction by David Harker (Newcastle upon Tyne: Frank Graham, 1971 [1812]), p. liii. See also Harker, *Fakesong*, p. 72.
35 Francis James Child, ed., *English and Scottish Ballads*, 8 vols (Boston: Little, Brown, 1857–58), I, xi.
36 Hales and Furnivall, eds, *Bishop Percy's Folio Manuscript*, I, xxiii.
37 See Gregory, *Victorian Songhunters*, pp. 325–58; Sigrid Rieuwerts, 'The Ballad Society: A Forgotten Chapter in the History of English Ballad Studies', in *Folk Song: Tradition, Revival, and Re-Creation*, ed. Ian Russell and David Atkinson (Aberdeen: Elphinstone Institute, University of Aberdeen, 2004), pp. 28–40.

attainable form' by collating, and occasionally altering, multiple copies.[38] 'In short,' he proclaims, somewhat romantically, 'the present editor, has dealt, as poet and critic, with a heap of confused materials, much as he would have dealt orally with the same materials, had fortune placed him in the world some three centuries ago in the condition of a ballad-minstrel (many worse conditions for a poet), singing in hall or cottage to groups of old and young.'[39] In his *Oxford Book of Ballads* of 1910, Arthur Quiller-Couch, writer, critic, and editor of several famous anthologies, known by his *nom de plume* as 'Q', explicitly acknowledges the editorial practice of Scott and Allingham as his model and offers the reader a single, and in many instances composite, 'best' copy of each ballad, albeit with the most significant interpolations enclosed within square brackets.[40] The poet and novelist Robert Graves, too, published ballad anthologies, in 1927 and 1957, and he again chose 'to give a version compressed from several surviving variants [. . .] and so show the potential completeness that the ballad had while it was still alive'.[41] Quiller-Couch's *Oxford Book of Ballads* was reprinted until eventually replaced in 1969 by James Kinsley's edition, who explicitly rejected his predecessor's method and instead reproduces each ballad from a single source, with emendation kept to a minimum.[42]

The contrasting Victorian (and later) approaches to ballad editing have been characterized as positivist and scientific (Child et al.), versus Romantic, idealist, and neo-Platonic (Allingham, Quiller-Couch, Graves).[43] More often than not, however, they reflect first and foremost a difference in the nature of the source materials and the editors' and publishers' intentions. On one side were those charged with editing a specified corpus, contained within a particular manuscript or collection of broadsides, for a largely scholarly readership; on the other, those whose project was to present the ballads at large to a general readership, drawing on a potentially unbounded corpus

---

38 William Allingham, ed., *The Ballad Book: A Selection of the Choicest British Ballads* (London and Cambridge: Macmillan, 1864), p. v (see also pp. xxvi–xxx).
39 Allingham, ed., *Ballad Book*, p. xxx.
40 Arthur Quiller-Couch, ed., *The Oxford Book of Ballads* (Oxford: Clarendon Press, 1910), pp. ix–xi.
41 Robert Graves, *The English Ballad: A Short Critical Survey* (London: Ernest Benn, 1927), p. 33; Robert Graves, ed., *English and Scottish Ballads* (London: Heinemann, 1957), pp. xxiv–xxv.
42 James Kinsley, ed., *The Oxford Book of Ballads* (Oxford: Oxford University Press, 1969), pp. vi–vii.
43 Gregory, 'In the Shadow of Child', p. 71; Gregory, *Victorian Songhunters*, p. 301.

that could include multiple iterations of the 'same' thing, and who were obliged to do so within constraints of space and budget.

Howbeit, Child's practice – that is to say, to edit at the level of the individual text – is held to represent the scholarly ideal. And yet (as with so many of the classic published ballad collections) there is actually no clear statement of editorial policy in *The English and Scottish Popular Ballads* at all. The reader is left to deduce, for example, that italic font in texts derived from early manuscripts represents the expansion of manuscript contractions – a convention that, to be fair, may have been more familiar in Child's time.[44] More importantly, though Child did not conflate texts in the Walter Scott manner, he did nonetheless collate texts; and on occasion he did adopt readings other than those of his source text, sometimes introducing emendations of his own. It is possible to substantiate these assertions by dipping into *The English and Scottish Popular Ballads* more or less at random, but a few examples will illustrate the main categories of editorial practice that demand consideration here.

Child 20 I is a text of 'The Cruel Mother', for which the base text (Child 20 I a) is found in the British Library manuscript of the Scottish ballad collector Peter Buchan.[45] Child did not live to see the same ballad in another Peter Buchan manuscript, formerly in the possession of Buchan's nephew, David Scott of Peterhead, and now at Harvard.[46] Variant readings are collated in the critical apparatus which is printed after all the texts of 'The Cruel Mother'.[47] The copies collated here are from Peter Buchan's *Ancient Ballads and Songs of the North of Scotland* (Child 20 I b);[48] and William Christie's *Traditional Ballad Airs*, where the words are 'epitomized [from Buchan's *Ancient Ballads and Songs*], and somewhat changed for this Work,

---

44 It is explained, for example, in Hales and Furnivall, eds, *Bishop Percy's Folio Manuscript*, I, xxiii.
45 London, British Library, Additional MS 29408–29409, vol. 2, pp. 111–13.
46 Cambridge, MA, Harvard University, Houghton Library, MS Eng 1491 (2) [recatalogued from 25241.10.5F*], pp. 718–21 [cited from microfilm copy in London, Vaughan Williams Memorial Library]. Buchan apparently copied out several different ballad manuscripts, of which the Harvard MS is the most comprehensive. See William Walker, *Peter Buchan and Other Papers on Scottish and English Ballads and Songs* (Aberdeen: D. Wyllie & Son, 1915), pp. 17–195; also Mary Ellen Brown, ed., *The Bedesman and the Hodbearer: The Epistolary Friendship of Francis James Child and William Walker* (Aberdeen: Aberdeen University Press, for the Elphinstone Institute, 2001), pp. 3–5. For an accessible account of the controversy surrounding Buchan's ballad collecting, see Sigrid Rieuwerts, 'The Case against Peter Buchan', in *The Flowering Thorn: International Ballad Studies*, ed. Thomas A. McKean (Logan: Utah State University Press, 2003), pp. 341–51.
47 The apparatus and other notes referred to here are at *ESPB*, I, 226, 504.
48 Peter Buchan, *Ancient Ballads and Songs of the North of Scotland*, 2 vols (Edinburgh: W. and D. Laing; J. Stevenson; Aberdeen: A. Brown & Co.; Glasgow: J. Wylie; Robertson and Atkinson; Perth: D. Morison & Co.; London: J. Darling, 1828), II, 217–20.

some of the changes being made according to the way the Editor has heard it sung', and matched with a melody collected in Banffshire (Child 20 I c).[49]

So, in line 3.1, 'She did her down to the greenwood gang', Child rejected 'green woods', the reading of the base text in the British Library MS, in favour of 'greenwood', which is the reading in *Ancient Ballads and Songs*, though the apparatus does not record this last point (the Harvard MS has 'green wood', though the space between the *n* of 'green' and the *w* of 'wood' is very slight). In lines 14.1 and 16.1, Child emended the word 'fool', which is the reading in the British Library MS (and the Harvard MS) and *Ancient Ballads and Songs* (and also in Christie's equivalent of 14.1, though this is not recorded) to 'fowl', even though 'fool' is a perfectly acceptable Scots spelling (Child notes against 'fool' in the apparatus: 'i.e. "fowl" spelt phonetically').[50] In lines 16.1 and 16.2, which in the British Library MS end with the words 'wood' and 'flood', respectively, Child chose to print 'wood[s]' and 'flood[s]', maintaining consistency with the plural forms of the same words in lines 14.1 and 14.2, but with only the presence of square brackets in the body of the Child 20 I text to indicate the emendation. The apparatus does not record it, and neither does it record that 'woods' and 'floods' are the readings in *Ancient Ballads and Songs* (and in the Harvard MS).

Further collation of Child 20 I against the two manuscripts (bearing in mind that Child did not have the opportunity to consult the Harvard manuscript) and *Ancient Ballads and Songs* reveals a number of variant readings (discounting minutiae of punctuation) not noted or only partially recorded in Child's apparatus (Table 6.1). Child also notes that the same ballad is found in a couple of other places: 'Printed as from the MS. in Dixon's *Scottish Traditional Versions of Ancient Ballads* [. . .] with a few arbitrary changes';[51] and in William Motherwell's manuscript.[52] These copies are not collated, though they do contain variant readings.

---

49 W. Christie, ed., *Traditional Ballad Airs*, 2 vols (Edinburgh: Edmonston & Douglas; David Douglas, 1876–81), I, 106–07. Christie's text begins with the equivalent of stanza 7 of Child 20 I and ends with the equivalent of stanza 14 (although this is perhaps not quite clear from Child's apparatus).

50 There is a further peculiarity to note here: in the British Library MS, someone has made a small number of pencil alterations, including the substitution of 'fowl' for 'fool' in these two lines (the other alterations do not correspond to anything in *ESPB*).

51 James Henry Dixon, ed., *Scottish Traditional Versions of Ancient Ballads* (London: Percy Society, 1845), pp. 50–52.

52 Glasgow University Library, MS Murray 501, pp. 475–76; transcribed copy in Cambridge, MA, Harvard University, Houghton Library, MS Eng 1556 [recatalogued from 25241.20*], 2 vols, pp. 558–60 [cited from microfilm copy in London, Vaughan Williams Memorial Library]. Several of the ballads in Motherwell's manuscript are duplicates of those in Peter Buchan's manuscripts.

	Child 20 I	British Library Additional MS 29408–29409	Harvard MS Eng 1491 (2)	Peter Buchan, Ancient Ballads and Songs (1828)	recorded in ESPB apparatus
2.2	belly did her betray	belly did her betray	belly it did her betray	belly it did her betray	yes
3.1	greenwood	green woods	green wood	greenwood	partially
4.1	lent	lent	lent	leant	no
5.2	bodyes	bodies	bodies	bodies	no
8.2	with the white bread and wine	with the white bread and wine	with white bread and wine	with white bread and wine	yes
9.1	wi	with	with	with	no
10.2	none of	none of	nane o'	nane o'	no
11.1	none of	none of	nane o'	nane o'	no
11.2	wore we of	wore we of	wear'd we o'	wear'd we o'	partially
13.2	sort of death you must die	sort of death you must die	sort o' death you maun die	sort of death you maun die	no
14.1	fowl	fool	fool	fool	yes
16.1	fowl wood[s]	fool wood	fool woods	fool woods	yes
16.2	flood[s]	flood	floods	floods	no

Table 6.1 Child 20 I variant readings

On occasion, too, Child was not averse to more radical conjectural emendation. Thus the first line of the final stanza of 'Bonnie Annie' (Child 24 A) reads: 'He made his love a coffin of the gowd sae yellow'.[53] However, the base text in George R. Kinloch's *Ancient Scottish Ballads* has: 'He made his love a coffin off the Goats of Yerrow'.[54] On the face of it, Child's emendation appears not unreasonable, and it is duly recorded in the apparatus. Kinloch, however, had satisfactorily explained 'Goats' as meaning inlets of the sea, and the usage is attested elsewhere,[55] though he was unable to give a location for 'Yerrow'. In a similar vein, Stephen Knight has commented on Child's (duly recorded) emendation in 'Robin Hood Rescuing Will Stutly' (Child 141) of the 'doubtless' of early printed copies to 'doughty', observing, 'he presumably did not note the ironical implication of *doubtles* in the sense of "fearless"'.[56] The adjective occurs in the context of the sheriff's men running away when assailed by Robin Hood and his companions. Knight's reading of 'doubtless' is indeed aesthetically attractive, but it should be noted that some of the later sources mentioned in Child's headnote, such as *A Collection of Old Ballads*, do in fact have 'doughty'.

Collation, emendation, and the exercise of editorial choice over variant readings constituted for Child perfectly respectable editorial practices, precedented in the editing of Shakespeare, for example. The collation of variants within an apparatus appended to a clear reading text was – and remains – standard practice, though it is not without consequences. As Peter Shillingsburg has intimated, one difficulty is that the method necessarily tends to privilege one set of readings, which provide the clear reading text, at the expense of all those collated in the apparatus – that is to say, it privileges one text over another.[57] This sort of privileging is an artefact of the editing process and has potentially serious consequences in that it may, for the general reader in particular, suppress an awareness of the intrinsic instability and variability of texts. The effect is especially pronounced when the apparatus is some pages removed from the reading text, as is often the case in *The English and Scottish Popular Ballads*.

---

53 *ESPB*, I, 245–47.

54 [Geo. R. Kinloch], *Ancient Scottish Ballads* (London: Longman, Rees, Orme, Brown, & Green; Edinburgh: John Stevenson, 1827), pp. 123–26.

55 *CSD* gote &c., *n*. 2; *DSL-SND1* gote, *n*. 2.

56 Stephen Knight, ed., *Robin Hood: The Forresters Manuscript, British Library Additional MS 71158* (Cambridge: D. S. Brewer, 1998), p. 92.

57 Peter L. Shillingsburg, *Resisting Texts: Authority and Submission in Constructions of Meaning* (Ann Arbor: University of Michigan Press, 1997), pp. 17–18. It remains to be seen whether electronic editions really can circumvent this difficulty.

Child's collations of variant texts, moreover, are not consistent, encompassing both (*i*) collations of texts that are genetically derived one from the other, and (*ii*) collations of texts that are merely quite similar. In the first of these categories are the many instances (like Child 20 I) where Child follows a base text in a manuscript but also records variant readings arising when it was subsequently published, recopied in manuscript, or reprinted elsewhere. In the second category are instances such as Child 10 R, where he simply brings together texts of 'The Two Sisters' from quite different sources but of a sufficient degree of similarity to permit collation.[58] Child 10 R a, which provides the base text, was published in *Notes and Queries* in 1852 as a '*Lancashire* ballad'.[59] Child 10 R b was written down by Lady Louisa Primrose at Wishaw House in 1861 for J. F. Campbell, who also cited parts of it in his *Popular Tales of the West Highlands*.[60] Child 10 R c was printed in 1859 in *The Scouring of the White Horse* by Thomas Hughes (author of *Tom Brown's Schooldays*), under the title of 'The Barkshire Tragedy', in a supposed representation of dialect speech, which Child interpreted as deriving from Berkshire.[61] Clearly, these three texts are most unlikely to be genetically related to one another in any immediate way.

Among the narrative differences that might be noted are the status of the sisters' father: a king of the north countree (Child 10 R a); a farmer in the north countree (Child 10 R b); a 'varmer' in the West Countree (Child 10 R c).[62] He gives his daughters gifts in Child 10 R a, apparently sparking off the jealousy between them; whereas in Child 10 R b it is the elder sister's lover who turns up in the second stanza, falls in love with the younger

---

[58] Later, Child printed a further copy, from New York, designated Child 10 Z, which he also considered 'a variety of [Child 10] R' (*ESPB*, II, 509).

[59] 'Ballad of "The Three Sisters"', *Notes and Queries*, 1st ser., 6 (1852), 102.

[60] J. F. Campbell, *Popular Tales of the West Highlands*, 4 vols (Edinburgh: Edmonston & Douglas, 1860–62), IV, 125–27. Child's location of Wishaw House in Lancashire, the same county as Child 10 R a, is an error for Lanarkshire (*ESPB*, I, 136). Campbell, incidentally, held decidedly to the 'neo-Platonic' school of editing: 'A ballad then bears the stamp of originality, and the traces of many minds; it may be of generations of singers of all classes of society, and of many districts; it may even be found in several different dialects, or even languages, and yet be the same ballad nevertheless. To strike out any bit of a genuine ballad is to mutilate it; to add anything to it is to disfigure it; but it is quite legitimate to fuse as many versions as can be got, so as to complete the story, and to select the best of several lines, if the fact be stated' (IV, 127).

[61] [Thomas Hughes], *The Scouring of the White Horse; or, The Long Vacation Ramble of a London Clerk* (Cambridge: Macmillan, 1859), pp. 158–60.

[62] Child's apparatus has 'west countree', while *The Scouring of the White Horse* has 'West Countree' with upper-case initials – in English usage there is potentially a difference of meaning.

sister, and gives her a gift; in Child 10 R c there are neither gifts nor lover. In Child 10 R a the miller fishes the drowning girl out of the stream, takes her gold chain from her, pushes her back in, and ends up being hanged for his pains. Child 10 R b goes on to recount that the elder sister sailed over the sea, 'And died an old maid of a hundred and three', while the lover became a beggar-man, 'And he drank out of a rusty tin can'. In Child 10 R c the miller is hunted down and hanged, while the elder sister fled the country 'And died an old maid among black savagees'. Child 10 R a more or less fits into the portmanteau story type A in Tristram Coffin's classification of ballad narrative variants, but he evidently felt the more or less burlesque 'old maid' ending was quite distinctive and Child 10 R b and c would fall within his story type P.[63]

Possibly the tactic of collating texts that can at best be described as 'generally similar' can be interpreted as thinking in terms of 'variants' (groupings of individual texts that share similar characteristics) as opposed to 'versions' (something closer to individual texts derived from distinct sources).[64] Presumably it was also driven at least in part by the requirement to conserve space in an edition that was already growing like Topsy. On the other hand, Child grouped together a copy of 'The Jolly Beggar' from David Herd's *Ancient and Modern Scots Songs* (Child 279 B a) with a broadside, *The Jolly Beggars*, from the British Library (Child 279 B b), which are similar in outline but differ so much in detail that they could not be conveniently collated, and instead the broadside text is printed in full in the critical apparatus.[65] Child thought the variant readings of the broadside were 'not the accidents of tradition, but deliberate alterations'.[66]

Where Child had access to more than one text from the same source he mostly collated the variant readings in the critical apparatus, except for one or two instances where he evidently judged the differences between

---

63 Tristram Potter Coffin, *The British Traditional Ballad in North America*, rev. edn, with supplement by Roger deV. Renwick (Austin: University of Texas Press, 1977), pp. 32, 34.
64 As noted in chapter 1, a degree of confusion between 'version' and 'variant' persists to the present day. See [Stith Thompson], 'Variant', in *Funk & Wagnalls Standard Dictionary of Folklore, Mythology, and Legend*, ed. Maria Leach, 2 vols (New York: Funk & Wagnalls, 1949–50), pp. 1154–55. Ballad scholars are currently more likely to think of Child 10 R a, b, and c as three distinct versions.
65 [David Herd], *The Ancient and Modern Scots Songs, Heroic Ballads, &c.* (Edinburgh: Martin & Wotherspoon, 1769), pp. 46–47; *The Jolly Beggars* ([1800?]) [London, British Library, 1078.m.24.(30.)].
66 *ESPB*, v, 109.

texts to be sufficient to warrant printing them in full.[67] An editor certainly has to bear in mind the possibility that different texts deriving from a single contributor might have been acquired from different sources and maintained their conceptual independence.[68] Nevertheless, allowing that it is very difficult to know for sure, in very many instances there most probably does exist some sort of direct genetic connection between variant texts of the same ballad deriving from the same contributor. What an editor is being called upon to do is to make a judgement concerning the significance of degrees of difference. Does each separate manifestation, rendering, or iteration invariably warrant entirely separate editorial treatment, or does this only become the case once a certain degree of difference has been attained, and if so where does the line of demarcation lie?

Likewise with broadside texts, which are often assumed to have been copied directly from one printing to another by the same and/or different printers, and yet can display just the same sorts of variation as are found among collected ballads.[69] Child tended to collate different broadside printings together and his practice may have contributed to a widespread impression of the intrinsic stability of printed texts. Of course, if they were copied one from another they would be genetically related in some degree, and their variant readings might appear semantically quite insignificant even while their bibliographic codes might be very different indeed. Conversely, the broadsides themselves might well have existed at quite different times and in quite different places, and it is therefore difficult not to allow that they are just as much different versions as ballads collected from contributors similarly separated by time and space. And if the argument holds for different printings, does it not then equally hold for

---

67 For example, Child 53 A, C and Child 76 D, E. Discussion of Child's treatment of the ballads from the Anna Brown repertoire is omitted here because the matter is quite complicated and there is now an excellent new edition of Anna Brown's ballads: Sigrid Rieuwerts, ed., *The Ballad Repertoire of Anna Gordon, Mrs Brown of Falkland*, Scottish Text Society, 5th ser., no. 8 (Woodbridge and Rochester, NY: Boydell Press, for the Scottish Text Society, 2011).

68 See, for example, David Atkinson and Julia C. Bishop, 'The Contributor as Collector: Ann Lyall and "The Fair Flower of Northumberland"', in *Emily Lyle: The Persistent Scholar*, ed. Frances J. Fischer and Sigrid Rieuwerts, BASIS, vol. 5 (Trier: WVT Wissenschaftlicher Verlag Trier, 2007), pp. 5–24.

69 Dianne M. Dugaw, 'Anglo-American Folksong Reconsidered: The Interface of Oral and Written Forms', *Western Folklore*, 43 (1984), 83–103. See also David Atkinson, 'Are Broadside Ballads Worth Editing?', *Variants*, 10 (2013), 235–55.

the individual sheets, even if they are to all intents and purposes lexically identical?

The decision is inevitably profoundly affected by the pragmatics of editing. One suspects that Child's judgements were influenced as much by the ease or otherwise of compiling collations of variant readings as by a coherent philosophical position concerning what constitutes an autonomous version. His system of designation using upper-case and lower-case lettering is certainly neither transparent nor consistent throughout *The English and Scottish Popular Ballads*. And while the trajectory from Percy, or at least from Scott, through to Child appears on the face of it to have determined that the locus of authority for ballad editing should lie not with the abstract ballad type but with the supposedly concrete, unitary version, and thence with its individual source, be that a person or a printing, the precise definition of version and source has remained elusive.

Child, then, was not editing in accordance with a single defined theory of text. Like Percy and Scott, Child was a pioneer, but since his time the theory of text for ballad editing has remained largely uncharted. In practice, the majority of editors of ballad materials have been concerned with the presentation of single texts derived from single sources, and have therefore been able to make policy on the fly, perpetuating the type/version paradigm even while version itself has remained undefined. A representative statement of policy is given by Arthur Kyle Davis in the introduction to *Traditional Ballads of Virginia*:

> No editorial liberties have been taken with the text. In every case, it is given as it was sent in, presumably as it was sung, essentially without emendation. Punctuation has, of course, been supplied where it was lacking or inaccurate; bad or unusual spelling, where it had no connection with the original pronunciation or rendition, has been corrected; stanza divisions have been provided, sometimes conjecturally, in order to present the words in a standard and readable form. But the essential folk quality of these ballads has not been tampered with. No attempt has been made to 'improve upon' oral tradition, after the manner of Bishop Percy, Sir Walter Scott, and others. The endeavor has been to present it as accurately as possible.[70]

As the second sentence in the quotation indicates, one reason why this approach appears non-problematical lies in the presumed closeness of the

---

70 Arthur Kyle Davis, Jr., ed., *Traditional Ballads of Virginia, collected under the auspices of the Virginia Folk-Lore Society* (Cambridge, MA: Harvard University Press, 1929), p. 21.

texts to what was taken down 'in the field'. In *More Traditional Ballads of Virginia*, Davis writes, 'the effort has been to present the song as it was actually sung, so far as can be determined'.[71]

This, however, turns out to be not without its difficulties. Collectors turn out to differ widely in their ability to take down music notations, so that 'it is ticklish business for an editor [. . .] to decide which aberrations are those of the transcriber, which of the singer. And the latter must be preserved at all cost, just as an obvious verbal intrusion (if one may speak of an "intrusion" here) must be preserved in the text, whether or not it makes sense, because it is preserved by the folk' – and yet at the same time, 'obvious musical errors have been eliminated; in a few instances, after consultation, the musical editors have made minor alterations which, in their considered opinion, bring the text nearer to what the singer must actually have sung'.[72] Moreover, problems arise when there is a discrepancy between the words as written down under the music transcription and those of the same stanza given in the separately written text. In *Traditional Ballads of Virginia*, such cases 'have not been altered as errors of copying, but left as interesting variants'.[73] *More Traditional Ballads of Virginia*, however, is seemingly a little more circumspect: 'The discrepancy arises chiefly from the fact that the musical transcriber has heard the words differently from the textual transcriber. Where one or the other was obviously in error, the two have been brought into conformity, but in a few cases, rather than make an arbitrary decision, the two readings have been allowed to stand as self-declared variants. The remaining differences are slight, and both readings are phonetically possible.'[74] Here, then, is what might be interpreted as a subtle shift of editorial policy, away from absolute documentary fidelity and towards critical emendation – implicitly towards the idea of recovering what the contributor intended.

What is beginning to become apparent is that the location of textual authority in the words and tune just as they were taken down 'in the field' from the individual contributor is not in itself sufficient. Not only are spelling and punctuation, and to a lesser extent line and stanza divisions, extraneous to 'the song as it was actually sung', but the possibility is there that the music

---

71 Davis, ed., *More Traditional Ballads of Virginia*, p. xvii.
72 Davis, ed., *Traditional Ballads of Virginia*, p. 16.
73 Davis, ed., *Traditional Ballads of Virginia*, p. 18.
74 Davis, ed., *More Traditional Ballads of Virginia*, p. xvii.

and words as transcribed could actually be a misrepresentation of what it is that the editor is seeking to recover. In other words, a degree of 'intentionalism' has begun to infiltrate the editorial process itself. Just as the 'social theory of text' acknowledges that non-authorial agents (printers, publishers, editors, and so forth) have the capacity to intervene between author and reader, and to alter the former's intentions, through deliberate and accidental alterations to literary texts, the inference here is that collectors, transcribers, and editors stand in the same relation vis-à-vis the source of any particular ballad – that is to say, they have a necessary role as agents.

For the would-be editor, there are seemingly both gains and losses to be had from the appearance of a tacit intentionalism in ballad editing. The gain may well be a seeming shift of the locus of textual authority away from documentary records and on to the contributor per se. This accords well with ethnographic perspectives on traditional singers and singing, and with the Romantic notion of the autonomy of the creative artist (though not with the fact that the contributor is most commonly *not* the original author or prime creator of the ballad in question). The loss is that the editor, faced with the diminished authority of documentary evidence, is then thrown back on his or her own inference as to what really constituted the contributor's intention. In fact, the seeming gain from the locating of textual authority with an autonomous source will turn out to be illusory and unattainable.

The problems are highlighted by the ballads in the collection made by James Madison Carpenter in Britain and Ireland (mostly in England and Scotland), and the USA, from the late 1920s onwards (he had probably ceased most of his collecting activity by the end of the 1930s).[75] Working under the auspices of Harvard, it is little surprise that (although his doctoral dissertation was on sea shanties) Carpenter accorded great weight to his discovery of Child ballads still current in England and Scotland, and that the ballads should represent the most complex and theoretically challenging part of his collection. Most of them exist in multiple iterations of the 'same' thing:

- a dictaphone recording of at least a few stanzas
- a rough copy text (mostly typescript, with handwritten alterations)

---

[75] Julia C. Bishop, '"Dr Carpenter from the Harvard College in America": An Introduction to James Madison Carpenter and his Collection', *Folk Music Journal*, 7.4 (1998), 402–20.

- a fair copy text (typescript)
- a lacquer disc copy of the dictaphone recording (sometimes more than one copy)
- Carpenter's transcription of the sound recording (often more than one attempt).

Carpenter described his method of ballad collecting in an interview with Alan Jabbour in 1972.[76] Initially, he asked his contributors to sing a few stanzas into the dictaphone, and then had them dictate the entire text, two lines at a time, which he took down on a portable typewriter. These texts typed 'in the field' are believed to constitute the rough copy texts. He made it clear, however, that he also discussed the songs with the contributors, asking them, for example, if they knew of further stanzas that he himself knew from printed sources (and on a few occasions he revisited a contributor after a lapse of time to go over the texts again). It is at this stage(s) that some of the handwritten amendments to the rough copy texts are thought to have been made. In a few instances, too, he noted words from the cylinder recordings on to the rough copy typescripts. Certainly, some of the amendments take the form of variant readings, additional stanzas, and the like. However, there are also many more mundane alterations – insertion of punctuation, standardization of spellings, and so forth – which look to have been made, quite possibly at a significantly later date, in anticipation of eventual publication of the ballad collection (which was never achieved in his lifetime).[77]

By and large, the fair copy texts then reproduce the rough copy texts with all their amendments in a neat form, but also with a large number of minor variants, especially concerning the spellings of Scots words, and a smaller number of more substantial variants, some of which do not have any evident precedent. In addition, the sound recordings frequently preserve sets of words that vary to a greater or lesser extent from the typescripts. The dictaphone recordings are generally of extremely poor quality. In some cases the disc copies, which were made at an earlier stage in the life of the wax cylinders, provide a better (though still not very good) signal. Carpenter's

---

[76] Washington, DC, Library of Congress, American Folklife Center, Archive of Folk Culture, AFC1972/001, James Madison Carpenter Collection, Reel tapes, AFS 14762–14765.

[77] The manuscripts and some of their challenges are described in a little more detail in David Atkinson, 'The Secret Life of Ballad Manuscripts', *Variants*, 8 (2012), 183–206 [and note the corrigendum in *Variants*, 10 (2013), 13].

own music transcriptions, with accompanying words, were made from the sound recordings; where they are available, they are invaluable for identifying and decoding the sound recordings, but at the same time inevitably they influence what the modern listener hears and writes down.

Carpenter's ballads, therefore, present the editor with manuscript materials of a complexity that has not faced – or at least has not been reported by – other ballad editors since Child's day. The editor is no longer dealing simply with single texts derived from single sources, but with dynamic texts that may derive from multiple sources – that is to say, from both the contributor and the collector, and from their unique interaction. Consequently, if an editor were to seek to pursue an intentionalist policy, he or she would have to be constantly making decisions as to what exactly was the contributor's intention. For example, where variant readings, or additional lines or stanzas, are inserted into the typescript by hand, should they be considered as the contributor's afterthoughts, or as the contributor's responses to Carpenter's suggestions, and in either case should they be included as constituting part of the contributor's own final intention?

In the interview with Alan Jabbour, Carpenter described this sort of situation in some detail:

> One thing that I attribute the value of my collection is the fact that . . . I have the ability to hold great masses of stuff in my memory. And I go over the ballads until I know them consecutively, straight through like that, and . . . after the person has finished singing, very often the excitement of singing on to a dictaphone makes him forget one or two or three stanzas that he knows. And so, with the thing in my mind, I say, 'Well, was there any stanza that began so-and-so?' He'll say, 'Oh yes!', and away he'd start with his things, you see. Now that's the difference between my collecting and that of just the haphazard collector. I . . . loved the stuff and was eager to get it . . . perfectly. And I'd always jog their memory after they'd finished: 'Was this in it? Was that in it?' Naturally, I didn't . . . pump him nor prime him nor put my stuff in, but if he knew a stanza or two or three that he had forgotten, and it comes, you see, and makes your collection complete. So many people, when you are trying to write for dictation . . . when you are waiting the two minutes for him to copy, then the sequence slips out of your mind and the next stanza that you were going to put in just slides through and you go to the third one instead.[78]

---

78 Author's transcription, with ellipses to edit out some of Carpenter's hesitations.

One might feel suspicious of Carpenter's insistence that he did not 'pump' or 'prime' his contributors, but if textual authority is to be located with the contributor's intention, then the correction of lapses of memory or other failures of execution would surely comply with that intention. No singer intends to stumble over or forget their words. But then, by the same token, where Carpenter's typescript has an ellipsis, should an editor fill that in too? The number and nature of variant readings among Carpenter's rough copies are perhaps sufficient to permit the inference that at least some of his contributors may not have been regular performers of the items they gave him and that they may have struggled on occasion to recall the words.[79]

Further points of decision arise where there occurs a 'nonsense' word. Should that be considered to be the contributor's error, or Carpenter's error, and should it be editorially emended? After all, an intentionalist policy permits the correction of 'evident' errors. For example, Sam Bennett, the remarkable singer and fiddle-player from Ilmington, Warwickshire, dictated a stanza of 'The Baffled Knight' (Child 112) in the following form:

> And as they rode upon the way
> They saw some poops of hay
> Oh is not this a pretty place
> For boys and girls to play?[80]

---

[79] Two points are worth making here. First, it is a not infrequent observation that singers can find it difficult to recall the words of a song other than in direct association with the melody, and vice versa, and that external interruptions can altogether disrupt the flow. Both Cecil Sharp and Percy Grainger allude to aspects of this phenomenon. See Cecil J. Sharp, *English Folk-Song: Some Conclusions* (London: Simpkin; Novello, 1907), p. 19; Percy Grainger, 'Collecting with the Phonograph', *Journal of the Folk-Song Society*, 3.3 (no. 12) (1908), 147–242 (p. 147). So it is certainly possible that Carpenter's method of taking down the words from spoken dictation, two lines at a time, may have been the inadvertent cause of certain lapses of memory. Secondly, some singers are on record as having been only too glad to be pointed towards fuller texts of songs they knew only in part. See, for example, Vic Gammon, *Desire, Drink and Death in English Folk and Vernacular Song, 1600–1900* (Aldershot and Burlington, VT: Ashgate, 2008), p. 245; Roy Palmer, 'George Dunn: Twenty-One Songs and Fragments', *Folk Music Journal*, 2.4 (1973), 275–96 (p. 275). So Carpenter's potential promptings, if such they were, need not necessarily be considered as being at odds with the contributors' own intentions.

[80] The full set of references is Carpenter Collection, Cylinders 107 12:07, 108 00:00; Disc sides 238 03:43, 04:24, 239 00:00; MS pp. 04267, 06451, 07861. The stanza in question is not on the sound recording or in Carpenter's transcription from it. It is presented here in accordance with orthographic principles developed for a critical edition of the Carpenter collection.

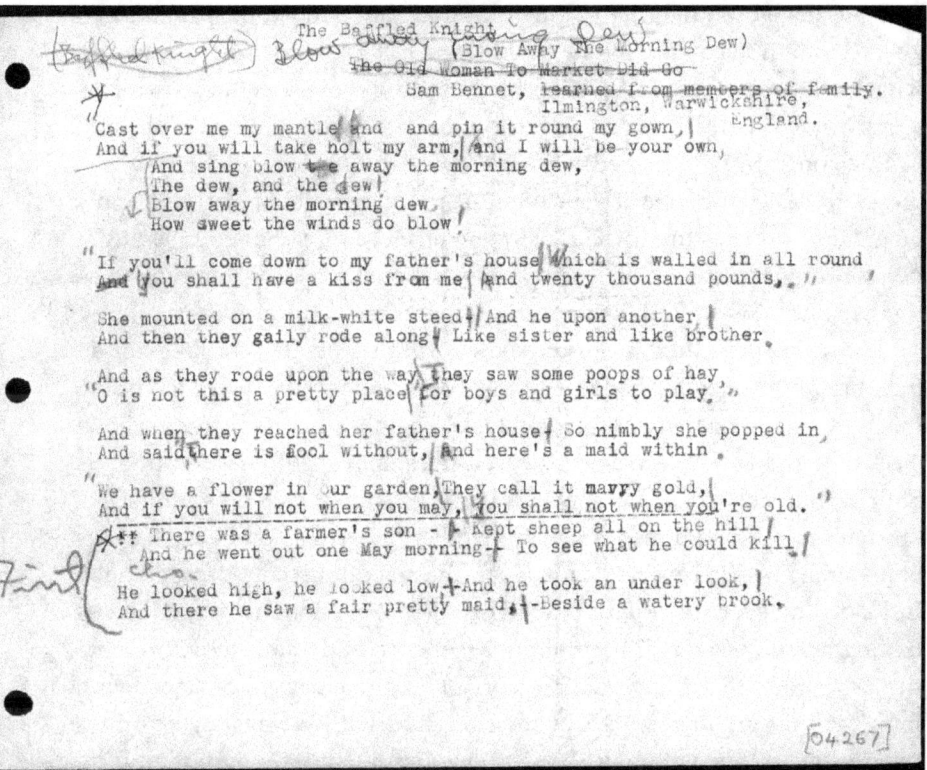

Fig. 6.1 Carpenter Collection, MS p. 04267. Courtesy of the American Folklife Center at the Library of Congress, Washington, DC, USA.

The word *poops*, which in none of its dictionary meanings has anything to do with hay, is unexpected. The anticipated reading would be *pooks*, which is found in other texts of 'The Baffled Knight'. The *Oxford English Dictionary* defines *pook* thus: 'A heap, *spec.* (*a*) a haycock; a roughly assembled heap of hay, oats, barley, or other unsheafed produce, not more than 5 feet high, pitched together for carting to a rick; (*b*) a tall stack of corn, wheat, etc., in the sheaf, in the form of a steep cone 9 or 10 feet high, built up temporarily in the harvest field to dry grain before it is carried to the main rick.'[81] There are at least four different possibilities here, of which the most obvious are the following: (*i*) that Carpenter simply misheard or mistyped the word *pooks* – a word that in any case, as an American and a native of Mississippi,

---

81 *OED* pook, *n.*

may not have been familiar to him;[82] (*ii*) that Sam Bennett mispronounced a word that in his own mind he understood as *pooks*; (*iii*) that Bennett said what he meant, *poops*, but that to his mind the word meant the same as *pooks*; (*iv*) that Bennett meant and said *poops*, knowing it to be nonsensical in this context, perhaps because he had learned the song that way and did not want to change it. The same sorts of considerations will apply wherever a word is misspelled in a manner that might, but equally might not, represent a genuine dialectal pronunciation: how is the intention to be divined and how should the word be rendered in a critical edition?[83]

The collection thus exposes some of the potential pitfalls of an intentionalist policy for ballad editing. There are possible ways of cutting this particular Gordian knot – for example, publishing the materials in an electronic archive. An archive, however, does not constitute an edition. As Shillingsburg observes, 'a "mere" archive of source materials will strike most new readers and researchers from other fields as an undigested chaos of material in which everyone must become an editor before proceeding'.[84] Instead, however, of attempting to counter objections to intentionalist editing by adopting a quite different practice, it is possible to incorporate the issues raised into a redefined theory of text. Literary editors faced with intractable layers of manuscript revision, and with the agency of others besides the author who have had various inputs into the published form of a text, which may or may not have met with the author's approval, have been drawn to the conclusion that authors are not altogether independent agents and that the production of texts necessarily takes place within a social, historical, and institutional context.[85] The locus of textual authority does not rest with the author alone, but is dispersed across a social nexus that includes authors, collaborators, friends, copyists, editors, printers,

---

82 The word does occur elsewhere in the collection, but in a manuscript that was supplied to Carpenter (Carpenter Collection, MS pp. 05118–05120, 06445).

83 See further Julia C. Bishop, '*Grouping, Grawping* and *Groping* towards a Critical Edition of the James Madison Carpenter Collection of Traditional Song and Drama', Dialect and Folk Life Studies in Britain: The Leeds Archive of Vernacular Culture in its Context, University of Leeds, 19 March 2005, available at http://library.leeds.ac.uk/multimedia/imu/2163/JuliaBishop2.pdf; Thomas A. McKean, 'The Dialect Conundrum in Transcribing Early Sound Recordings', in *From 'Wunderhorn' to the Internet: Perspectives on Conceptions of 'Folk Song' and the Editing of Traditional Songs*, ed. Eckhard John and Tobias Widmaier, BASIS, vol. 6 (Trier: WVT Wissenschaftlicher Verlag Trier, 2010), pp. 209–24.

84 Shillingsburg, *Scholarly Editing*, p. 165.

85 Jerome J. McGann, *A Critique of Modern Textual Criticism* (Charlottesville: University Press of Virginia, 1992 [1983]); Jerome J. McGann, *The Textual Condition* (Princeton: Princeton University Press, 1991), pp. 19–47.

publishers, censors, reviewers, critics, and the reading public – so that it might, for instance, support the choice of a published text as a base text even where a manuscript survives.

The social theory of text has considerable attractions for the editing of ballad texts in light of the problems raised by the Carpenter collection. For one thing, it will justify the straightforward choice of fair copy as base text, against which variants can be collated. This will have certain advantages in terms of reducing, or at least systematizing, editorial guesswork or inference, and ensuring some degree of consistency of treatment – it renders the editing process more transparent. The corollary is that textual authority is located not with the contributor as autonomous source, but with the social nexus that brought that particular text into being. In particular, the necessary agency of the collector is brought fully into the equation. Ballad texts edited in this light embody an awareness of multiple agency which is essential to literary or musical production of any kind.

While it can be objected that the social theory of text downplays the creative input of the artist – in the ballad case, the contributor (singer) – the theory remains focused on multiple sorts of agency, among which that of the author or equivalent must be acknowledged at least as a major organizing principle.[86] Nevertheless, it is difficult to imagine the appearance of such a theory in textual criticism prior to the decentring of the author brought about by literary theory during the second half of the twentieth century. The crucial corollary of the 'death of the author', however, was the 'birth of the reader' – the recognition that the process of reading, or reception, is essential for a work to be fully realized.[87] The reader thus becomes a prime point of agency in literary production. Applied to the ballad, the social theory renders the collector no longer as unreliable agent or mediator but instead as the necessary representative of an essential process of textual reception. And this is *not* because the collector is simply the individual who translates vocalized sound into writing. Rather, it is because the role of the collector stands for that of *every* listener/reader.

At the root of this is the fact that the ballad medium, as argued in chapter one, is language and music. The task of the ballad singer is one of *textualization* – the 'inscription' of language into sound, just as that of the literary author is to 'inscribe' language into written marks on paper

---

[86] Shillingsburg, *Scholarly Editing*, p. 30; Shillingsburg, *Resisting Texts*, pp. 152, 154.
[87] Roland Barthes, 'The Death of the Author', in *Image – Music – Text*, trans. Stephen Heath (London: Fontana, 1977), pp. 142–48.

or electronic signs in a word processor. The task of the listener is one of *reception* – the 'translation' of vocalized sound into language, just as the reader of a literary text 'translates' written or printed marks into language. That is to say, the ballad, rendered either as sound or as writing, comprises a semiotic code through which language and music are represented in tangible, material form. So although the ballad collector does subsequently give physical form to language once again – a further textualization or inscription, this time into writing or recorded sound – his or her initial role in textual reception is not intrinsically different from that of any other reader/listener. What the collector does is simply to provide a reification of the process of reception and to bring it to the attention of the editor (who may, of course, be the same person), who then has to locate it within a theory of text and deal with it accordingly.

Now it should be evident that this process of 'inscription' and 'reinscription' is by no means an objective one, and that its products will be inherently variable. This instability finds its immediate reification in such things as the rendering of spelling, punctuation, and word, line, and stanza divisions. These are all products of the reception process. Unlike the literary author, the ballad singer has virtually no authority whatsoever over such matters. Here is Carpenter's description (in the interview with Alan Jabbour) of the way in which he exercised control over the dictation of the ballad texts:

> Then, after his, after his singing, then I'd, I'd take the . . . the little portable typewriter on my knees, and say to him, 'Now, now, dictate that song to me, two, two lines at the time.' And . . . he'd say, for instance, '. . . The king sut in Dunfermline toun / Drinking the blude reid wine', and I'd stop him and then type that out, and then hold up my finger for him, and . . . he would finish, 'Says whaur'll I get a skeely skipper / To sail this ship o mine?' in other words, give me the second two lines, and I'd type that right straight through . . . There was no conversation went on at all, I'd just hold up my finger and he'd sing, he'd dictate another two lines, and then I'd record that, and, right straight through.[88]

Textual reception is necessarily dependent upon such things as pronunciation and hearing, knowledge and expectation, understanding and interpretation, and these all find their eventual reification in the received text. A word such as *poops* is a visible instance of the process, which is best accounted for, if not necessarily explained, in terms of the operation of multiple agencies in ballad textualization.

---

88 Author's transcription.

Not only different collectors, but each different listener, will therefore engage with the same initial rendering in different ways, and should they then reproduce it as text they might do so differently.[89] That is why a sound recording (even an idealized one capable of introducing no artefacts of its own), though it can certainly carry information of a different and more extensive kind than writing, comes no closer to providing a definitive text. Neither does the work of the ballad editor. Instead, what the editor can do is to present a text that is necessarily a product of multiple agencies, including both editor and reader, and of concomitant textualizations of an underlying medium of language and music into different tangible semiotic codes, such as sound and writing, in the course of its passage into print. The ballad does not bear the authority of an autonomous source.

To that extent, Walter Scott's first instinct was correct. The contributor, like the collector, like anyone else, also represents an agency within a continuous process of textual reception, which has moments of textualization in material form. In this manner, it might be argued, variance (and even the quality of 'tradition' itself) is built into the ballad because it depends for its very existence upon multiple agencies and cannot be referred back to the authority or intention of a unitary source. The answer to the question about the nature of the version is that, at least from the perspective of textual criticism, the unitary version can only ever be the representation of the momentary rendering of a ballad's reception, necessarily mediated through whatever channel(s) of agency has enabled its textualization.

---

89 Exemplified by so-called 'mondegreens' – phrases that have been misheard or misunderstood and consequently written down incorrectly, amounting to a kind of aural malapropism. The term comes from the lines in 'The Bonny Earl of Murray' (Child 181) 'They hae slain the Earl o Moray / An laid him on the green' rendered as 'They hae slain the Earl o Moray / An Lady Mondegreen'.

7. Palimpsest or *texte génétique*

The ballad, whatever else it may be, is an aesthetic artefact. Like other works, literary and musical alike, the same ballad can be presented in a number (perhaps any number) of different ways, in manuscript, print, recording, or performance. Of course, what constitutes the 'same' is potentially problematic, but common practice is to link ballad type with source and to fall into the habit of speaking of 'so-and-so's version of such-and-such a ballad'. Notwithstanding the fact that the ballad, a genre associated with performance, is amenable to unlimited successive and evanescent renditions, and can quite readily vary between one and the next, a silent equation is thus being made between the collected item and the agency or intention of its contributor.

Implicit in this standard approach is the tolerance of a degree – but only a quite limited degree – of variance in what one is talking about. Commonly, all that is extant is a single sound recording or set of music and words taken down by a collector, and the name of the contributor stands as a, seemingly unproblematic, organizing principle. The contributor is deemed well-nigh equivalent to the author or composer of a conventional literary or musical work. And yet that is not the case. However ethnographically and artistically important the individual might be, the whole point of most of the ballads under discussion here is that the individual is not its originator.[1]

An earlier version of this chapter was published as 'Genetic Foundations for a Palimpsest Model of the Anglo-Scottish Ballad Text: Evidence from the J. M. Carpenter Collection', *Folklore*, 121 (2010), 245–67, and the material is reused with permission.

1 That is not wilfully to neglect altogether the role of local ballad composers. See, for example, Edward D. Ives, *Larry Gorman: The Man Who Made the Songs* (Bloomington: Indiana University Press, 1964); Edward D. Ives, *Lawrence Doyle, The Farmer-Poet of Prince Edward Island: A Study in Local Songmaking*, University of Maine Studies, no. 92 (Orono: University of Maine Press, 1971); Edward D. Ives, *Joe Scott: The Woodsman-Songmaker* (Urbana: University of Illinois Press, 1978); Thomas A. McKean, *Hebridean Song-Maker: Iain MacNeacail of the Isle of Skye* (Edinburgh: Polygon, [1997?]).

http://dx.doi.org/10.11647/OBP.0041.07

And however creative the contributor, the ballad remains a palimpsest of precedent and current words and melody – 'palimpsest' in its technical sense being 'A parchment or other writing surface on which the original text has been effaced or partially erased, and then overwritten by another; a manuscript in which later writing has been superimposed on earlier (effaced) writing', and in less formal, extended use 'a thing likened to such a writing surface, esp. in having been reused or altered while still retaining traces of its earlier form; a multilayered record'.[2]

Mostly, this is something of an abstract idea, revealed in part by historical research into ballad words and melodies, but still requiring exercise of the imagination. However, the J. M. Carpenter ballad collection, described in the previous chapter, offers something of a special case, where manuscript materials show evidence of possibly multiple layers of revision, and sound recordings differ sometimes substantially from their manuscript equivalents, so that it is suddenly no longer so easy to make the instinctive equation between item and contributor intention. Some editing of the confusing layers of materials seems essential if the collection is to be of value to those who might be expected to want to make use of it – as potential performers, family and social historians, scholars wanting to carry out comparative and other kinds of studies.

The Carpenter ballads have shown themselves amenable to the social theory of text, but they also offer a possibly unique opportunity to consider the ballads in relation to the insights of another area of editing theory, the French school of genetic criticism, or *critique génétique*.[3] The defining characteristic of genetic criticism, or textual genetics as it is sometimes called, is that the work, as manifest in documents such as literary manuscripts (most of the manifesto statements about *critique génétique* refer to literary texts and works, but the theory has wide-ranging application across the creative arts), is envisaged not just as product but as a *process*. Thus the preference of the genetic critic is for 'production over the product, writing over what is written, textualization over the text, multiplicity over uniqueness, possibility over the finite, virtuality over the *ne varietur*, the

---

[2] *OED* palimpsest, *n.* 2 a, b.
[3] See, for example, Almuth Grésillon, *Éléments de critique génétique: Lire les manuscrits modernes* (Paris: Presses Universitaires de France, 1994); Pierre-Marc de Biasi, *La Génétique des textes* (Paris: Nathan, 2000). In English, see Jed Deppman, Daniel Ferrer, and Michael Groden, eds, *Genetic Criticism: Texts and Avant-textes* (Philadelphia: University of Pennsylvania Press, 2004); essays in *Yale French Studies*, no. 89 'Drafts' (1996).

dynamic over the static, the operation over the opus, genesis over structure, the strength of the act of writing over the form of the printed word'.⁴ Genetic criticism ties the material basis of literature (the text in the document) to what can be inferred about the process that brought it into being:

> Like old-fashioned philology or textual criticism, it examines tangible documents such as writers' notes, drafts, and proof corrections, but its real object is something much more abstract – not the existing documents but the movement of writing that must be inferred from them. Then, too, it remains concrete, for it never posits an ideal text beyond those documents but rather strives to reconstruct, from all available evidence, the chain of events in a writing process.⁵

The *critique génétique* project endeavours to recover, or elucidate, the dynamics seemingly obscured within texts, written, typed, printed, or mechanically recorded. 'Its vision is of literature as a *doing* ("*un 'faire'*"), as an activity, as a movement.'⁶

The general approach is not, in fact, an entirely unique or recent one, and it has some eminent forerunners. Samuel Johnson, for example, observes in his 'Life of Milton', 'it is pleasant to see great works in their seminal state, pregnant with latent possibilities of excellence; nor could there be any more delightful entertainment than to trace their gradual growth and expansion, and to observe how they are sometimes suddenly advanced by accidental hints, and sometimes slowly improved by steady meditation'.⁷ Edgar Allan Poe's 1846 essay on 'The Philosophy of Composition', considered a foundational text of French genetic criticism,⁸ considers how valuable it would be were an author to 'detail, step by step, the processes by which any one of his compositions attained its ultimate point of completion' – and then proceeds to do just that for his own poem 'The Raven'.⁹ Genetic criticism, however, really gained traction, in France especially, in the last quarter of the twentieth century, partly as a response to the potential

---

4 Almuth Grésillon, 'Slow: Work in Progress', *Word & Image* 13 (1997), 106–23 (p. 106).
5 Deppman, Ferrer, and Groden, eds, *Genetic Criticism*, p. 2.
6 Grésillon, 'Slow: Work in Progress', p. 106.
7 Samuel Johnson, *The Lives of the Most Eminent English Poets, with critical observations on their works*, introduction and notes by Roger Lonsdale, 4 vols (Oxford: Clarendon Press, 2006), I, 261.
8 Deppman, Ferrer, and Groden, eds, *Genetic Criticism*, p. 3.
9 Edgar Allan Poe, 'The Philosophy of Composition', in *Selected Writings of Edgar Allan Poe: Poems, Tales, Essays and Reviews*, ed. David Galloway (Harmondsworth: Penguin, 1967), pp. 480–92 (p. 481).

apparent in the vast array of surviving manuscript materials relating to important modern authors such as Zola, Balzac, Hugo, Valéry, Flaubert, and Proust, and, in English, Joyce, Yeats, Beckett, and Eliot. In this respect, genetic criticism stands in acute contrast to the mid-century New Critical insistence on the integrity of the finished work, to which earlier drafts were considered as, at best, marginal, discarded, alternative versions.[10]

Genetic criticism considers together all of the different, interdependent, dynamic states of a work that are available, up to and including the point of publication. These may be comprised, variously, in such things as manuscript drafts, notebooks, outlines, sketches, letters, corrected proofs, which all belong temporally prior to the 'achieved', published text. These are conceived of not as superseded matter that is external to the literary work, but as an integral part of its ontology, designated accordingly by the new term *avant-texte*, originally coined in 1972 by Jean Bellemin-Noël.[11] Generally, genetic critics do acknowledge a dividing line between this system of *avant-texte* and the 'frozen shape of a published text', marked by that moment when the author signs off the text as *bon à tirer*, or 'passed for press'.[12] At that moment the endlessly pliable *avant-texte* gives way to a particular manifestation that passes into the public domain, after which the reality of its existence cannot be altered, although that fact need not in itself preclude subsequent modifications in the form of further published editions, author's handwritten annotations, and so forth. In practice, though, genetic criticism offers a somewhat ambiguous perspective on the relationship between *avant-texte* and the supposed authority of the published text, between process and product.[13]

Now, it is true that a tradition of Anglo-American textual editing deriving from nineteenth-century philology has long been concerned with recording variant readings. However, variant readings have characteristically been subordinated to an idea of the author's 'final

---

10 René Wellek and Austin Warren, *Theory of Literature*, 3rd edn (Harmondsworth: Penguin, 1963), pp. 90–91.
11 Jean Bellemin-Noël, *Le Texte et l'avant-texte: Les Brouillons d'un poème de Milosz* (Paris: Larousse, 1972). See also Jean Bellemin-Noël, 'Reproduire le manuscrit, présenter les brouillons, établir un avant-texte', *Littérature*, no. 28 (1977), 3–18.
12 Pierre-Marc de Biasi, 'What Is a Literary Draft? Toward a Functional Typology of Genetic Documentation', *Yale French Studies*, no. 89 (1996), 26–58 (p. 37).
13 Grésillon, 'Slow: Work in Progress', p. 115; Laurent Jenny, 'Genetic Criticism and its Myths', *Yale French Studies*, no. 89 (1996), 9–25 (p. 14).

intentions' as embodied in one particular state of the text.¹⁴ The variants themselves are recorded in a suitably subordinate position, usually in a critical apparatus at the back of the book or the foot of the page. Genetic criticism, in contrast, is concerned not so much with the variants per se, though it may take account of the aesthetics of different textual states, as with what Daniel Ferrer calls the 'injunctions' that appear in the acts of accretion, deletion, and superimposition that the variants represent.¹⁵ Together, the variants establish a matrix of binary on/off switches as each variant modifies and is modified by its context. Thus in genetic criticism the object of study becomes the dynamic process of artistic 'invention'. In that sense, it entirely reverses the perspective of Anglo-American textual criticism geared towards the ultimate shape of the text that best embodies the author's final intentions.¹⁶ Instead, textual genetics seeks to grasp the inherent fluidity, and, as a corollary, the diachronicity, of the literary work. Pierre-Marc de Biasi refers to the way in which literary genetics restores the temporal dimension to criticism, so that 'the text of the work reclaims possession of its history'.¹⁷

Though scarcely on the scale of, for example, the Flaubert or Joyce manuscripts, it is nonetheless the fact of the presence of a mass of *avant-texte* among the Carpenter ballads, as described in the previous chapter, that has prompted the idea of applying some of the principles of genetic criticism to the investigation of a theory of text for the Anglo-Scottish ballad. And while the Child ballads in the collection provide the most compelling case, many of the other collected items exist in more than one iteration of the 'same' thing, and further examples could be drawn, for example, from among the folk plays. So the textual model described below as a 'palimpsest' potentially has a broader application.

---

14 Jerome J. McGann, *A Critique of Modern Textual Criticism* (Charlottesville: University Press of Virginia, 1992 [1983]), pp. 37–49; Peter L. Shillingsburg, *Scholarly Editing in the Computer Age: Theory and Practice*, 3rd edn (Ann Arbor: University of Michigan Press, 1996), pp. 29–39; G. Thomas Tanselle, 'The Editorial Problem of Final Authorial Intention', *Studies in Bibliography*, 29 (1976), 167–211; G. Thomas Tanselle, *A Rationale of Textual Criticism* (Philadelphia: University of Pennsylvania Press, 1989), esp. pp. 75–78.
15 Cited in D. C. Greetham, *Theories of the Text* (Oxford: Oxford University Press, 1999), p. 60.
16 Hans Walter Gabler, 'The Text as Process and the Problem of Intentionality', *Text: Transactions of the Society for Textual Scholarship*, 3 (1987), 107–16.
17 de Biasi, 'What Is a Literary Draft?', p. 58.

Now, as already observed (and notwithstanding the objections raised in chapter six), a particular song as taken down from a particular contributor is most usually said to constitute that person's version of that particular song type. It would be normal practice to speak of, say, Sam Bennett's 'version' of 'Our Goodman' (Child 274),[18] or of Sarah Phelps's 'version' of 'The Outlandish Knight' (Child 4),[19] when they are in fact represented by several variant iterations. But none of those written or recorded iterations are texts 'intended' for publication or for issue as recordings, and there is nothing definitive about any one particular rendering of either words or tune. The words on the sound recordings might differ more or less noticeably from those the contributors dictated, and the user of the collection is therefore obliged to consider the two as being at least as distinct – in principle, if not in degree – as the acknowledged versions of certain literary texts – say, the second quarto and folio *Hamlet*. To minimize potential confusion over terminology, the sound recording and the dictated text could be referred to as different 'renditions' of the 'same' thing, which are to be considered of equivalent status – this despite the fact that their genesis may be separated in time by no more than a matter of a minute or two. In contrast, the fair copy typescripts derive directly from the rough copy typescripts, even though their genesis may have been separated in time by a space of several years, so those texts need to be considered as further iterations of the same renditions, albeit characteristically in a variant textual state. Much the same can be said of the relationship between the sound recordings and Carpenter's own music transcriptions, and between the sound recordings and modern transcriptions that can be made from them.

The folk plays, likewise, are in typescript but with handwritten alterations, which appear to reflect corrections of a nature more or less comparable to those in the ballad rough copies.[20] At least one play (the Lower Heyford play) was recorded in its entirety, as well as taken down from dictation, once again providing different renditions of equivalent status. In other instances, a play from a particular location was taken down from more

---

18 Washington, DC, Library of Congress, American Folklife Center, Archive of Folk Culture, AFC1972/001, James Madison Carpenter Collection, Cylinder 031 00:00; Disc sides 064 02:17, 065 00:00; MS pp. 05701–05703, 07592–07593, 08622–08623.

19 Carpenter Collection, Cylinder 131 04:21; Disc side 310 03:05; MS pp. 04924–04926, 06997–06998, 08480–08481, 11721–11722.

20 For a general introduction to Carpenter's folk play collection, see Eddie Cass, 'The James Madison Carpenter Collection of British Folk Plays', *Folklore*, 123 (2012), 1–22.

Palimpsest or texte génétique   155

than one contributor (the Hunton sword dance play, for example). This latter situation is not, however, directly comparable to that of the same ballad type taken down from different contributors, because the implicit demands of collaborative dramatic performance can be presumed to imbue the text-as-learned with much greater authority than in the ballad case. Rather, these instances might be considered again as multiple renditions of the same play.

Some of the difficulties of taking an intentionalist approach to this sort of material have been outlined in chapter six, so here, instead, it will be useful to turn to a specific example to explore the nature and potential of the ballad *avant-texte*. The range of choice among the ballads is huge and it should be emphasized that this one may or may not be the best, or the most characteristic, example. It is, however, one that displays a good range of kinds and concentrations of textual variants. The ballad in question is 'The Bonnie Banks o Fordie' (Child 14) and the contributor Mrs Alexander McEwan (spelling unconfirmed).[21] Although he does not name names, in the course of several drafts of essays present in the collection, Carpenter writes about a couple who, on the basis of the repertoire items mentioned, must be Mr and Mrs McEwan. Apparently, they were Scottish Travellers, and his description of them becomes more than a little romantic: 'She was a lithe attractive creature, with her quick animation and flashing black eyes. When I first saw her, in the morning, wandering along a green country lane, glancing swiftly from side to side as she laughed and bant[er]ed with her elderly husband, I had thought, somehow, of a wild animal – perhaps a deer.'[22]

The ballad in question exists in a characteristic number of renditions and iterations:
- a rough copy typescript (designated *T1*) (Fig. 7.1)
- a fair copy typescript (designated *T2*)
- a cylinder recording, comprising three stanzas
- a lacquer disc copy of the recording
- a transcription of one stanza from the sound recording
- stanzas quoted in draft essays.

---

21 The full set of references is Carpenter Collection, Cylinder 130 11:12; Disc sides 308 04:25, 309 00:00; MS pp. 04384–04387, 06539–06541, 07930, 10333–10334, 11180–11181, 12187–12189, 12272–12273, 12395–12396.
22 Carpenter Collection, MS p. 10333.

156 The Anglo-Scottish Ballad

```
The Bonnie Banks o Fordie    Bubbl'n Johnnie    (Lived in Inverness, Scotland.
[Bonnie Banks o Fordie]      (Bubblin Johnnie)
[Bubblin Johnnie]                    Mrs. Alexander Mc Ewan,
                                     Learned from her father and grandfath
There were three sisters walkin alone  Wm. and John Newlands, 46 years ago
On the bonnie banks o Eldrie Chielens, taix Inverness and Falls o Foyers)
As this young man come up on them,
On the bonny banks o Eldrie O.

He catched the older siter by the hand
And wheeled her round and he gart her stand,   [Seven sisters on roadside
He wheeled her round and he gart her stand,    on Lunnummmmm Fort Augustus
On the bonny banks o Eldrie O.                 and Inverness road.—
                                               see seven rocks on side
It's will ye be a rank robbers wife,                of road]
Or will ye die by my penknife,
Or will ye die by my penknife
On the bonny banks o Eldrie O?

I will not be a rank robbers wife,
But I will die by your penknife,
But I will die by your penknife
On the bonny banks o Eldrie O.

He took the second sister by the hand,
He wheeled her round and he gart her stand,
He wheeled her round and he gart her stand
On the bonny banks o Eldrie O.

It's wid ye be a rank rober's wife,
Or wid ye die by my penknife,
Or wid ye be a rank robers' wife?
On the bonny banks o Eldrie O?"

I will not be a rank robbers wife,
But I shall die by your penknife,
But I shall die by your pen knife
On the bonny banks o Eldrie O.                        [04384]
```

```
He's catched the third sister by the hand
And he wheeled her round and he gart her stand,
He wheeled her round and he gart her stand
On the bonny banks o Eldrie O.

O will ye be a rank bobber's wife,
Or will ye die by my penknife,
Or will ye die by my penknife
On the Bonnie Banks o Eldrie O?

I will not be a rank robber's wife,
Or wh I will not die by your penknife,
Or I will not die by your pen knife
On the bonny banks o Eldrie O.

For if you kill me, I've a brother will kill you
On the bonny banks o Eldrie O.

Come tell to me what is your brother's name,
On the bonnie banks o Eldrie O.
Bubblin Johnnie is his name,
On the Bonnie banks o Eldrie O.

He catched his sister, he kissed her again
On the bonny banks o Eldrie O.

They kissed one another and sore set down,
And sore set down and sore set down, and lamenting
On the bonny banks o Eldrie O.
                                                       [04385]
```

Fig. 7.1 Carpenter Collection, MS pp. 04384–04387. Courtesy of the American Folklife Center at the Library of Congress, Washington, DC, USA.

Bubblin Johnnie

"My
~~This~~ two sisters I have slain
On the bonnie banks o Eldrie O.
I am sure I will have revenge
On the bonnie banks o Eldrie o.

He catched his youngest sister by the hand, walked
The tears they wiped, and walked on, | The tears they wiped and they ~~walk~~ on
~~On the bonny bans~~ To the coves up abeen the birks o Eldrie O. coves
What's the Calder ~~gave~~ ~~mantha~~ into the birk, bubblin
Where the robers had their nest in Eldrie O?
This where the coves and the rank robbers bides
Up abeen the banks o Eldrie O.
Says Bubblin Johnnie, Come wie me
And I'll have revenge on Eldrie O.
Thays
There theyre settin waitin till Johnnie will come home
~~Up in the cove men abeen Eldrie O~~ Up abeen the banks o Eldrie O
When in goes Bubblin Johnnie and there's none got a chance,
~~Gambles~~ Up ~~manten~~ abeen the banks o Eldrie O.

I have killed my sisters and I have got revenge,
Up abeen the banks o Eldrie O."

(He killed them as they ran out, one by one)

over

[04386]

Story. The seven robbers induced Bubblin Johnnie, who was a herd boy whom they thought was silly, to rob for them. Put him up to attack sisters. When he found that he had murdered his sisters, he went back to murder them.

Singer seemed almost trembling
and eyes shining as she sang, (strain
~~broken~~ (at last, like lines) as if under
some strange spell. Evidently afraid to
sing concluding verse. Had "Too heavy
awful." Had heard ballad preached against
in pulpit.

[04387]

The manuscript pages carry several different titles – 'The Bonnie Banks o Fordie', 'The Banks o Eldrie', 'Bubblin Johnnie' – the last of which, taking the name of the outlaw character, is possibly unique as an identifier for this particular ballad. For ease of reference, a critical edition text, founded on *T2* as base text and with a simplified critical apparatus, is given in Appendix 1 at the end of this chapter. Stanza and line numbers cited below are keyed to this text, indicated by *crit. ed.*

The assumption is that *T1* represents what Carpenter took down on his portable typewriter and amended in consultation with Mrs McEwan. The sound recording is evidently of a somewhat different nature, not just because it was created at a different, albeit probably quite close, moment in time, but more importantly because it derives from the process of singing as opposed to that of dictation. Pragmatically, these can be treated as separate renditions and therefore presented independently, which conveniently circumvents the difficulty posed by differences between the words as sung and as dictated. A transcription from the sound recording, alongside the corresponding lines from the critical text, is given in Appendix 2.

The rough copy *T1* carries alterations made both in ink and in red pencil, the cautious assumption (founded upon general impressions drawn from increasing familiarity with the entire collection) being that alterations in ink were made more or less at the time of dictation, while those in red pencil *may* have been made at a later date.[23] As far as stanza 10 – that is to say, over the part of the ballad that is essentially incremental and hence presumably easier to recall – *T1* is quite clean and has been copied into *T2* largely without difficulty (the spelling *bonnie* regularly replacing *bonny*). The missing *o* at the end of 1.2 in *T1* is easily explained by the stanza running into the contributor information typed at the top of the page. At 2.2 the typist of *T2* has added the pronoun *he*, not present in *T1*, following *And* at the beginning of the line *And he wheeled her round and he gart her stand*. This might be either an accident of the copying process (8.2 also begins *And he*, while 5.2 begins *He*), or a recollection of the way the ballad was actually dictated – there is no way of knowing. At 6.3, there is one substantial handwritten amendment, in ink, correcting *Or wid ye be a rank rob[b]er's wife*, apparently a mistaken repetition of the wording of 6.1, to the expected repetition of 6.2 *Or wid ye die by my penknife*. This could represent the correction of an error on the part of either contributor or collector – perhaps,

---

23 David Atkinson, 'The Secret Life of Ballad Manuscripts', *Variants*, 8 (2012), 183–206 (esp. pp. 186–87) [and note the corrigendum to this article in *Variants*, 10 (2013), 13].

given the extent of the correction and evident irregularity of what was initially typed (compare 3.3 and 9.3), the former seems more likely. At 10.2 Carpenter began typing *Or wi[ll]*, before making the correction to *Or I will*, again an evident slip which could be readily charged to either contributor or collector.

Thus far, nine out of the first ten stanzas have held to a regular, four-stress line, rhyming *aaae* (where *e* represents the *Eldrie, o* refrain); the exception being stanza 1 which rhymes *aebe* (or, if *alone/them* is allowed as a half-rhyme, *aeae*). Stanza 10 of *T1* is followed by a two-line stanza comprising an extrametrical line, *For if you kill me, I've a brother will kill you*, and the *bonny banks o Eldrie, o* refrain line. In *T2*, these two lines have been closed up to stanza 10 to give a six-line stanza, rhyming *aaaebe*. The following stanza (*crit. ed.* 11) reverts to the *aeae* rhyme scheme suggested in stanza 1, with an apparently extrametrical first line. Here it is worth noting that, though extrametrical lines might indicate something that is going on with regard to the dictating of the text, in practice they are likely to present no special difficulty to a ballad singer.[24] The next stanza (*crit. ed.* 12) is typed as an unrhymed two-line stanza in *T1*, with an intervening line, *And the tears ran down in sorrow*, handwritten in ink (*crit. ed.* 12.2).

Continuing the romantic vein of the draft essays already noted, Carpenter describes Mrs McEwan's demeanour when singing this ballad as 'a striking example of the eerie enchantment once exercised over the minds of primitive folk by ancient ballad lore'.[25] Then he types out *crit. ed.* 1–3, after which he describes Mrs McEwan 'half-chanting, half-dramatizing the sister's reply' (i.e. *crit. ed.* 4), and goes on to give *crit. ed.* 12 (filled out to a quatrain by repetition of the second line). Then he writes:

> At this point in the ballad her voice seemed somehow to catch in her throat. Then suddenly her English melted into her native Doric, and for several stanzas my Dictaphone recorded, in the half-chanted rhythm of the ancient Gaels, the words of this strange story, crooned to a somber Gaelic melody that sounded like a song of lament. I am not sure that her husband, trying to calm her, did not break off her story. At all events, after gaining time to collect herself, she explained that 'Bubblin Johnnie' was under the power of

---

24 M. J. C. Hodgart, *The Ballads*, 2nd edn (London: Hutchinson, 1962), pp. 56–57; Hugh Shields, 'Textual Criticism and Ballad Studies', in *Dear Far-Voiced Veteran: Essays in Honour of Tom Munnelly*, ed. Anne Clune (Miltown Malbay: Old Kilfarboy Society, 2007), pp. 287–94 (p. 293). More generally, see Hugh Shields, 'Supplementary Syllables in Anglo-Irish Folk Singing', *Yearbook of the International Folk Music Council*, 5 (1973), 62–71.

25 Carpenter Collection, MS p. 10333.

a robber band, who had set him on to do the deed, but that in the end he avenged himself, as follows: [quotes *crit. ed.* 16–17].[26]

There are certain difficulties with this account (which may have been written well after the event). This part of the ballad is not in fact on the dictaphone recording; the rough copy *T1* has the appearance of having been taken down from dictation, not singing, in accordance with Carpenter's usual practice; and the description appears to skip over *crit. ed.* 13–15 and to conflate the prose explanation given separately at the end of *T1* (see below) with the story as it can be gleaned from the ballad verses. Nevertheless, the indications of a change of language register, and of a break in concentration at this point in the ballad (perhaps prompted by the presence of an 'audience' in the form of her husband and/or the collector), are highly suggestive in relation to what follows.

There follows in *T1* another unrhymed three-line stanza, the second line of which has a repetition of the phrase *and sore sat down*, making the line extrametrical, which repetition is simply omitted from *T2* (*crit. ed.* 13.2). Quite possibly influenced by the previous occurrence of the same phrase at the end of the immediately preceding line (*crit. ed.* 13.1), the assumption was presumably made in the preparation of *T2* that this was simply an accidental repetition. On the other hand, the handwritten alteration in *T1*, in ink, of the last two words of the same line, *and lamenting*, to *with sorrow*, is most probably attributable to self-correction on the part of the contributor. Conversely, the handwritten alteration, this time in red pencil, of *set* to *sat* in three places in this and the preceding line would seem to be the work of the collector, favouring the standard English form over what is a plausible older Scots and/or dialect form.[27] It is not possible to know whether either form has any bearing on what Carpenter thought he had heard – in general, he was more likely to 'Scotticize' than to standardize words during the preparation of the fair copies, but there are instances in both directions.

The next stanza picks up the *aeae* rhyme scheme again, and has a handwritten alteration, in ink, of *This* to *My* (*crit. ed.* 14.1). This is followed by a stanza rhyming *abbe*, with a missing word, *they*, written in, in ink, in the second line (*crit. ed.* 15.2). The final line initially began *On the bonny ban[k]s*, presumably in anticipation of the usual refrain line, but this was subsequently typed through with hyphens (and later crossed through

---

26 Carpenter Collection, MS p. 10334.
27 *DSL-DOST* sit, *v.*; *EDD* sit, *v.*; *OED* sit, *v.*

again by hand) and replaced by an extrametrical line, *To the coves up abeen the banks o Eldrie, o*; subsequently *banks* was altered by hand, in ink, to *birks* (*crit. ed.* 15.4). The *coves*, it would seem, are caves or caverns, specifically recesses worn out of a river bank (the verb *cove* refers to the action of a river hollowing out its banks).[28] So *birks* (birch trees) seems to shy away from the more obvious connection and further to increase the complexity of idea in this line.

This is sustained, to the point of confusion, in the next stanza, which initially began *What's the calder cave on the*, altered in typescript to *What's the calder coves into the birk* (*crit. ed.* 16.1). Although *calder* is possible as a comparative form of Scots *cald/cauld* (cold), the word is also common as a personal or place name, and in *T1* the typed lower-case initial *c* has been raised by hand, in ink, to upper-case. When quoting this stanza in the essay drafts, Carpenter typed *Calder Coves*, with upper-case C for both words. But the meaning remains unclear. Also, the *birk* of *T1* has become *birks* in the preparation of *T2*, possibly under the influence of the plural form in the last line of the preceding stanza (*crit. ed.* 15.4). The correction in *T1* of *bides* to *bide* (*crit. ed.* 16.3), and the replacement of the older spelling *wie* with *wi* in the preparation of *T2* (*crit. ed.* 16.5), in contrast, require little notice. This is a six-line stanza of difficult syntax, where the rhyme scheme is largely lost.

That apparent loss is continued into the penultimate stanza. The first two lines are typed as a single line in *T1* and split into two in the preparation of *T2* (*crit. ed.* 17.1–2). The epithet *Bubblin* is handwritten in, in ink, to correct a presumably accidental omission. The essay drafts quote a single, variant, line, *There they're settin waitin till Bubblin Johnnie comes home*. Given the absence of easy syntax and predictable lines in this part of the ballad, the next line, initially beginning *Up in the cove of*, then altered, in typescript, to read *Up in the cove abeen Eldrie, o*, then typed through with hyphens and replaced, still in typescript, with *Up abeen the banks o Eldrie, o*, seems on the face of it likely to be attributable to the contributor's self-correction (*crit. ed.* 17.3). In the draft essays, it is given as *Up in the Coves abeen Eldrie, o*. There then follows a long extrametrical line, *When in goes Bubblin Johnnie and there's none got a chance* (*crit. ed.* 17.4). A fifth line contains some further presumed self-correction, all in typescript, of *On the* to *Up on t[he?] to*, finally, *Up abeen the banks o Eldrie, o* (*crit. ed.* 17.5).

---

28 *CSD* cove &c, *n., vt.*; *DSL-SND1* cove, *n.* 1; *DSL-SNDS* cove, *v.*³.

The final stanza then comprises just two lines: another extrametrical line, *I have killed my sisters and I have got revenge* (crit. ed. 18.1); and the *Up abeen the banks o Eldrie, o* refrain (crit. ed. 18.2), which by this stage has emerged as the regular form (crit. ed. 16.4, 17.3, 17.5, 18.2), replacing *On the bonnie banks o Eldrie, o*. Notwithstanding the caveat entered above, the increasing prevalence of extrametrical lines in this latter part of the ballad can be read as modulating towards what, judging by the fact that the typed line is indented and within parentheses in *T1* and *T2*, must have been a spoken explanation following the ballad proper: 'He killed them as they ran out, one by one.'

If the impression derived from *T1* of some self-correction on the part of the contributor, followed by further necessary correction during the preparation of *T2*, is at all correct, then both metre and rhyme do appear to be giving way over the more complicated, non-incremental, and seemingly more emotional, part of the ballad story. Following the ballad there is, on a new page in both *T1* and *T2*, a prose summary which contains some details that cannot be deduced from the text as it stands, along with some comments on Mrs McEwan's demeanour and her attitude to the ballad:

> Story: The seven robbers induced Bubblin Johnnie, a herd boy whom they thought to be silly, to rob for them. They put him up to attack sisters. When he found that he had murdered his sisters, he went back and murdered them.
>
> The singer was trembling and eyes were shining as she sang (strong face, like lioness) as if under some strange spell. She was loath to sing concluding verses. 'Too heavy, awful.' She had heard the ballad preached against in pulpit.

The implication is that she did have a coherent outline in mind, even if it was not confidently realized in the dictated text.

The raw materials of this ballad thus contain the potential for its representation either as process or as product. The fair copy (and, by and large, the critical edition text) presents the ballad as product. But it would be equally possible to present it in a genetic edition, representing the matrix of various forms that embody the ballad as it occurs across the manuscripts *T1* and *T2*. In somewhat simplified form, a genetic edition of stanzas 12–18 might look rather like the following.[29]

---

29 Pointed brackets ◇ mark deletions, and arrows ↑↓ mark insertions other than direct substitutions. For the sake of clarity, mere corrections of typing errors and the marking of line divisions are ignored, and an editorial system of minimal punctuation has been applied (on punctuation, see further chapter 8 below). The annotation is loosely

He catched his sister, he kissed her again
↑And the tears ran down in sorrow↓
On the <bonny> bonnie banks o Eldrie, o.

They kissed one another and sore <set> sat down
And sore <set> sat down <and sore <set> sat down> <and lamenting> with sorrow
On the <bonny> bonnie banks o Eldrie, o.

<This> My two sisters I have slain
On the bonnie banks o Eldrie, o
I am sure I will have revenge
On the bonnie banks o Eldrie, o.

He catched his youngest sister by the hand
The tears they wiped, and ↑they↓ walked on
The tears they wiped and they walked on
<On the bonny ban[k]s> To the coves up abeen the <banks> birks o Eldrie, o.

What's the <calder> Calder <cave on the> coves into the birk↑s↓
Where the robbers had their nest in Eldrie, o?
This where the coves and the rank robbers bide<s>
Up abeen the banks o Eldrie, o
Says Bubblin Johnnie, Come wi<e> me
And I'll have revenge on Eldrie, o.

There they're settin waitin
Till ↑Bubblin↓ Johnnie will come home
<Up in the cove <of> abeen Eldrie, o> Up abeen the banks o Eldrie, o
When in goes Bubblin Johnnie and there's none got a chance
<On the> Up <on t[he]> abeen the banks o Eldrie, o.

I have killed my sisters and I have got revenge
Up abeen the banks o Eldrie, o.

A genetic text along these lines presents simultaneously the matrix of variant possibilities preserved within the extant documentary evidence. What it depicts on the page is Mrs McEwan endeavouring to reconstruct the ballad for Carpenter, and Carpenter endeavouring to represent her recitation. He may also have prompted her at various points – the evidence for or against this is not recorded – and he might himself have begun to type lines, anticipating what he thought she was going to say, so that traces of his own contribution may be present, albeit unmarked as such. The

---

borrowed from genetic examples in D. C. Greetham, *Textual Scholarship: An Introduction* (New York: Garland, 1994), pp. 408–10. This is just the kind of editing, however, that most obviously lends itself to the electronic environment.

genetic text, therefore, also represents a social text. Even more than as an editorial procedure, this way of representing the 'coming into being' of a ballad text captures something of the process by which it was achieved in the historically situated interaction between contributor and collector. And although it is not quite so easy to envisage what it would look like, there is no reason in principle why the same approach should not be applied to the music transcription (both words and melody), especially as the (poor quality) raw material of the sound recordings relate to a modern interpretation of what is going on therein.

What the genetic approach offers, therefore, is two things, simultaneously: (*i*) it depicts the ballad as a process, embodying intentions that are relative and in flux throughout; and (*ii*) it depicts something of the social interaction involved in (verbal and musical) text creation. The exercise is designed to demonstrate that genetic editing, which is possible in this particular instance of Mrs McEwan's 'Bubblin Johnnie' because renditions in various different states have been preserved, can bring out into the open principles that are most often suppressed on the printed page or in sound recordings. Ultimately there is unlikely to be sufficient practical justification for a genetic edition of ballads, but the *potential* for such presentation alongside more conventional editing methods remains important to the opening up of ballad ontology and the establishment of a theory of text.

There might, however, still be a problem. Genetic criticism, as noted above, generally does recognize that moment when the author signs off a text as *bon à tirer*, passed for press, when a particular state of the work passes into the public domain. The observance of this moment permits the crucial distinction between *avant-texte* and the 'frozen shape of a published text'. In doing so it also facilitates the recognition of a temporal and logical ordering within the matrix of *avant-texte* – a teleology that represents the genesis of a state signalled by the declaration 'passed for press'.[30] Emphatically, this is not a hierarchical, evolutionary, or 'finalist' ordering, since chronology is by no means necessarily synonymous with progress or improvement.[31] Indeed, the genetic approach can seem to undermine the finality, or at least the 'sacrosanct *auctoritas*', of the published text.[32] Nevertheless, it is difficult in practice not to perceive the published text

---

30 de Biasi, 'What Is a Literary Draft?', p. 33.
31 G. Thomas Tanselle, 'Textual Criticism at the Millennium', *Studies in Bibliography*, 54 (2001), 1–80 (p. 27).
32 Grésillon, 'Slow: Work in Progress', p. 115.

as a point from which to orient the discussion of *avant-texte*. In the case of the ballad, however, although Carpenter's fair copy typescript may be the nearest thing to the 'passed for press' state that can be identified, clearly it does not bear Mrs McEwan's metaphorical signature any more or less than do, say, the variant stanzas that she sang for the sound recording. It may be that with materials that are not in a conventional sense 'authored', there never actually is a 'passed for press' moment.

In consequence, while the process of artistic 'invention' rendered visible in this way can illuminate the collecting of ballads and suchlike materials, it might not provide the most exact analogy for thinking both about potential multiplicities of ballad renditions, and about a putative 'conceptual text' that might lie behind them.[33] It is quite reasonable to suppose that a ballad never is 'passed for press', in the sense that at least its vocal rendition may be perceived as – indeed, may be intended to be – evanescent. So each rendition attributable to the same source will be of equivalent, independent status; each is, so to speak, an equivalent part of a matrix of something akin to *avant-texte*, but lacking either logical or even temporal ordering. Of course, there necessarily will be a chronology among such renditions, but that temporal arrangement is without teleological significance. Each rendition represents, more or less accurately, an intention that can be attributed to a particular passing moment in time and the circumstances then prevailing. Variation among such renditions represents merely the relativity of those momentary intentions.

An alternative way of looking at the same body of renditions, of course, is simply to consider everything as 'passed for press', since once rendered aloud, however transiently, the ballad has entered the public domain (regardless of the actual physical presence or absence of some kind of audience). Each rendition momentarily achieves the 'frozen shape

---

33 This term 'conceptual text' alludes in part to the notion of 'mental text' in Lauri Honko, *Textualising the Siri Epic*, FF Communications, no. 264 (Helsinki: Suomalainen Tiedeakatemia/Academia Scientiarum Fennica, 1998), pp. 92–99; Lauri Honko, 'Thick Corpus and Organic Variation: An Introduction', in *Thick Corpus, Organic Variation and Textuality in Oral Tradition*, ed. Lauri Honko (Helsinki: Finnish Literature Society, 2000), pp. 3–28 (pp. 18–19). I would not, however, want to draw anything like a direct analogy between the English-language ballads and the oral epics studied by Honko. In substituting 'conceptual' for 'mental' I am hoping, too, to avoid locating this abstract textual idea solely with the contributor. The conceptual text refers simultaneously to the contributor's dynamic mental image of the ballad, the social interaction that has enabled it to be collected in a particular form(s), and its ongoing (and changing) reception over time – but organized by its identification with the named contributor.

of a "published" [my added quotes] text', which could potentially be recorded or written down. This is to draw the analogy not so much with manuscript genetics as with the genetics of published editions – although a temporal and logical ordering is still lacking, since each rendition has an exactly equivalent status and their chronology is again without teleological significance. Literary and musical editors are most used to thinking of versions of works as something insubstantial, a form of the work as the author intended it at one particular moment. In the ballad scenario, however, intention is made momentarily explicit by the act of recitation, singing, or writing.

Nevertheless, it still seems counter-intuitive to consider these renditions just as discrete units, because they do all testify to a single, though not necessarily fixed, conceptual text. It is the felt presence of this emergent conceptual text – largely analogous to the idea of the literary work – that imposes a pattern on to the distinct renditions. In other words, it would be possible, in theory at least, to order ballad renditions rather in the manner of a genetic edition – not so much by establishing the usually unknown *avant-texte* that underlies a known 'passed for press' state, as by assembling the known physical texts and so enabling a more fluid conceptual text to emerge. One way of describing such a combined text would be as the representation of a palimpsest of material texts.[34]

The notion of palimpsest is being invoked here in a manner close to its technical meaning for manuscript studies. Ballad renditions can be imagined as layers superimposed upon one another, while each is still able to be read and/or heard. Where a thick corpus of material is physically available, the editorial representation of such a palimpsest might begin to permit the depiction of a putative conceptual text with a certain amount of depth. Whether such an exercise would actually be intellectually fruitful is perhaps more questionable. Certainly, if one considers simply mapping Mrs McEwan's third stanza from the sound recording on to the dictated text, the fact that, to put it crudely, when singing the ballad she conflated two stanzas of the text she subsequently dictated, is scarcely surprising and probably not particularly culturally or psychologically significant.

---

34 There is a possible analogy here with the discussion in Jerome J. McGann, *The Textual Condition* (Princeton: Princeton University Press, 1991), p. 30, of 'evolutionary texts' combining the entire extant corpus of materials relating to a work into an edition representing a single, continuous historical project. In the ballad case, while the notion of continuity is useful, that of 'evolution' should be resisted, although change is certainly possible.

Where the model is perhaps more illuminating is in disentangling the conventional language of 'versions'. The recognition that, generally, when one speaks of a contributor's version of a ballad what one is really referring to is a palimpsest of material texts that equate, with greater or lesser accuracy, to a putative conceptual text, is salutary.[35] At the very least, a degree of caution is required when discussing ballad and folk song aesthetics and repertoires, especially at a historical distance, based on limited evidence. Most of the manuscript, printed, and recorded ballad collections – the extant physical texts – offer a mere snapshot, a single layer of the palimpsest.[36] If nothing else, the iconic status of great ballad collections is being challenged here.

This palimpsest, presumed or actual, is complemented by the perspective derived analogically from genetic criticism, whereby 'the text remains inseparable from its pre-textual realization',[37] and which therefore posits, so to speak, 'versions within versions'. The relativity of the notion of intention is highly pertinent to ballads that are always amenable to being variously learned, reconstructed, transmitted, modified. For instance, although when a ballad is first learned, regardless of the nature of its source, the intention may well be to achieve a form that reproduces that source with some accuracy, subsequently that intention might become modified towards a rendering that resembles it much less closely, as the performer seeks to make the song 'their own'.[38] The genetic perspective would nonetheless recognize the earlier, learned form as still integral to that later form, in the manner of *avant-texte*. The Carpenter collection, with its mass of amended typescripts, seems to indicate that carriers of traditions are not always confident, accomplished performers, but that they may well seek consciously to recover or reconstruct texts. In that case, the contribution of the collector/editor may be both a necessary and a welcome intervention. The reconstructed text, too, would itself then be integral to any subsequent rendition that might emerge.

---

35 Quite independently, Peter Harrop, 'The Antrobus Soulcakers: A Consideration of Site, Mobility and Time as Components of Traditional Performance', *Contemporary Theatre Review*, 22 (2012), 267–73, has employed 'palimpsest' as a way of describing the cumulative effect of repetition in folk play performances.

36 Nevertheless, the possibilities presented by, for example, the Sabine Baring-Gould manuscripts should not be overlooked.

37 de Biasi, 'What Is a Literary Draft?', p. 58.

38 Thomas A. McKean, 'The Stewarts of Fetterangus and Literate Oral Tradition', in *The Singer and the Scribe: European Ballad Traditions and European Ballad Cultures*, ed. Philip E. Bennett and Richard Firth Green (Amsterdam: Rodopi, 2004), pp. 181–207 (p. 198).

The idea of palimpsest and the genetic perspective together offer a textual model for the ballad more or less equivalent to that of the literary work, and more fluid than any of the ballad's individual manifestations. The model posits a matrix of variance and connectedness, implying at any one moment both its preceding and succeeding variations. The ballad as received is conceived both as a process of accretion, deletion, and superimposition, and as a product that exists, even if only ephemerally, relative to its own contexts of production, collection, publication, and reception.

Appendix 1

1   There were three sisters walkin alone
    On the bonnie banks o Eldrie, o
    As this young man come up on them
    On the bonnie banks o Eldrie, o.

2   He catched the older sister by the hand
    And he wheeled her round and he gart her stand
    He wheeled her round and he gart her stand
    On the bonnie banks o Eldrie, o.

3   It's will ye be a rank robber's wife?
    Or will ye die by my penknife?
    Or will ye die by my penknife
    On the bonnie banks o Eldrie, o?

4   I will not be a rank robber's wife
    But I will die by your penknife
    But I will die by your penknife
    On the bonnie banks o Eldrie, o.

5   He took the second sister by the hand
    He wheeled her round and he gart her stand
    He wheeled her round and he gart her stand
    On the bonnie banks o Eldrie, o.

6   It's wid ye be a rank robber's wife?
    Or wid ye die by my penknife?
    Or wid ye die by my penknife
    On the bonnie banks o Eldrie, o?

7   I will not be a rank robber's wife
    But I shall die by your penknife
    But I shall die by your penknife
    On the bonnie banks o Eldrie, o.

8   He's catched the third sister by the hand
    And he wheeled her round and he gart her stand
    He wheeled her round and he gart her stand
    On the bonnie banks o Eldrie, o.

9   Oh will ye be a rank robber's wife?
    Or will ye die by my penknife?
    Or will ye die by my penknife
    On the bonnie banks o Eldrie, o?

10   I will not be a rank robber's wife
     Or I will not die by your penknife
     Or I will not die by your penknife
     On the bonnie banks o Eldrie, o
     For if you kill me, I've a brother will kill you
     On the bonnie banks o Eldrie, o.

11   Come tell to me what is your brother's name
     On the bonnie banks o Eldrie, o
     Bubblin Johnnie is his name
     On the bonnie banks o Eldrie, o.

12   He catched his sister, he kissed her again
     And the tears ran down in sorrow
     On the bonnie banks o Eldrie, o.

13   They kissed one another and sore sat down
     And sore sat down with sorrow
     On the bonnie banks o Eldrie, o.

14   My two sisters I have slain
     On the bonnie banks o Eldrie, o
     I am sure I will have revenge
     On the bonnie banks o Eldrie, o.

15   He catched his youngest sister by the hand
     The tears they wiped and they walked on
     The tears they wiped and they walked on
     To the coves up abeen the birks o Eldrie, o.

16   What's the Calder coves into the birks
     Where the robbers had their nest in Eldrie, o?
     This where the coves and the rank robbers bide
     Up abeen the banks o Eldrie, o.
     Says Bubblin Johnnie, Come wi me
     And I'll have revenge on Eldrie, o.

17   There they're settin waitin
     Till Bubblin Johnnie will come home
     Up abeen the banks o Eldrie, o
     When in goes Bubblin Johnnie and there's none got a chance
     Up abeen the banks o Eldrie, o.

18   I have killed my sisters and I have got revenge
     Up abeen the banks o Eldrie, o.

     'He killed them as they ran out, one by one.'

Palimpsest or texte génétique 171

Key: *del – deleted; ins – inserted; om – omitted*

recurrent variant: bonnie] *T2*; bonny *T1* (1.4, 2.4, 3.4, 4.4, 5.4, 6.4, 7.4, 8.4, 9.4, 10.4, 10.6, 12.3, 13.3)

1.2	(*after* Eldrie) o] *T2, ins T1*
2.2	(*after* And) he] *T2*; *om T1*
6.3	die by my penknife] *T2, T1*; be a rank rob[b]er's wife *del T1*
10.2	*after* Or] wi[ll] *del T1*
10.4–5	] *stanza break T1*
12.2	] *T2, ins T1*
13.1	sat] *T2, T1*; set *del T1*
13.2	sat] *T2, T1*; set *del T1* *after* down] and sore sat down (sat] *T1*; set *del T1*) *T1* with sorrow] *T2, T1*; and lamenting *del T1*
14.1	My] *T2, T1*; This *del T1*
15.2	(*after* and) they] *T2, ins T1*
15.4	*before* To] On the bonny ban[k]s *del T1* birks] *T2, T1*; banks *del T1*
16.1	Calder] *T2, T1*; calder *del T1* coves] *T2, T1*; cave on the *del T1* birks] *T2*; birk *T1*
16.3	bide] *T2, T1*; bides *del T1*
16.5	wi] *T2*; wie *T1*
17.1–2	*line break*] *T2*; *om T1*
17.2	Bubblin] *T2, ins T1*
17.3	*before* Up] Up in the cove abeen Eldrie, o (*after* cove] of *del T1*) *del T1*
17.5	*before* Up] On the *del T1* *after* Up] on t[he?] *del T1*

Appendix 2

cylinder recording

... was walking alone
On the bonnie banks of Eldrie, o [*cylinder skips*]
... was walking alone
On the bonnie banks of Eldrie, o
Fan [there?] was a gentleman comin his lone
On the bonnie, bonnie banks o Eldrie, o.

He catched the older sister by the han
He feeled her round and he gart
    her stand
He feeled her round and he gart
    her stand
On the bonnie banks o Eldrie, o.

Will you be a rank robber's wife?
Or will you die by my penknife?
I will not be a rank robber's wife
On the bo ...
But I will die by your penknife
On the bonnie banks o Eldrie, o.

[transcription by Thomas A. McKean and author]

critical edition

There were three sisters walkin alone
On the bonnie banks o Eldrie, o
As this young man come up on them
On the bonnie banks o Eldrie, o.

He catched the older sister by the hand
And he wheeled her round and he gart
    her stand
He wheeled her round and he gart
    her stand
On the bonnie banks o Eldrie, o.

It's will ye be a rank robber's wife?
Or will ye die by my penknife?
Or will ye die by my penknife
On the bonnie banks o Eldrie, o?

I will not be a rank robber's wife
But I will die by your penknife
But I will die by your penknife
On the bonnie banks o Eldrie, o.

8. Afterword: 'All her friends cried out for shame'

Editing is all about making choices. Thomas Percy, as we have seen, was judged by later generations to have made the wrong choices and condemned in consequence to Albert Friedman's 'special hell reserved for bad editors'.[1] Others, too – Sabine Baring-Gould, for example – have come in for the same sort of criticism.[2] Ralph Vaughan Williams, who often neglected to write down more than just a few of the words of the songs he collected, seems to have attracted rather less opprobrium.[3] Perhaps sins of commission are held in greater disdain than sins of omission. The issue remains alive and well with the controversies surrounding A. L. Lloyd's way with folk songs.[4] The scarcely veiled implication behind the almost ritual condemnation of 'bad editors' is that there is an alternative, 'scientific', practice capable of delivering an 'authentic' text – which they deliberately eschewed but that today's more enlightened scholars would unhesitatingly, indeed instinctively, adopt.

But a Manichaean view of ballad editing is insidious because it encourages complacency – not only towards the pioneers of the field but

---

1 Albert B. Friedman, *The Ballad Revival: Studies in the Influence of Popular on Sophisticated Poetry* (Chicago: University of Chicago Press, 1961), p. 205.
2 See, for example, Steve Gardham, '"The Brown Girl" (Child 295B): A Baring-Gould Concoction?', in *Folk Song: Tradition, Revival, and Re-Creation*, ed. Ian Russell and David Atkinson (Aberdeen: Elphinstone Institute, University of Aberdeen, 2004), pp. 363–76. For a more sympathetic treatment, see Christopher James Bearman, 'The English Folk Music Movement, 1898–1914' (unpublished doctoral thesis, University of Hull, 2001), pp. 169–71.
3 Roy Palmer, ed., *Bushes and Briars: Folk Songs Collected by Ralph Vaughan Williams*, 2nd edn ([Burnham-on-Sea]: Llanerch, 1999), pp. xi–xii.
4 See, for example, Graham Seal, 'A. L. Lloyd in Australia: Some Conclusions', *Folk Music Journal*, 9.1 (2006), 56–71; Stephen D. Winick, 'A. L. Lloyd and Reynardine: Authenticity and Authorship in the Afterlife of a British Broadside Ballad', *Folklore*, 115 (2004), 286–308.

http://dx.doi.org/10.11647/OBP.0041.08

174 The Anglo-Scottish Ballad

towards the ballad itself. As we have seen, the ballad text – words and music alike – is transmitted and preserved only by means of sets of instructions for its repetition, and it is in the nature of sets of instructions that they can be imprecise, incomplete, or incorrect as representations of the sequential patterns that constitute the work that lies behind them. Thomas Tanselle has written:

> Although the traditional term for the evaluation of the makeup of texts, 'textual criticism', suggests the fundamental role of judgment, readers and critics in modern times have predominantly regarded textual criticism (and the editing that emerges from it) as a relatively objective and mechanical activity anticipatory to literary criticism. The inseparability of editing and literary criticism has been more evident in recent debates, but there is not as yet any widespread recognition of textual criticism as a part of the process of reading [. . .] Yet the necessity of questioning the constitution of the texts of documents is sensed, at some level, by all thoughtful people. The antiquity of textual criticism and the prominent position it once held in humanistic scholarship are testimony to the elemental fascination exerted by the mystery of how verbal messages are passed across time.[5]

Arguably, the recognition he is asking for has begun to emerge in some branches at least of the study of canonical literature and music (to his 'process of reading', add 'and listening').[6] The present volume has been an attempt to move ballad scholarship in the same direction – beyond the notion of an authentic text and a good editor/bad editor dichotomy. Like any other literary or musical work, the ballad is unstable and the artefact the listener/reader might think of as *the* ballad is of necessity a convenient construct. Nevertheless, it is still true that on the whole editors do not like making decisions – they can be held to account and might be judged to have been wrong. Yet in the end something has to go into print, or into an electronic edition, and it would be an abrogation of responsibility not to do one's best (if only for the benefit of readers and listeners whose interests are not primarily textual – historians, performers, critics of poetry and music).

This can be neatly illustrated from three copies of 'Barbara Allen' (Child 84) that Carpenter collected in the Gloucestershire/Warwickshire area probably in the early 1930s. The first ballad is from Charles Terry, Long

---

5 G. Thomas Tanselle, 'The Varieties of Scholarly Editing', in *Scholarly Editing: A Guide to Research*, ed. D. C. Greetham (New York: Modern Language Association of America, 1995), pp. 9–32 (p. 28).

6 This could certainly be claimed in relation to the Shakespeare canon, for example. See John Jowett, *Shakespeare and Text* (Oxford: Oxford University Press, 2007). Another instance might be found in the early music/historically informed performance movement.

Compton, Warwickshire.[7] Here, stanza 7 of the fair copy typescript reads as follows:

> The more she looked, the more she laughed,
> The farther she drew from him;
> Till all her friends cried out, "For shame!
> Hardhearted Barbara Ellen!"

Close inspection of the rough copy typescript (Fig. 8.1), however, reveals that what was first typed was as follows:

> The more she looked, the more she laughed,
> The farther she drew from him;
> Till all her friends cried out for shame,
> Hard hearted Barbara Ellen!

But, apparently while the sheet of paper was still in his portable typewriter (that the above was indeed the initial reading is indicated by the spacing of the typed characters, and their alignment suggests the paper was not removed from the machine in the interim), Carpenter went back over line 3, changing it to read: 'Till all her friends cried out, For shame'. Subsequently, he added handwritten quotation marks and inserted a hyphen into 'Hard hearted' to give a stanza that corresponds, more or less, with the fair copy:

> The more she looked, the more she laughed,
> The farther she drew from him;
> Till all her friends cried out, "For shame,
> Hard-hearted Barbara Ellen!"

Now, in line with the discussion in the previous chapter, the alteration of line 3 might be attributable to contributor, or collector, or both – but clearly it signifies a change of meaning. In the line as initially typed, 'for shame' is an adverbial phrase and it is Barbara Ellen's friends (probably in the sense of kin, relatives, family connections, as well as close acquaintances) who experience shame, sharing in a sense of what they consider she should also feel. In the fair copy, however, 'For shame' has become an exclamation (= 'For shame's sake') directed entirely at Barbara Ellen, urging her to a sense of her own reprehensible conduct.

---

7 Washington, DC, Library of Congress, American Folklife Center, Archive of Folk Culture, AFC1972/001, James Madison Carpenter Collection, MS pp. 04403–04404, 06555–06556 (there is no identified sound recording). (Double quotation marks in the quotations that follow are Carpenter's.)

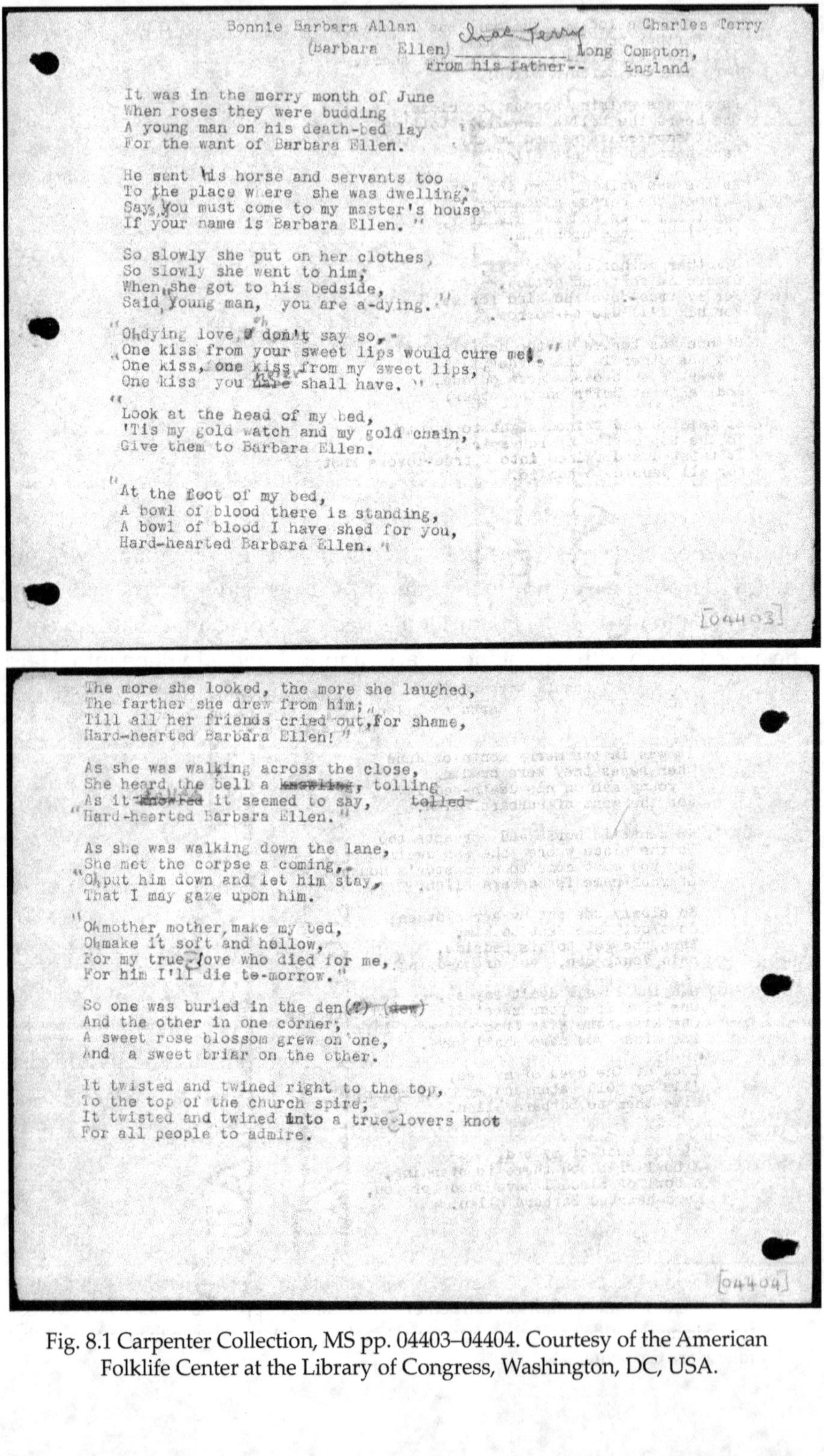

Bonnie Barbara Allan Chas Terry Charles Terry
(Barbara Ellen) from his father-- Long Compton, England

It was in the merry month of June
When roses they were budding
A young man on his death-bed lay
For the want of Barbara Ellen.

He sent his horse and servants too
To the place where she was dwelling,
Says,You must come to my master's house
If your name is Barbara Ellen."

So slowly she put on her clothes,
So slowly she went to him;
When she got to his bedside,
Said young man, you are a-dying."

"Oh dying love, don't say so,
One kiss from your sweet lips would cure me."
"One kiss, one kiss from my sweet lips,
One kiss you ne'er shall have."

"Look at the head of my bed,
'Tis my gold watch and my gold chain,
Give them to Barbara Ellen.

"At the foot of my bed,
A bowl of blood there is standing,
A bowl of blood I have shed for you,
Hard-hearted Barbara Ellen."

[04403]

The more she looked, the more she laughed,
The farther she drew from him;
Till all her friends cried out,For shame,
Hard-hearted Barbara Ellen!"

As she was walking across the close,
She heard the bell a knelling, tolling
As it answered it seemed to say, tolled
"Hard-hearted Barbara Ellen."

As she was walking down the lane,
She met the corpse a coming,
"Oh,put him down and let him stay,
That I may gaze upon him."

"Oh mother, mother, make my bed,
Oh make it soft and hollow,
For my true-love who died for me,
For him I'll die te-morrow."

So one was buried in the den(?) (dew)
And the other in one corner;
A sweet rose blossom grew on one,
And a sweet briar on the other.

It twisted and twined right to the top,
To the top of the church spire;
It twisted and twined into a true-lovers knot
For all people to admire.

[04404]

Fig. 8.1 Carpenter Collection, MS pp. 04403–04404. Courtesy of the American Folklife Center at the Library of Congress, Washington, DC, USA.

The second ballad is from Thomas Bunting, Sherborne, Gloucestershire.[8] Here, stanza 8 of the fair copy reads:

> The more she gazed, the more she laughed,
> Till she came nearer to him;
> Till all her friends cried out, "For shame!
> Hardhearted Barbara Allan!"

The rough copy, however, reads as follows (the quotation marks and the upgrading of the final point to an exclamation mark are handwritten):

> The more she gazed, the more she laughed,
> Till she came nearer to him;
> Till all her friends cried out for shame,
> "Hard-hearted Barbara Allen!"

This time, the crux has been resolved in the move from rough copy to fair copy (at which time also 'Allen' became 'Allan').

The third ballad is from Mrs Cobb, Sapperton, Gloucestershire, and apparently exists only as a rough copy typescript.[9] Here, the equivalent stanza reads:

> The more she looked, the more she laughed,
> The nearer she got to him,
> Until her parents cried out for shame,
> Hard hearted Barbara Allan.

There is no way of knowing which of these is the 'correct' reading. Nineteenth-century broadsides (of which there are a great number) tend to print 'cried out for shame',[10] while earlier printed copies have the unambiguously adverbial 'cried out amain'.[11] The typesetter might

---

8 Carpenter Collection, MS pp. 04400–04401, 06553, 07936 (although there is a music transcription, no sound recording has been identified).
9 Carpenter Collection, MS p. 06549.
10 For example, *Barbara Allen* ([London]: J. Catnach, [1813–38]) [London, British Library, L.R.271.a.2., vol. 4, no. 248]; *Barbara Allen* ([London]: Pitts, [1819–44]) [Oxford, Bodleian Library, Harding B 25(115)]; *Barbara Allen* (London: H. Such, [1849–62]) [Oxford, Bodleian Library, Firth c.17(71), Harding B 11(729), Harding B 11(730)]; *Barbara Allen* ([Manchester]: Swindells, [1796–1853]) [Oxford, Bodleian Library, 2806 c.17(19), Harding B 16(14a)].
11 For example, *Barbara Allen's Cruelty; or, The Young-Man's Tragedy* ([London]: P. Brooksby, J. Deacon, J. Blare, J. Back, [1688–92]) [ESTC R226987]; *Barbara Allen's Cruelty; or, The Young Man's Tragedy* ([London?, 1750?]) [ESTC T21370]; *Barbara Allen's Cruelty; or, The Young Man's Tragedy* ([Edinburgh?, 1775]) [ESTC T21372]; *The Old Ballad of Cruel Barbara Allen* (Salisbury: Fowler, [1785?]) [ESTC T223848]; *Barbara Allen's Cruelty; or, The Young Man's Tragedy* (London: J. Davenport, [1800?]) [ESTC T188670].

simply have taken the path of least resistance. 'Barbara Allen' has been very widely collected and both interpretations can be found among collectors' manuscripts (in some instances there are niceties of wording or syntax that favour one reading over the other).[12] It might, of course, be argued that the semantic difference is really quite slight, especially in the context of one of the less intellectually challenging of the Child ballads. But in a sense that is just the point – whether or not it is held to 'matter', the ambiguity means that the precise constitution of what we identify as Charles Terry's, or Thomas Bunting's, or Mrs Cobb's 'Barbara Allen' remains forever conjectural.

The point is particularly well illustrated by ballads, since melody tends to mask punctuation. It is very difficult to sing, with any consistency, the appropriate pauses marked by a comma or a semi-colon, and, unless deliberately adopting different voices, probably impossible to sing a quotation mark. Even so, punctuation in English is not an altogether scientific or mechanical exercise.[13] Conventions and habits vary substantially with time and geography, and with purpose and personal preference, and especially over the use of marks such as the comma and semi-colon. Broadly speaking, a general trend over time can be discerned away from a rhetorical system, which indicates varying lengths of pauses to facilitate vocal delivery, towards a syntactic system, which employs punctuation to give visual guidance to the syntactic relations of the sentence in order to facilitate reading. But elements of both systems coexisted for a very long time – and still do.

A couple of historical examples will be useful further to illustrate the fluidity of punctuation practice. Manuscripts of John Donne's poems that circulated for recitation among a contemporary literary coterie display a more rhetorical system of pointing, providing instructions for speaking the verse out loud, than early printed editions, designed for more personal reading, which are punctuated to provide more guidance to the syntactical relations of the poetry.[14] In the nineteenth century, W. M. Thackeray wrote

---

12 For example, Chippenham, Wiltshire and Swindon Archives, 2598/36, Alfred Williams Folk Song Collection, Wt. 388; London, EFDSS Archives, Anne Gilchrist Collection, AGG/8/4; Hammond Collection, HAM/3/18/28; Ralph Vaughan Williams Collection, RVW1/1/90 [all accessible via the Full English Digital Archive at http://www.vwml.org.uk].

13 M. B. Parkes, *Pause and Effect: An Introduction to the History of Punctuation in the West* (Aldershot: Scolar Press, 1992). For a useful summary, see E. A. Levenston, *The Stuff of Literature: Physical Aspects of Texts and their Relation to Literary Meaning* (Albany: State University of New York Press, 1992), esp. pp. 65–72.

14 Ted-Larry Pebworth, 'Manuscript Transmission and the Selection of Copy-Text in

using primarily a rhetorical system of punctuation, at a time when his early nineteenth-century printers had largely switched to a syntactic system, creating substantial difficulties for his modern editors.[15] The editor of *Vanity Fair* (Peter Shillingsburg) was faced with an especially unenviable decision, for while it is possible to argue persuasively in favour of reproducing either the author's punctuation or that imposed by the publisher, Thackeray's manuscript survives for only about one sixth of the novel. In the end, he chose to retain as much of Thackeray's writing style as possible, warning readers that the compositorial style of pointing prevailed throughout the remaining bulk of the book. The decision may have been controversial, but it certainly foregrounds the inherently conjectural and contested nature of the text – not only of that particular work, but of all works.

Scholars have struggled to make some sense of the mostly very light (even to the point of absence), often erratic, and essentially rhetorical pointing of medieval manuscripts. Although there is some evidence of systematic punctuation emerging among certain scribes or scriptoria prior to the invention of printing, it is often assumed that it was largely left to the printers to mandate coherent systems of spelling and punctuation.[16] Many subsequent editors have simply imposed modern conventions of punctuation, capitalization, word division, and the like, with the needs of the modern reader in mind. Katherine O'Brien O'Keeffe, however, argues strenuously that the punctuation of manuscript texts of Old English verse does make sense.[17] Pointing, she maintains, and other visual characteristics of the written text such as capitalization, spacing, lineation, paragraphing, and page layout, are visual cues for decoding and are therefore less important when a text is conceived primarily as something to be read aloud. In such texts, the little pointing that is present serves more of an expressive than an analytical or syntactic function. Accordingly, the extant pointing of much Old English manuscript verse, along with other visual markers and the occurrence of variant readings, can be taken as evidence of what can be described as an oral (though one might prefer 'rhetorical') mode of reception on the part of the scribes. The contrast is with the manuscript

---

Renaissance Coterie Poetry', *Text: Transactions of the Society for Textual Scholarship*, 7 (1994), 243–61.

15 Peter L. Shillingsburg, *Scholarly Editing in the Computer Age: Theory and Practice*, 3rd edn (Ann Arbor: University of Michigan Press, 1996), pp. 56–70 (see also pp. xi–xiii).

16 D. C. Greetham, *Textual Scholarship: An Introduction* (New York: Garland, 1994), pp. 223–24.

17 Katherine O'Brien O'Keeffe, *Visible Song: Transitional Literacy in Old English Verse* (Cambridge: Cambridge University Press, 1990), esp. pp. 138–54.

writing of Latin verse, which was certainly intended to be read visually, and where scribes were employing a much more systematic method of pointing and layout from a much earlier date. After, perhaps, the late tenth century, there is a greater appearance of conventional visual graphic cues and evidence of more coherent pointing practices, indicative of a shift towards the reading rather than the speaking of verse.

Scribes are envisaged as committing blocks of texts to short-term memory, and drawing on their knowledge of the conventions of the verse they were copying, while writing it down; they are also believed to have worked by reading aloud, or sub-vocalizing, and therefore 'hearing' at least a part of their texts.[18] (It is intriguing to speculate whether the compositors of broadside and chapbook ballads ever also worked in this way.) This mode of reception was operative quite regardless of the possible oral or written origins of the works in question. For example, in the verse dialogue *Solomon and Saturn I*, which is almost certainly a product of writing, O'Keeffe characterizes the manuscript pointing as a visual analogue of the speaker's drop in voice. Thus the scribe – a necessarily literate reader of the copy-text – was also an active participant in the reception and transmission of the verse. Embodying the roles of active reader and passive copyist, 'language-producer and visual-reproducer', as receiver of the text the scribe can be considered as a special kind of audience, and as reproducer of the text as a special kind of performer.[19] All of this then has implications for the modern editor's role. Evidence of scribal participation in the making of texts on the one hand provides historical and social context for their reception and (re)production, while on the other hand it distances texts from any notion of authorial intention.[20] Idealist editing, for example, which delivers a remade text, largely purged of scribal intervention, clarified and rendered accessible to the modern reader – a text that never actually existed but that encapsulates an editor's conception of the author's work – may, ironically, be less historically accurate and useful than the reproduction of a text that shows traces of the scribe's own activity.[21] On the other hand, the impenetrability for the

---

18 H. J. Chaytor, *From Script to Print: An Introduction to Medieval Literature* (Cambridge: Cambridge University Press, 1945), pp. 13–21; O'Keeffe, *Visible Song*, pp. 40–41.
19 O'Keeffe, *Visible Song*, pp. 66–67, 75, 192.
20 O'Keeffe, *Visible Song*, pp. 193–94.
21 O'Keeffe, *Visible Song*, pp. 115–16, 193.

modern reader of Old English pointing can in practice be held to reduce the usefulness of such texts in the grand sweep of history.

Like the scribe of Old English poetry, the folk song collector/editor can be envisaged as both a special kind of audience and a special kind of performer. The collector/editor's documentary text, which represents the moment of reception of the contributor's song, may well be the most historically precise artefact that will ever be available. This is an argument for the digital archive approach. Equally, though, there is an argument for publishing some kind of edited text which might be of greater use to the modern user – resolving, or at least addressing, matters such as the crux in 'Barbara Allen'. The analogy with the Anglo-Saxon scribe, however, is not quite an exact one. Unlike the scribe, the nineteenth-/twentieth-century folk song collector/editor will have approached the task with a received set of conventions governing such matters as spelling and punctuation, and the rules of music notation. Carpenter's punctuation is unremarkable for an early twentieth-century American; his slips tend to be self-evident, and where verbal ambiguities remain there is no real evidence that he was using punctuation in an attempt to resolve them. The challenge for the editor is to make some sense of his various additions and alterations, to determine whether they do really provide evidence for the reception of the ballads in a manner analogous to the Old English scribe, and to alight on a consistent manner of dealing with them. There would be nothing inherently unreasonable in reproducing Carpenter's own punctuation; the visible signs of the editing hand would certainly be his rather than those of a modern editor. But it is not clear that the resultant texts would not be more of a witness to convention and precedent than to a historically situated act of reception reflecting the speaker's own pauses and inflections – and the crux in 'Barbara Allen' would remain.

So there is an argument for stripping out the 1930s American-English punctuation as far as possible. The stanza from 'Barbara Allen' would then read:

> The more she looked, the more she laughed
> The farther she drew from him
> Till all her friends cried out for shame
> Hard-hearted Barbara Ellen.

Ostensibly the editor will have chosen the reading that imposes the least in the way of interpretation by means of punctuation – trusting the reader to sense the inherent instability, not to say ambiguity, of the text, which then goes at least some way towards representing the stream of evanescent language that lies behind the material ballad, and foregrounding the necessity for conjecture in reconstituting it. Applied to ballads and folk songs at large, such an approach has the advantage that it admits the influence upon phrasing of melody and/or verse rhythm.

Pragmatically, one would probably not wish to present the ballad as a conglomerate of discrete lines of verse with little sense of syntactic continuity and a reduced sense of story-telling. Accordingly, a system of minimal punctuation can be conveniently combined with conventional verse lineation and division into stanzas, which themselves serve as a form of visual punctuation directing the way the words are read, spoken, or sung. Ballad lineation and stanza division are usually syntactic as well as rhetorical. Line endings, for example, signal a pause, most frequently equivalent to a comma – which, accordingly, is not required in addition. However, the ends of sentences still require to be marked with full stops. Commas are required in a few other instances: to break up verbal repetitions and listed items, to switch from indirect to direct speech and vice versa, to precede or follow direct forms of address. But with a comma and an initial capital letter, quotation marks are not needed in addition around direct speech. The effect is to suppress, though not to eliminate, the visual rhetoric of punctuation and to shift the burden of interpretive reception and conjecture on to the modern reader.

The visual intrusiveness of the editing hand is reduced, even while the resultant text is still a construct. The editorial procedure can be thought of as akin to the choice of a prescriptive over a descriptive level of music transcription (see chapter five). It is perhaps the best the editor can do, but in the end the editor – and the reader and the listener – does have to make a choice. The ballad text, in words and music, is inherently unstable, and there is at least a logic to an approach to its representation that seeks to maintain and even to emphasize that instability.

Select Bibliography

Abrahams, Roger D., and George Foss, *Anglo–American Folklsong Style* (Englewood Cliffs, NJ: Prentice–Hall, 1968).

Adams, Thomas R., and Nicolas Barker, 'A New Model for the Study of the Book', in *A Potencie of Life: Books in Society*, ed. Nicolas Barker (London: British Library; New Castle, DE: Oak Knoll Press, 1993), pp. 5–43.

Allen, Don Cameron, ed., *Essayes by Sir William Cornwallis, the Younger* (Baltimore: Johns Hopkins Press, 1946).

Allingham, William, ed., *The Ballad Book: A Selection of the Choicest British Ballads* (London and Cambridge: Macmillan, 1864).

Andersen, Flemming G., 'From Tradition to Print: Ballads on Broadsides', in Flemming G. Andersen, Otto Holzapfel, and Thomas Pettitt, *The Ballad as Narrative: Studies in the Ballad Traditions of England, Scotland, Germany and Denmark* (Odense: Odense University Press, 1982), pp. 39–58.

—, '"All There Is . . . As It Is": On the Development of Textual Criticism in Ballad Studies', *Jahrbuch für Volksliedforschung*, 39 (1994), 28–40.

—, and Thomas Pettitt, 'Mrs. Brown of Falkland: A Singer of Tales?', *Journal of American Folklore*, 92 (1979), 1–24.

Atkinson, David, '"George Collins" in Hampshire', in *The Flowering Thorn: International Ballad Studies*, ed. Thomas A. McKean (Logan: Utah State University Press, 2003), pp. 193–204.

—, 'The English "Maid" and the Ballad Idea', in *Singing the Nations: Herder's Legacy*, ed. Dace Bula and Sigrid Rieuwerts, BASIS, vol. 4 (Trier: WVT Wissenschaftlicher Verlag Trier, 2008), pp. 298–308.

—, 'The Secret Life of Ballad Manuscripts', *Variants*, 8 (2012), 183–206 [and corrigendum in *Variants*, 10 (2013), 13].

—, 'Are Broadside Ballads Worth Editing?', *Variants*, 10 (2013), 235–55.

—, '"William and Margaret": An Eighteenth-Century Ballad', *Folk Music Journal*, 10.4 (2014), 478–511.

—, and Julia C. Bishop, 'The Contributor as Collector: Ann Lyall and "The Fair Flower of Northumberland"', in *Emily Lyle: The Persistent Scholar*, ed. Frances J. Fischer and Sigrid Rieuwerts, BASIS, vol. 5 (Trier: WVT Wissenschaftlicher Verlag Trier, 2007), pp. 5–24.

—, and Steve Roud, eds, *Street Ballads in Nineteenth-Century Britain, Ireland, and North America: The Interface between Print and Oral Traditions* (Farnham and Burlington, VT: Ashgate, 2014).

Baring Gould, S., and H. Fleetwood Sheppard, *Songs and Ballads of the West* (London: Methuen, [1891–95]).

Barry, Jonathan, 'Literacy and Literature in Popular Culture: Reading and Writing in Historical Perspective', in *Popular Culture in England, c.1500–1850*, ed. Tim Harris (Basingstoke: Macmillan, 1995), pp. 69–94.

Barry, Phillips, 'The Part of the Folk Singer in the Making of Folk Balladry', in *The Critics & the Ballad*, ed. MacEdward Leach and Tristram P. Coffin (Carbondale: Southern Illinois University Press, 1961), pp. 59–76.

Barthes, Roland, 'The Death of the Author', in *Image – Music – Text*, trans. Stephen Heath (London: Fontana, 1977), pp. 142–48.

Bateson, F. W., 'Modern Bibliography and the Literary Artifact', in *English Studies Today*, 2nd ser., ed. G. A. Bonnard (Bern: Francke, 1961), pp. 67–77.

—, 'The New Bibliography and the "New Criticism": A Lecture at Lausanne', in *Essays in Critical Dissent* (London: Longman, 1972), pp. 1–15.

Baugh, Albert C., 'Improvisation in the Middle English Romance', *Proceedings of the American Philosophical Society*, 103 (1959), 418–54.

Bayard, Samuel P., 'Prolegomena to a Study of the Principal Melodic Families of British-American Folk Song', *Journal of American Folklore*, 63 (1950), 1–44; reprinted in *The Critics & the Ballad*, ed. MacEdward Leach and Tristram P. Coffin (Carbondale: Southern Illinois University Press, 1961), pp. 103–50.

Bayard, Samuel P., 'The "Johnny Collins" Version of "Lady Alice"', *Journal of American Folklore*, 58 (1945), 73–103.

Bearman, C. J., 'Who Were the Folk? The Demography of Cecil Sharp's Somerset Folk Singers', *Historical Journal*, 43 (2000), 751–75, http://dx.doi.org/10.1017/s0018246x99001338.

—, 'The English Folk Music Movement 1898–1914' (unpublished doctoral thesis, University of Hull, 2001).

—, 'Cecil Sharp in Somerset: Some Reflections on the Work of David Harker', *Folklore*, 113 (2002), 11–34, http://dx.doi.org/10.1080/00155870220125426.

—, 'Percy Grainger, the Phonograph, and the Folk Song Society', *Music & Letters*, 84 (2003), 434–55, http://dx.doi.org/10.1093/ml/84.3.434.

—, 'The Folk-Song Society and the Phonograph', *Folk Music Journal*, 10.3 (2013), 370–74.

Bell, John, ed., *Rhymes of Northern Bards*, introduction by David Harker (Newcastle upon Tyne: Frank Graham, 1971 [1812]).

Bellemin-Noël, Jean, *Le Texte et l'avant-texte: Les Brouillons d'un poème de Milosz* (Paris: Larousse, 1972).

—, 'Reproduire le manuscrit, présenter les brouillons, établir un avant-texte', *Littérature*, no. 28 (1977), 3–18, http://dx.doi.org/10.3406/litt.1977.2072.

Ben-Amos, Dan, 'The Seven Strands of *Tradition*: Varieties in its Meaning in American Folklore Studies', *Journal of Folklore Research*, 21 (1984), 97–131.

Benjamin, Walter, 'The Work of Art in the Age of its Technological Reproducibility', in *Selected Writings*, vol. 3, 1935–1938, trans. Edmund Jephcott, Howard Eiland, et al., ed. Howard Eiland and Michael W. Jennings (Cambridge, MA: The Belknap Press of Harvard University Press, 2002), pp. 101–33.

Bennett, Anthony, 'Sources of Popular Song in Early Nineteenth-Century Britain: Problems and Methods of Research', *Popular Music*, 2 (1982), 69–89, http://dx.doi.org/10.1017/s0261143000001239.

Bishop, Julia C., '"Dr Carpenter from the Harvard College in America": An Introduction to James Madison Carpenter and his Collection', *Folk Music Journal*, 7.4 (1998), 402–20.

—, '*Grouping, Grawping* and *Groping* towards a Critical Edition of the James Madison Carpenter Collection of Traditional Song and Drama', Dialect and Folk Life Studies in Britain: The Leeds Archive of Vernacular Culture in its Context, University of Leeds, 19 March 2005, available at http://library.leeds.ac.uk/multimedia/imu/2163/JuliaBishop2.pdf.

Bogatyrëv, Peter, and Roman Jakobson, 'Folklore as a Special Form of Creativity', trans. Manfred Jacobson, in *The Prague School: Selected Writings, 1929–1946*, ed. Peter Steiner (Austin: University of Texas Press, 1982), pp. 32–46.

Bohlman, Philip V., *The Study of Folk Music in the Modern World* (Bloomington and Indianapolis: Indiana University Press, 1988).

Bold, Valentina, '"Nouther right spelled nor right setten down': Scott, Child and the Hogg Family Ballads', in *The Ballad in Scottish History*, ed. Edward J. Cowan (East Linton: Tuckwell Press, 2000), pp. 116–41.

Bornstein, George, *Material Modernism: The Politics of the Page* (Cambridge: Cambridge University Press, 2001).

Bownde, Nicholas, *The Doctrine of the Sabbath* (London: printed by the Widdow Orwin, for Iohn Porter, and Thomas Man, 1595) [ESTC S113231].

Boyes, Georgina, *The Imagined Village: Culture, Ideology and the English Folk Revival* (Leeds: No Masters Co-operative, 2010 [1993]).

Bradbury, Nancy Mason, *Writing Aloud: Storytelling in Late Medieval England* (Urbana and Chicago: University of Illinois Press, 1998).

Bradley, Kevin, *Risks Associated with the Use of Recordable CDs and DVDs as Reliable Storage Media in Archival Collections – Strategies and Alternatives*, Memory of the World Programme, Sub-Committee on Technology (Paris: UNESCO, 2006), available at unesdoc.unesco.org/images/0014/001477/147782E.pdf.

Bradtke, Elaine, 'Fiddle Tunes from under the Bed: Extracting Music from Carpenter's Recordings', in *Crossing Over: Fiddle and Dance Studies from around the North Atlantic*, 3, ed. Ian Russell and Anna Kearney Guigné (Aberdeen: Elphinstone Institute, University of Aberdeen, in association with the Department of Folklore, MMaP and the School of Music, Memorial University of Newfoundland, 2010), pp. 35–48.

Brady, Erika, *A Spiral Way: How the Phonograph Changed Ethnography* (Jackson: University Press of Mississippi, 1999).

Bronson, Bertrand Harris, *The Traditional Tunes of the Child Ballads*, 4 vols (Princeton: Princeton University Press, 1959–72).

—, *The Ballad as Song* (Berkeley and Los Angeles: University of California Press, 1969).

Brown, Carleton, ed., *English Lyrics of the XIIIth Century* (Oxford: Clarendon Press, 1932).

Brown, Mary Ellen, 'Mr. Child's Scottish Mentor: William Motherwell', in *Ballads into Books: The Legacies of Francis James Child*, ed. Tom Cheesman and Sigrid Rieuwerts (Bern: Peter Lang, 1997), pp. 29–39.

—, ed., *The Bedesman and the Hodbearer: The Epistolary Friendship of Francis James Child and William Walker* (Aberdeen: Aberdeen University Press, for the Elphinstone Institute, 2001).

—, *William Motherwell's Cultural Politics, 1797–1835* (Lexington: University Press of Kentucky, 2001).

—, 'Child's Ballads and the Broadside Conundrum', in *Ballads and Broadsides in Britain, 1500–1800*, ed. Patricia Fumerton and Anita Guerrini (Farnham and Burlington, VT: Ashgate, 2010), pp. 57–72.

—, *Child's Unfinished Masterpiece: The English and Scottish Popular Ballads* (Urbana, Chicago, and Springfield: University of Illinois Press, 2011).

—, and Bruce A. Rosenberg, eds, *Encyclopedia of Folklore and Literature* (Santa Barbara: ABC-CLIO, 1998).

Buchan, David, *The Ballad and the Folk* (London: Routledge & Kegan Paul, 1972).

—, 'History and Harlaw', in *Ballad Studies*, ed. E. B. Lyle (Cambridge: D. S. Brewer; Totowa, NJ: Rowman and Littlefield, for the Folklore Society, 1976), pp. 29–40.

Buchan, Peter, *Ancient Ballads and Songs of the North of Scotland*, 2 vols (Edinburgh: W. and D. Laing; J. Stevenson; Aberdeen: A. Brown & Co.; Glasgow: J. Wylie; Robertson and Atkinson; Perth: D. Morison & Co.; London: J. Darling, 1828).

Burke, Peter, *Popular Culture in Early Modern Europe* (Aldershot: Wildwood House, 1988 [1978]).

Burns, Tom, 'A Model for Textual Variation in Folksong', *Folklore Forum*, 3 (1970), 49–56.

Burstow, Henry, *Reminiscences of Horsham, being Recollections of Henry Burstow, the Celebrated Bellringer & Songsinger*, [ed. William Albery] (Horsham: Free Christian Church Book Society, 1911).

Campbell, J. F., *Popular Tales of the West Highlands*, 4 vols (Edinburgh: Edmonston & Douglas, 1860–62).

Cass, Eddie, 'The James Madison Carpenter Collection of British Folk Plays', *Folklore*, 123 (2012), 1–22.

Cerquiglini, Bernard, *In Praise of the Variant: A Critical History of Philology*, trans. Betsy Wing (Baltimore: Johns Hopkins University Press, 1999).

Chambers, E. K., *English Literature at the Close of the Middle Ages* (Oxford: Clarendon Press, 1945).

Chandler, Daniel, 'Biases of the Ear and Eye: "Great Divide" Theories, Phonocentrism, Graphocentrism & Logocentrism' (1994), available at http://www.aber.ac.uk/media/Documents/litoral/litoral.html.

—, 'The Transmission Model of Communication' (1994), available at http://www.aber.ac.uk/media/Documents/short/trans.html.

Chappell, W., *The Ballad Literature and Popular Music of the Olden Time*, 2 vols (London: Chappell and Co., [1859]).

Chartier, Roger, *The Order of Books: Readers, Authors, and Libraries in Europe between the Fourteenth and Eighteenth Centuries*, trans. Lydia G. Cochrane (Stanford: Stanford University Press, 1994).

Chaytor, H. J., *From Script to Print: An Introduction to Medieval Literature* (Cambridge: Cambridge University Press, 1945).

Cheesman, Tom, '*Bänkelsang*: Seeing, Hearing, Telling and Singing in the German Ballad Picture Show', *Lore and Language*, 12 (1994), 41–57.

—, *The Shocking Ballad Picture Show: German Popular Literature and Cultural History* (Oxford and Providence, RI: Berg, 1994).

Child, Francis James, ed., *English and Scottish Ballads*, 8 vols (Boston: Little, Brown, 1857–58).

—, 'Ballad Poetry', in *Johnson's New Universal Cyclopædia*, eds-in-chief Frederick A. P. Barnard and Arnold Guyot, 4 vols (New York: A. J. Johnson, 1881 [1874]), I, 365–68.

—, ed., *The English and Scottish Popular Ballads*, 5 vols (Boston: Houghton, Mifflin, 1882–98).

Christie, W., ed., *Traditional Ballad Airs*, 2 vols (Edinburgh: Edmonston & Douglas; David Douglas, 1876–81).

Christophersen, Paul, *The Ballad of Sir Aldingar: Its Origin and Analogues* (Oxford: Clarendon Press, 1952).

Clanchy, M. T., *From Memory to Written Record: England 1066–1307*, 3rd edn (Oxford and Malden, MA: Wiley-Blackwell, 2013).

Coffin, Tristram Potter, *The British Traditional Ballad in North America*, rev. edn, with supplement by Roger deV. Renwick (Austin: University of Texas Press, 1977).

Copper, Bob, *Songs and Southern Breezes: Country Folk and Country Ways* (London: Heinemann, 1973).

[Copper Family, The], *The Copper Family Song Book: A Living Tradition* (Peacehaven: Coppersongs, 1995).

Cra'ster, Barbara M., 'George Collins', *Journal of the Folk-Song Society*, 4.2 (no. 15) (1910), 106–09.

Crain, Patricia, 'New Histories of Literacy', in *A Companion to the History of the Book*, ed. Simon Eliot and Jonathan Rose (Oxford and Malden, MA: Wiley-Blackwell, 2007), pp. 467–79, http://dx.doi.org/10.1002/9780470690949.ch34.

Cressy, David, *Literacy and the Social Order: Reading and Writing in Tudor and Stuart England* (Cambridge: Cambridge University Press, 1980), http://dx.doi.org/10.1017/cbo9780511560484.

Culler, Jonathan, *Structuralist Poetics: Structuralism, Linguistics and the Study of Literature* (London: Routledge, 2002 [1975]), http://dx.doi.org/10.4324/9780203449769.

—, 'Prolegomena to a Theory of Reading', in *The Reader in the Text: Essays on Audience and Interpretation*, ed. Susan R. Suleiman and Inge Crosman (Princeton: Princeton University Press, 1980), pp. 46–66.

Darnton, Robert, 'What Is the History of Books?', *Daedalus*, 111.3 (1982), 65–83.

Davis, Arthur Kyle, Jr., ed., *Traditional Ballads of Virginia, collected under the auspices of the Virginia Folk-Lore Society* (Cambridge, MA: Harvard University Press, 1929).

—, ed., *More Traditional Ballads of Virginia, collected with the cooperation of members of the Virginia Folklore Society* (Chapel Hill: University of North Carolina Press, 1960).

de Biasi, Pierre-Marc, 'What Is a Literary Draft? Toward a Functional Typology of Genetic Documentation', *Yale French Studies*, no. 89 (1996), 26–58, http://dx.doi.org/10.2307/2930337.

—, *La Génétique des textes* (Paris: Nathan, 2000).

de la Torre Bueno, Lillian, 'Was Ambrose Philips a Ballad Editor?', *Anglia*, 59 (1935), 252–70, http://dx.doi.org/10.1515/angl.1935.1935.59.252.

'Definition of Folk Music', *Journal of the International Folk Music Council*, 7 (1955), 23.

Deppman, Jed, Daniel Ferrer, and Michael Groden, eds, *Genetic Criticism: Texts and Avant-textes* (Philadelphia: University of Pennsylvania Press, 2004).

Derrida, Jacques, *Of Grammatology*, corrected edn, trans. Gayatri Chakravorty Spivak (Baltimore: Johns Hopkins University Press, 1997).

Deutscher, Penelope, *How to Read Derrida* (London: Granta, 2005).

Dixon, James Henry, ed., *Scottish Traditional Versions of Ancient Ballads* (London: Percy Society, 1845).

Donatelli, Joseph, 'The Percy Folio Manuscript: A Seventeenth-Century Context for Medieval Poetry', *English Manuscript Studies, 1100–1700*, 4 (1993), 114–33.

Dorson, Richard M., *Buying the Wind: Regional Folklore in the United States* (Chicago: University of Chicago Press, 1964).

Dragstra, Henk, '"Before woomen were Readers": How John Aubrey Wrote Female Oral History', in *Oral Traditions and Gender in Early Modern Literary Texts*, ed. Mary Ellen Lamb and Karen Bamford (Aldershot and Burlington, VT: Ashgate, 2008), pp. 41–53.

Dronke, Peter, "Learned Lyric and the Popular Ballad in the Early Middle Ages," *Studi Medievali*, 3rd ser., 17 (1976), 1–40.

Dugaw, Dianne M., 'Anglo-American Folksong Reconsidered: The Interface of Oral and Written Forms', *Western Folklore*, 43 (1984), 83–103.

Duncan, Thomas G., ed., *Medieval English Lyrics and Carols* (Cambridge: D. S. Brewer, 2013).

Eggert, Paul, 'The Way of All Text: The Materialist Shakespeare', in *Voice, Text, Hypertext: Emerging Practices in Textual Studies*, ed. Raimonda Modiano, Leroy F. Searle, and Peter Shillingsburg (Seattle: Walter Chapin Simpson Center for the Humanities in association with University of Washington Press, 2004), pp. 162–76.

Eisenstein, Elizabeth L., *The Printing Revolution in Early Modern Europe*, 2nd edn (Cambridge: Cambridge University Press, 2005), http://dx.doi.org/10.1017/cbo9781139197038.

Ellis, Bill, 'Why Are Verbatim Texts of Legends Necessary?', in *Perspectives on Contemporary Legend*, vol. 2, ed. Gillian Bennett, Paul Smith, and J. D. A. Widdowson (Sheffield: Sheffield Academic Press, for the Centre for English Cultural Tradition and Language, 1987), pp. 31–60.

Entwistle, William J., *European Balladry* (Oxford: Clarendon Press, 1939).

—, '"Sir Aldingar" and the Date of English Ballads', *Saga-Book of the Viking Society*, 13 (1946–53), 97–112.

Fine, Elizabeth, 'In Defense of Literary Dialect: A Response to Dennis R. Preston', *Journal of American Folklore*, 96 (1983), 323–30.

—, *The Folklore Text: From Performance to Print* (Bloomington and Indianapolis: Indiana University Press, 1984).

Finnegan, Ruth, *Oral Traditions and the Verbal Arts: A Guide to Research Practices* (London: Routledge, 1992).

Fish, Stanley, *Is There a Text in This Class? The Authority of Interpretive Communities* (Cambridge, MA: Harvard University Press, 1980).

Foucault, Michel, 'What Is an Author?', in *The Foucault Reader*, ed. Paul Rabinow (Harmondsworth: Penguin, 1984), pp. 101–20.

Fox, Adam, *Oral and Literate Culture in England, 1500–1700* (Oxford: Clarendon Press, 2000), http://dx.doi.org/10.1093/acprof:oso/9780199251032.001.0001.

—, and Daniel Woolf, eds, *The Spoken Word: Oral Culture in Britain, 1500–1850*, ed. Adam Fox and Daniel Woolf (Manchester: Manchester University Press, 2002).

Fox Strangways, A. H., in collaboration with Maud Karpeles, *Cecil Sharp* (London: Oxford University Press, 1933).

Franco Vázquez, Alfonso, 'The Galician Fiddle Style', in *Crossing Over: Fiddle and Dance Studies from around the North Atlantic, 3*, ed. Ian Russell and Anna Kearney Guigné (Aberdeen: Elphinstone Institute, University of Aberdeen, in association with the Department of Folklore, MMaP and the School of Music, Memorial University of Newfoundland, 2010), pp. 200–14.

Freeman, Graham, '"That chief undercurrent of my mind": Percy Grainger and the Aesthetics of English Folk Song', *Folk Music Journal*, 9.4 (2009), 581–617.

—, '"It wants all the creases ironing out": Percy Grainger, the Folk Song Society, and the Ideology of the Archive', *Music & Letters*, 92 (2011), 410–36, http://dx.doi.org/10.1093/ml/gcr075.

Friedman, Albert B., *The Ballad Revival: Studies in the Influence of Popular on Sophisticated Poetry* (Chicago: University of Chicago Press, 1961).

—, 'The Oral-Formulaic Theory of Balladry – A Re-rebuttal', in *The Ballad Image: Essays Presented to Bertrand Harris Bronson*, ed. James Porter (Los Angeles: Center for the Study of Comparative Folklore & Mythology, University of California, Los Angeles, 1983), pp. 215–40.

Fumerton, Patricia, and Anita Guerrini, eds, *Ballads and Broadsides in Britain, 1500–1800* (Farnham and Burlington, VT: Ashgate, 2010).

Furnivall, Frederick J., ed., *Bishop Percy's Folio Manuscript: Loose and Humorous Songs* (London: printed by and for the editor, 1868).

Gabler, Hans Walter, 'The Text as Process and the Problem of Intentionality', *Text: Transactions of the Society for Textual Scholarship*, 3 (1987), 107–16.

Gammon, Vic, *Desire, Drink and Death in English Folk and Vernacular Song, 1600–1900* (Aldershot and Burlington, VT: Ashgate, 2008).

Garbáty, Thomas J., 'Rhyme, Romance, Ballad, Burlesque, and the Confluence of Form', in *Fifteenth-Century Studies: Recent Essays*, ed. Robert F. Yeager (Hamden, CT: Archon Books, 1984), pp. 283–301.

Gardham, Steve, '"The Brown Girl" (Child 295B): A Baring-Gould Concoction?', in *Folk Song: Tradition, Revival, and Re-Creation*, ed. Ian Russell and David Atkinson (Aberdeen: Elphinstone Institute, University of Aberdeen, 2004), pp. 363–76.

Gaskill, Malcolm, 'Reporting Murder: Fiction in the Archives in Early Modern England', *Social History*, 23 (1998), 1–30, http://dx.doi.org/10.1080/03071029808568018.

—, *Crime and Mentalities in Early Modern England* (Cambridge: Cambridge University Press, 2000), http://dx.doi.org/10.1017/ccol0521572754.

Gelbart, Matthew, *The Invention of 'Folk Music' and 'Art Music': Emerging Categories from Ossian to Wagner* (Cambridge: Cambridge University Press, 2007), http://dx.doi.org/10.1017/cbo9780511481918.

Genette, Gérard, *Figures of Literary Discourse*, trans. Alan Sheridan (Oxford: Blackwell, 1982).

Georges, Robert A., 'The Universality of the Tale-Type as Concept and Construct', *Western Folklore*, 42 (1983), 21–28.

—, and Michael Owen Jones, *Folkloristics: An Introduction* (Bloomington and Indianapolis: Indiana University Press, 1995).

Goehr, Lydia, *The Imaginary Museum of Musical Works: An Essay in the Philosophy of Music*, rev. edn (New York: Oxford University Press, 2007), http://dx.doi.org/10.1093/0198235410.001.0001.

Grainger, Percy, 'Collecting with the Phonograph', *Journal of the Folk-Song Society*, 3.3 (no. 12) (1908), 147–242.

Graves, Robert, *The English Ballad: A Short Critical Survey* (London: Ernest Benn, 1927).

—, ed., *English and Scottish Ballads* (London: Heinemann, 1957).

Green, Richard Firth, 'Textual Production and Textual Communities', in *The Cambridge Companion to Medieval English Literature, 1100–1500*, ed. Larry Scanlon (Cambridge: Cambridge University Press, 2009), pp. 25–36, http://dx.doi.org/10.1017/ccol9780521841672.003.

Greetham, D. C., *Textual Scholarship: An Introduction* (New York: Garland, 1994).

—, *Theories of the Text* (Oxford: Oxford University Press, 1999), http://dx.doi.org/10.1093/acprof:oso/9780198119937.001.0001.

Greg, W. W., 'A Ballad of Twelfth Day', *Modern Language Review*, 8 (1913), 64–67; 9 (1914), 235–36, http://dx.doi.org/10.2307/3712650 http://dx.doi.org/10.2307/3713003.

Gregory, E. David, 'In the Shadow of Child: Other Victorian Perspectives on Ballad Editing', in *Ballad Mediations: Folksongs Recovered, Represented, and Reimagined*, ed. Roger deV. Renwick and Sigrid Rieuwerts, BASIS, vol. 2 (Trier: WVT Wissenschaftlicher Verlag Trier, 2006), pp. 69–77.

—, *Victorian Songhunters: The Recovery and Editing of English Vernacular Ballads and Folk Lyrics, 1820–1883* (Lanham, MD: Scarecrow Press, 2006).

—, 'Fakesong in an Imagined Village? A Critique of the Harker–Boyes Thesis', *Canadian Folk Music/Musique folklorique canadienne*, 43.3 (2009), 18–26.

—, *The Late Victorian Folksong Revival: The Persistence of English Melody, 1878–1903* (Lanham, MD: Scarecrow Press, 2010).

Grésillon, Almuth, *Éléments de critique génétique: Lire les manuscrits modernes* (Paris: Presses Universitaires de France, 1994).

—, 'Slow: Work in Progress', *Word & Image* 13 (1997), 106–23, http://dx.doi.org/10.10 80/02666286.1997.10434276.

Grier, James, *The Critical Editing of Music: History, Method, and Practice* (Cambridge: Cambridge University Press, 1996).

Groom, Nick, *The Making of Percy's Reliques* (Oxford: Clarendon Press, 1999), http://dx.doi.org/10.1093/acprof:oso/9780198184591.001.0001.

Grundtvig, Svend, et al., eds, *Danmarks gamle Folkeviser*, 12 vols (København: Samfundet til den danske Literaturs Fremme, Universitets-Jubilæets danske Samfund, et al., 1853–1976).

Hales, John W., and Frederick J. Furnivall, eds, *Bishop Percy's Folio Manuscript: Ballads and Romances*, 3 vols (London: Trübner, 1867–68).

Hall, Peter A., 'Farm Life and the Farm Songs', in *The Greig-Duncan Folk Song Collection*, ed. Patrick Shuldham-Shaw, Emily B. Lyle, et al., 8 vols (Aberdeen: Aberdeen University Press; Edinburgh: Mercat Press, for the University of Aberdeen in association with the School of Scottish Studies, University of Edinburgh, 1981–2002), III, xxi–xxxiv.

Halpert, Herbert, and J. D. A. Widdowson, 'Folk-Narrative Performance and Tape Transcription: Theory versus Practice', *Lore & Language*, 5.1 (1986), 39–50.

—, *Folktales of Newfoundland: The Resilience of the Oral Tradition*, 2 vols (New York: Garland, 1996).

Harker, Dave, *Fakesong: The Manufacture of British 'Folksong', 1700 to the Present Day* (Milton Keynes: Open University Press, 1985).

Harlow, Ilana, 'Tale-Type', in *Encyclopedia of Folklore and Literature*, ed. Mary Ellen Brown and Bruce A. Rosenberg (Santa Barbara: ABC-CLIO, 1998), pp. 641–43.

Harrop, Peter, 'The Antrobus Soulcakers: A Consideration of Site, Mobility and Time as Components of Traditional Performance', *Contemporary Theatre Review*, 22 (2012), 267–73, http://dx.doi.org/10.1080/10486801.2012.666739.

[Herd, David], *The Ancient and Modern Scots Songs, Heroic Ballads, &c.* (Edinburgh: Martin & Wotherspoon, 1769).

Hindley, Charles, *The Life and Times of James Catnach, (Late of Seven Dials), Ballad Monger* (London: Reeves and Turner, 1878).

Hints to Collectors of Folk Music ([London: Folk-Song Society, 1898]).

Hirsh, John C., 'The Earliest Known English Ballad: A New Reading of "Judas"', *Modern Language Review*, 103 (2008), 931–39, http://dx.doi.org/10.2307/20468022.

Hobsbawm, Eric, and Terence Ranger, eds, *The Invention of Tradition* (Cambridge: Cambridge University Press, 1983).

Hodgart, M. J. C., *The Ballads*, 2nd edn (London: Hutchinson, 1962).

Hogg, James, *Memoir of the Author's Life* and *Familiar Anecdotes of Sir Walter Scott*, ed. Douglas S. Mack (Edinburgh: Scottish Academic Press, 1972).

Holcroft, Thomas, *Memoirs of the Late Thomas Holcroft*, 3 vols (London: Longman, Hurst, Rees, Orme, and Brown, 1816).

Honko, Lauri, *Textualising the Siri Epic*, FF Communications, no. 264 (Helsinki: Suomalainen Tiedeakatemia/Academia Scientiarum Fennica, 1998).

—, 'Thick Corpus and Organic Variation: An Introduction', in *Thick Corpus, Organic Variation and Textuality in Oral Tradition*, ed. Lauri Honko (Helsinki: Finnish Literature Society, 2000), pp. 3–28.

Houston, R. A., *Scottish Literacy and the Scottish Identity: Illiteracy and Society in Scotland and Northern England, 1600–1800* (Cambridge: Cambridge University Press, 1985), http://dx.doi.org/10.1017/cbo9780511522598.

Hudson, Nicholas, '"Oral Tradition": The Evolution of an Eighteenth-Century Concept', in *Tradition in Transition: Women Writers, Marginal Texts, and the Eighteenth-Century Canon*, ed. Alvaro Ribeiro and James G. Basker (Oxford: Clarendon Press, 1996), pp. 161–76, http://dx.doi.org/10.1093/acprof:oso/9780198182887.003.0010.

—, 'Constructing Oral Tradition: The Origins of the Concept in Enlightenment Intellectual Culture', in *The Spoken Word: Oral Culture in Britain, 1500–1850*, ed. Adam Fox and Daniel Woolf (Manchester: Manchester University Press, 2002), pp. 240–55.

[Hughes, Thomas], *The Scouring of the White Horse; or, The Long Vacation Ramble of a London Clerk* (Cambridge: Macmillan, 1859).

Hustvedt, Sigurd Bernhard, *Ballad Books and Ballad Men: Raids and Rescues in Britain, America, and the Scandinavian North since 1800* (Cambridge, MA: Harvard University Press, 1930).

Innis, Harold A., *The Bias of Communication* ([Toronto]: University of Toronto Press, 1951).

Ives, Edward D., *Larry Gorman: The Man Who Made the Songs* (Bloomington: Indiana University Press, 1964).

—, *Lawrence Doyle, The Farmer-Poet of Prince Edward Island: A Study in Local Songmaking*, University of Maine Studies, no. 92 (Orono: University of Maine Press, 1971).

—, *Joe Scott: The Woodsman-Songmaker* (Urbana: University of Illinois Press, 1978).

Jenny, Laurent, 'Genetic Criticism and its Myths', *Yale French Studies*, no. 89 (1996), 9–25, http://dx.doi.org/10.2307/2930336.

Johnson, Samuel, *The Lives of the Most Eminent English Poets, with critical observations on their works*, introduction and notes by Roger Lonsdale, 4 vols (Oxford: Clarendon Press, 2006).

Jones, James H., 'Commonplace and Memorization in the Oral Tradition of the English and Scottish Popular Ballads', *Journal of American Folklore*, 74 (1961), 97–112.

Jowett, John, *Shakespeare and Text* (Oxford: Oxford University Press, 2007).

Ker, W. P., *Form and Style in Poetry: Lectures and Notes*, ed. R. W. Chambers (London: Macmillan, 1966 [1928]).

[Kinloch, Geo. R.], *Ancient Scottish Ballads* (London: Longman, Rees, Orme, Brown, & Green; Edinburgh: John Stevenson, 1827).

Kinsley, James, ed., *The Oxford Book of Ballads* (Oxford: Oxford University Press, 1969).

Klobčar, Marija, 'Itinerant Singers in Slovenia: Views on a Distinct Phenomenon', in *Songs of People on the Move*, ed. Thomas A. McKean, BASIS, vol. 8 (Trier: WVT Wissenschaftlicher Verlag Trier, 2012), pp. 3–15.

Knapman, Zinnia, 'A Reappraisal of Percy's Editing', *Folk Music Journal*, 5.2 (1986), 202–14.

Knight, Stephen, ed., *Robin Hood: The Forresters Manuscript, British Library Additional MS 71158* (Cambridge: D. S. Brewer, 1998).

Kunej, Drago, '"We have plenty of words written down; we need melodies!": The Purchase of the First Recording Device for Ethnomusicological Research in Slovenia', *Traditiones* [Ljubljana], 34.1 (2005), 125–40.

—, 'Digitised Early Sound Recordings as Scholarly Resources', in *Trapped in Folklore? Studies in Music and Dance Tradition and their Contemporary Transformations*, ed. Drago Kunej and Urša Šivic (Wien: Lit Verlag, 2013), pp. 181–96.

Lakoff, George, *Women, Fire, and Dangerous Things: What Categories Reveal about the Mind* (Chicago: University of Chicago Press, 1987).

Laqueur, Thomas, 'The Cultural Origins of Popular Literacy in England, 1500–1850', *Oxford Review of Education*, 2 (1976), 255–75, http://dx.doi.org/10.1080/0305498760020304.

Laws, G. Malcolm, Jr., *American Balladry from British Broadsides: A Guide for Students and Collectors of Traditional Song* (Philadelphia: American Folklore Society, 1957).

Levenston, E. A., *The Stuff of Literature: Physical Aspects of Texts and their Relation to Literary Meaning* (Albany: State University of New York Press, 1992).

Levin, Richard, 'Negative Evidence', *Studies in Philology*, 92 (1995), 383–410.

Lockhart, J. G., *Memoirs of Sir Walter Scott*, 5 vols (London: Macmillan, 1900).

Long, Eleanor, *'The Maid' and 'The Hangman': Myth and Tradition in a Popular Ballad* (Berkeley and Los Angeles: University of California Press, 1971).

—, 'Ballad Singers, Ballad Makers, and Ballad Etiology', *Western Folklore*, 32 (1973), 225–36.

Lord, Albert Bates, *The Singer Resumes the Tale*, ed. Mary Louise Lord (Ithaca, NY: Cornell University Press, 1995).

—, *The Singer of Tales*, 2nd edn, ed. Stephen Mitchell and Gregory Nagy (Cambridge, MA: Harvard University Press, 2000).

Lyle, E. B., ed., *Andrew Crawfurd's Collection of Ballads and Songs*, 2 vols (Edinburgh: Scottish Text Society, 1975, 1996).

—, 'Parity of Ignorance: Child's Judgment on "Sir Colin" and the Scottish Verdict "Not Proven"', in *The Ballad and Oral Literature*, ed. Joseph Harris (Cambridge, MA: Harvard University Press, 1991), pp. 109–15.

Macaulay, Ronald K. S., '"Coz it izny spelt when they say it": Displaying Dialect in Writing', *American Speech*, 66 (1991), 280–91, http://dx.doi.org/10.2307/455800.

Machan, Tim William, *Textual Criticism and Middle English Texts* (Charlottesville: University Press of Virginia, 1994).

Marsh, Christopher, *Music and Society in Early Modern England* (Cambridge: Cambridge University Press, 2010).

McCarthy, William B., 'William Motherwell as Field Collector', *Folk Music Journal*, 5.3 (1987), 295–316.

McGann, Jerome J., *A Critique of Modern Textual Criticism* (Charlottesville: University Press of Virginia, 1992 [1983]).

—, *The Textual Condition* (Princeton: Princeton University Press, 1991).

McKean, Thomas A., *Hebridean Song-Maker: Iain MacNeacail of the Isle of Skye* (Edinburgh: Polygon, [1997?]).

—, 'The Stewarts of Fetterangus and Literate Oral Tradition', in *The Singer and the Scribe: European Ballad Traditions and European Ballad Cultures*, ed. Philip E. Bennett and Richard Firth Green (Amsterdam: Rodopi, 2004), pp. 181–207.

—, 'The Dialect Conundrum in Transcribing Early Sound Recordings', in *From 'Wunderhorn' to the Internet: Perspectives on Conceptions of 'Folk Song' and the Editing of Traditional Songs*, ed. Eckhard John and Tobias Widmaier, BASIS, vol. 6 (Trier: WVT Wissenschaftlicher Verlag Trier, 2010), pp. 209–24.

McKenzie, D. F., *Bibliography and the Sociology of Texts* (Cambridge: Cambridge University Press, 1999), http://dx.doi.org/10.1017/cbo9780511483226.

—, *Making Meaning: 'Printers of the Mind' and Other Essays*, ed. Peter D. McDonald and Michael F. Suarez (Amherst and Boston: University of Massachusetts Press, 2002).

McLaverty, James, 'The Mode of Existence of Literary Works of Art: The Case of the *Dunciad Variorum*', *Studies in Bibliography*, 37 (1984), 82–105.

McLuhan, Marshall, *Understanding Media: The Extensions of Man* (London: Routledge & Kegan Paul, 1964).

McShane, Angela, 'Typography Matters: Branding Ballads and Gelding Curates in Stuart England', in *Book Trade Connections from the Seventeenth to the Twentieth Centuries*, ed. John Hinks and Catherine Armstrong (New Castle, DE: Oak Knoll Press; London: British Library, 2008), pp. 19–44.

McShane Jones, Angela, '"Rime and Reason": The Political World of the English Broadside Ballad, 1640–1689' (unpublished doctoral thesis, University of Warwick, 2004).

Mish, Charles C., 'Black Letter as a Social Discriminant in the Seventeenth Century', *PMLA*, 68 (1953), 627–30, http://dx.doi.org/10.2307/459873.

Motherwell, William, *Minstrelsy: Ancient and Modern* (Glasgow: John Wylie, 1827).

—, *The Poetical Works of William Motherwell*, with memoir by James M'Conechy, Esq., 2nd edn (Glasgow: David Robertson, 1847).

Newman, David V., 'Chaos, Classification, and Intelligence/Caos, classificazione e intelligenza', in *Origine della vita intelligente nell'universo/Origin of Intelligent Life in the Universe*, ed. Roberto Colombo, Giulio Giorello, Gioachino Rigamonti, Elio Sindoni, and Corrado Sinigaglia (Como: Edizioni New Press, 1999), pp. 93–106.

Nicolaisen, W. F. H., 'On the Internationality of Ballads', in *Gender and Print Culture: New Perspectives on International Ballad Studies*, ed. Maria Herrera-Sobek ([n.p.]: Kommission für Volksdichtung, 1991), pp. 99–104.

Nygard, Holger Olof, *The Ballad of 'Heer Halewijn', its Forms and Variations in Western Europe: A Study of the History and Nature of a Ballad Tradition* (Knoxville: University of Tennessee Press, 1958).

—, 'Popular Ballad and Medieval Romance', in *Ballad Studies*, ed. E. B. Lyle (Cambridge: D. S. Brewer; Totowa, NJ: Rowman and Littlefield, for the Folklore Society, 1976), pp. 1–19.

—, 'Mrs. Brown's Recollected Ballads', in *Ballads and Ballad Research*, ed. Patricia Conroy (Seattle: University of Washington, 1978), pp. 68–87.

O'Keeffe, Katherine O'Brien, *Visible Song: Transitional Literacy in Old English Verse* (Cambridge: Cambridge University Press, 1990).

Olson, Ian, 'The Folk Song Society's *Hints for Collectors* (1898)', *English Dance & Song*, 57.1 (1995), 2–5.

Onderdonk, Julian, 'The Revised (1904) Version of the Folk Song Society's *Hints to Collectors*', *English Dance & Song*, 62.3 (2000), 21–23.

Ong, Walter J., *Orality and Literacy: The Technologizing of the Word* (London: Routledge, 1988 [1982]).

—, 'Writing Is a Technology that Restructures Thought', in *The Written Word: Literacy in Transition*, ed. Gerd Baumann (Oxford: Clarendon Press, 1986), pp. 23–50.

Palmer, Roy, 'George Dunn: Twenty-One Songs and Fragments', *Folk Music Journal*, 2.4 (1973), 275–96.

—, ed., *Bushes and Briars: Folk Songs Collected by Ralph Vaughan Williams*, 2nd edn ([Burnham-on-Sea]: Llanerch, 1999).

Parker, Harbison, 'The "Clerk Colvill" Mermaid', *Journal of American Folklore*, 60 (1947), 265–85.

Parkes, M. B., *Pause and Effect: An Introduction to the History of Punctuation in the West* (Aldershot: Scolar Press, 1992).

Parry, Edward Abbott, ed., *The Love Letters of Dorothy Osborne to Sir William Temple, 1652–54* (New York: Dodd, Mead, 1901).

Pearsall, Derek, 'Middle English Romance and its Audiences', in *Historical & Editorial Studies in Medieval & Early Modern English for Johan Gerritsen*, ed. Mary-Jo Arn and Hanneke Wirtjes, with Hans Jansen (Groningen: Wolters-Noordhoff, 1985), pp. 37–47.

Pebworth, Ted-Larry, 'Manuscript Transmission and the Selection of Copy-Text in Renaissance Coterie Poetry', *Text: Transactions of the Society for Textual Scholarship*, 7 (1994), 243–61.

Peirce, Charles S., 'What Is a Sign?', in *The Essential Peirce: Selected Philosophical Writings*, vol. 2 (1893–1913), ed. the Peirce Edition Project (Bloomington and Indianapolis: Indiana University Press, 1998), pp. 4–10, available at http://www.iupui.edu/~peirce/ep/ep2/ep2book/ch02/ep2ch2.htm.

[Percy, Thomas], *Reliques of Ancient English Poetry*, 3 vols (London: J. Dodsley, 1765).

[—], *Reliques of Ancient English Poetry*, 2nd edn, 3 vols (London: J. Dodsley, 1767).

[—], *Reliques of Ancient English Poetry*, 4th edn, 3 vols (London: F. and C. Rivington, 1794).

Pettitt, Thomas, 'Journalism vs. Tradition in the English Ballads of the Murdered Sweetheart', in *Ballads and Broadsides in Britain, 1500–1800*, ed. Patricia Fumerton and Anita Guerrini (Farnham and Burlington, VT: Ashgate, 2010), pp. 75–89.

—, 'Mediating Maria Marten: Comparative and Contextual Studies of the Red Barn Ballads', in *Street Ballads in Nineteenth-Century Britain, Ireland, and North America: The Interface between Print and Oral Traditions*, ed. David Atkinson and Steve Roud (Farnham and Burlington, VT: Ashgate, 2014), forthcoming.

Poe, Edgar Allan, 'The Philosophy of Composition', in *Selected Writings of Edgar Allan Poe: Poems, Tales, Essays and Reviews*, ed. David Galloway (Harmondsworth: Penguin, 1967), pp. 480–92.

Popper, Karl, *The Logic of Scientific Discovery* (London: Routledge, 2002 [1959]).

Preston, Dennis R., ''Ritin' Fowklower Daun 'Rong: Folklorists' Failures in Phonology', *Journal of American Folklore*, 95 (1982), 304–26.

—, 'Mowr Bayud Spellin': A Reply to Fine', *Journal of American Folklore*, 96 (1983), 330–39.

Putter, Ad, and Jane Gilbert, eds, *The Spirit of Medieval English Popular Romance* (Harlow: Longman, 2000).

Quiller-Couch, Arthur, ed., *The Oxford Book of Ballads* (Oxford: Clarendon Press, 1910).

Raven, James, 'New Reading Histories, Print Culture and the Identification of Change: The Case of Eighteenth-Century England', *Social History*, 23 (1998), 268–87, http://dx.doi.org/10.1080/03071029808568038.

Reay, Barry, 'The Context and Meaning of Popular Literacy: Some Evidence from Nineteenth-Century Rural England', *Past and Present*, no. 131 (1991), 89–129, http://dx.doi.org/10.1093/past/131.1.89.

—, *Popular Cultures in England, 1550–1750* (London: Longman, 1998).

Reeves, James, ed., *The Idiom of the People: English Traditional Verse* [. . .] *from the manuscripts of Cecil J. Sharp* (London: Heinemann, 1958).

Renwick, Roger deV., *Recentering Anglo/American Folksong: Sea Crabs and Wicked Youths* (Jackson: University Press of Mississippi, 2001).

Rieuwerts, Sigrid, 'The Case against Peter Buchan', in *The Flowering Thorn: International Ballad Studies*, ed. Thomas A. McKean (Logan: Utah State University Press, 2003), pp. 341–51.

—, 'The Ballad Society: A Forgotten Chapter in the History of English Ballad Studies', in *Folk Song: Tradition, Revival, and Re-Creation*, ed. Ian Russell and David Atkinson (Aberdeen: Elphinstone Institute, University of Aberdeen, 2004), pp. 28–40.

—, ed., *The Ballad Repertoire of Anna Gordon, Mrs Brown of Falkland*, Scottish Text Society, 5th ser., no. 8 (Woodbridge and Rochester, NY: Boydell Press, for the Scottish Text Society, 2011).

[Ritson, Joseph], *A Select Collection of English Songs*, 3 vols (London: J. Johnson, 1783).

[—], *Ancient Songs, from the Time of King Henry the Third, to the Revolution* (London: J. Johnson, 1790).

Rollins, Hyder E., 'The Black-Letter Broadside Ballad', *PMLA*, 34 (1919), 258–339, http://dx.doi.org/10.2307/457063.

Ross, Angus, ed., *Selections from The Tatler and The Spectator of Steele and Addison* (Harmondsworth: Penguin, 1982).

Rothenbuhler, Eric W., and John Durham Peters, 'Defining Phonography: An Experiment in Theory', *Musical Quarterly*, 81 (1997), 242–64, http://dx.doi.org/10.1093/mq/81.2.242.

Roud, Steve, 'Introduction', in *Street Ballads in Nineteenth-Century Britain, Ireland, and North America: The Interface between Print and Oral Traditions*, ed. David Atkinson and Steve Roud (Farnham and Burlington, VT: Ashgate, 2014), forthcoming.

Russell, Ian, 'Stability and Change in a Sheffield Singing Tradition', *Folk Music Journal*, 5.3 (1987), 317–58.

—, 'The Singer's the Thing: Individual and Group Identity in a Pennine Singing Tradition', *Folk Music Journal*, 8.3 (2003), 266–81.

St Clair, William, *The Reading Nation in the Romantic Period* (Cambridge: Cambridge University Press, 2004).

Sandys, William, *Christmas Carols, Ancient and Modern* (London: Richard Beckley, 1833).

Schlauch, Margaret, *Chaucer's Constance and Accused Queens* (New York: New York University Press, 1927).

Schofield, Derek, 'Sowing the Seeds: Cecil Sharp and Charles Marson in Somerset in 1903', *Folk Music Journal*, 8.4 (2004), 484–512.

Schofield, R. S., 'The Measurement of Literacy in Pre-Industrial England', in *Literacy in Traditional Societies*, ed. Jack Goody (Cambridge: Cambridge University Press, 1968), pp. 311–25.

Scott, Sir Walter, *Minstrelsy of the Scottish Border*, ed. T. F. Henderson, 4 vols (Edinburgh: Oliver and Boyd, 1932 [1902]).

Seal, Graham, 'A. L. Lloyd in Australia: Some Conclusions', *Folk Music Journal*, 9.1 (2006), 56–71.

Seeger, Charles, 'Prescriptive and Descriptive Music-Writing', *Musical Quarterly*, 44 (1958), 184–95, http://dx.doi.org/10.1093/mq/xliv.2.184.

Shannon, Claude E., and Warren Weaver, *The Mathematical Theory of Communication* (Urbana: University of Illinois Press, 1949).

Sharp, Cecil J., *English Folk-Song: Some Conclusions* (London: Simpkin; Novello, 1907).

Shepard, Leslie, *John Pitts: Ballad Printer of Seven Dials, London, 1765–1844* (London: Private Libraries Association, 1969).

Shields, Hugh, 'Supplementary Syllables in Anglo-Irish Folk Singing', *Yearbook of the International Folk Music Council*, 5 (1973), 62–71, http://dx.doi.org/10.2307/767495.

—, 'Textual Criticism and Ballad Studies', in *Dear Far-Voiced Veteran: Essays in Honour of Tom Munnelly*, ed. Anne Clune (Miltown Malbay: Old Kilfarboy Society, 2007), pp. 287–94.

Shillingsburg, *Scholarly Editing in the Computer Age: Theory and Practice*, 3rd edn (Ann Arbor: University of Michigan Press, 1996).

—, *Resisting Texts: Authority and Submission in Constructions of Meaning* (Ann Arbor: University of Michigan Press, 1997).

—, *From Gutenberg to Google: Electronic Representations of Literary Texts* (Cambridge: Cambridge University Press, 2006), http://dx.doi.org/10.1017/cbo9780511617942.

Shorrocks, Graham, 'Reflections on the Problems of Transcribing Contemporary Legends', *Contemporary Legend*, 2 (1992), 93–117.

Simons, John, 'Romance in the Eighteenth-Century Chapbook', in *From Medieval to Medievalism*, ed. John Simons (Basingstoke: Macmillan, 1992), pp. 122–43.

Simpson, Claude M., *The British Broadside Ballad and its Music* (New Brunswick, NJ: Rutgers University Press, 1966).

Simpson, Jacqueline, and Steve Roud, *A Dictionary of English Folklore* (Oxford: Oxford University Press, 2000), http://dx.doi.org/10.1093/acref/9780198607663.001.0001.

Small, Christopher, *Musicking: The Meanings of Performing and Listening* (Middletown, CT: Wesleyan University Press, 1998).

Smout, T. C., 'Born Again at Cambuslang: New Evidence on Popular Religion and Literacy in Eighteenth-Century Scotland', *Past and Present*, no. 97 (1982), 114–27, http://dx.doi.org/10.1093/past/97.1.114.

Spufford, Margaret, *Small Books and Pleasant Histories: Popular Fiction and its Readership in Seventeenth-Century England* (Cambridge: Cambridge University Press, 1981).

—, 'The Pedlar, the Historian and the Folklorist: Seventeenth Century Communications', *Folklore*, 105 (1994), 13–24, http://dx.doi.org/10.1080/0015587x.1994.9715870.

Sterne, Jonathan, *The Audible Past: Cultural Origins of Sound Reproduction* (Durham, NC: Duke University Press, 2003), http://dx.doi.org/10.1215/9780822384250.

Stock, Brian, *The Implications of Literacy: Written Language and Models of Interpretation in the Eleventh and Twelfth Centuries* (Princeton: Princeton University Press, 1983).

—, *Listening for the Text: On the Uses of the Past* (Philadelphia: University of Pennsylvania Press, 1996 [1990]).

Stone, Lawrence, 'Literacy and Education in England, 1640–1900', *Past and Present*, no. 42 (1969), 69–139, http://dx.doi.org/10.1093/past/42.1.69.

Swain, Joseph P., *Musical Languages* (New York: W. W. Norton, 1997).

Sykes, Richard, 'The Evolution of Englishness in the English Folksong Revival, 1890–1914', *Folk Music Journal*, 6.4 (1993), 446–90.

Tanselle, G. Thomas, 'The Editorial Problem of Final Authorial Intention', *Studies in Bibliography*, 29 (1976), 167–211.

—, *A Rationale of Textual Criticism* (Philadelphia: University of Pennsylvania Press, 1989).

—, 'The Varieties of Scholarly Editing', in *Scholarly Editing: A Guide to Research*, ed. D. C. Greetham (New York: Modern Language Association of America, 1995), pp. 9–32.

—, 'Textual Criticism at the Millennium', *Studies in Bibliography*, 54 (2001), 1–80.

Taylor, Andrew, 'Fragmentation, Corruption, and Minstrel Narration: The Question of the Middle English Romances', *Yearbook of English Studies*, 22 (1992), 38–62, http://dx.doi.org/10.2307/3508375.

—, *The Songs and Travels of a Tudor Minstrel: Richard Sheale of Tamworth* (York: York Medieval Press, 2012).

Taylor, Archer, *'Edward' and 'Sven i Rosengård': A Study in the Dissemination of a Ballad* (Chicago: University of Chicago Press, 1931).

Taylor, Donald S., 'The Lineage and Birth of Sir Aldingar', *Journal of American Folklore*, 65 (1952), 139–47.

Thigpen, Kenneth A., Jr., 'A Reconsideration of the Commonplace Phrase and Commonplace Theme in the Child Ballads', *Southern Folklore Quarterly*, 37 (1973), 385–408.

Thomas, Keith, *Man and the Natural World: Changing Attitudes in England, 1500–1800* (London: Allen Lane, 1983).

—, 'The Meaning of Literacy in Early Modern England', in *The Written Word: Literacy in Transition*, ed. Gerd Baumann (Oxford: Clarendon Press, 1986), pp. 97–131.

Thompson, Raymond H., '"Muse on þi mirrour...": The Challenge of the Outlandish Stranger in the English Arthurian Verse Romances,' *Folklore*, 87 (1976), 201–08, http://dx.doi.org/10.1080/0015587x.1976.9716035.

Thompson, Stith, 'Type', in *Funk & Wagnalls Standard Dictionary of Folklore, Mythology, and Legend*, ed. Maria Leach, 2 vols (New York: Funk & Wagnalls, 1949–50), pp. 1137–38.

[—], 'Variant', in *Funk & Wagnalls Standard Dictionary of Folklore, Mythology, and Legend*, ed. Maria Leach, 2 vols (New York: Funk & Wagnalls, 1949–50), pp. 1154–55.

Thomson, Robert S., 'The Development of the Broadside Ballad Trade and its Influence upon the Transmission of English Folksongs' (unpublished doctoral thesis, University of Cambridge, 1974).

Titon, Jeff Todd, 'Text', in *Eight Words for the Study of Expressive Culture*, ed. Burt Feintuch (Urbana and Chicago: University of Illinois Press, 2003), pp. 69–98.

Todorov, Tzvetan, *Introduction to Poetics*, trans. Richard Howard (Brighton: Harvester, 1981).

Toelken, Barre, *Morning Dew and Roses: Nuance, Metaphor, and Meaning in Folksongs* (Urbana and Chicago: University of Illinois Press, 1995).

Treitler, Leo, 'History and the Ontology of the Musical Work', in *With Voice and Pen: Coming to Know Medieval Song and How It Was Made* (Oxford: Oxford University Press, 2003), pp. 298–316, http://dx.doi.org/10.1093/acprof:oso/9780199214761.003.0012.

Universal Songster, The; or, Museum of Mirth, 3 vols (London: John Fairburn; Simpkin and Marshall; Sherwood, Gilbert, and Piper, 1825–26).

Vargyas, Lajos, *Researches into the Mediaeval History of Folk Ballad*, trans. Arthur H. Whitney (Budapest: Akadémiai Kiadó, 1967).

Vincent, David, *Literacy and Popular Culture: England 1750–1914* (Cambridge: Cambridge University Press, 1989), http://dx.doi.org/10.1017/cbo9780511560880.

Walker, William, *Peter Buchan and Other Papers on Scottish and English Ballads and Songs* (Aberdeen: D. Wyllie & Son, 1915).

Wallace, David, ed., *The Cambridge History of Medieval English Literature* (Cambridge: Cambridge University Press, 1999), http://dx.doi.org/10.1017/chol9780521444200.

[Walton, Izaak], *The Compleat Angler; or, The Contemplative Man's Recreation* (London: printed by T. Maxey, for Rich. Marriot, 1653) [ESTC R202374].

Watt, Tessa, *Cheap Print and Popular Piety, 1550–1640* (Cambridge: Cambridge University Press, 1991).

Wehse, Rainer, 'Broadside Ballad and Folksong: Oral Tradition versus Literary Tradition', *Folklore Forum*, 8 (1975), 324–34 [2–12].

Weir, W., 'St. Giles's, Past and Present', in *London*, ed. Charles Knight, 6 vols (London: Charles Knight, 1841–44), III, 257–72.

Wellek, René, and Austin Warren, *Theory of Literature*, 3rd edn (Harmondsworth: Penguin, 1963).

Whisnant, David E., *All That Is Native & Fine: The Politics of Culture in an American Region* (Chapel Hill: University of North Carolina Press, 1983).

Wilgus, D. K., *Anglo-American Folksong Scholarship since 1898* (New Brunswick, NJ: Rutgers University Press, 1959).

—, 'The Text Is the Thing', *Journal of American Folklore*, 86 (1973), 241–52.

Williams, R. Vaughan, and A. L. Lloyd, eds, *The Penguin Book of English Folk Songs* (Harmondsworth: Penguin, 1959).

—, eds, *Classic English Folk Songs*, rev. Malcolm Douglas (London: EFDSS, 2003).

Williams, Raymond, *Keywords: A Vocabulary of Culture and Society*, rev. edn (London: Fontana, 1988).

Winick, Stephen D., 'A. L. Lloyd and Reynardine: Authenticity and Authorship in the Afterlife of a British Broadside Ballad', *Folklore*, 115 (2004), 286–308, http://dx.doi.org/10.1080/0015587042000284275.

Wright, Chris, 'Forgotten Broadsides and the Song Tradition of the Scots Travellers', in *Street Ballads in Nineteenth-Century Britain, Ireland, and North America: The Interface between Print and Oral Traditions*, ed. David Atkinson and Steve Roud (Farnham and Burlington, VT: Ashgate, 2014), forthcoming.

Würzbach, Natascha, *The Rise of the English Street Ballad, 1550–1650*, trans. Gayna Walls (Cambridge: Cambridge University Press, 1990).

Yates, Michael, 'Percy Grainger and the Impact of the Phonograph', *Folk Music Journal*, 4.3 (1982), 265–75.

Zug, Charles G., III, 'The Ballad Editor as Antiquary: Scott and the *Minstrelsy*', *Journal of the Folklore Institute*, 13 (1976), 57–73, http://dx.doi.org/10.2307/3813814.

Zumthor, Paul, *Essai de poétique médiévale* (Paris: Éditions du Seuil, 1972).

—, *La lettre et la voix: De la 'littérature' médiévale* (Paris: Éditions du Seuil, 1987).

Index

Aarne, Antti, 120
Addison, Joseph, 57, 70
Allingham, William, 128–129
Appalachia, 52
Aristotle, 96
avant-texte, 152, 153, 155, 164, 165, 166, 167

Bach, J. S.
  Toccata and Fugue in D minor, 5, 6, 13, 18, 23
ballad singers, semi-professional, 57
Ballad Society, 128
Ballad Warehouse, 29, 31
ballads and songs
  As I me rode this endre dai, 42
  Barbara Allan/Allen (Child 84), 20, 65, 174–178, 181
  Bloody Miller (Roud 263), 43
  Bonnie Annie (Child 24), 133
  Chevy Chase (Child 162), 64
  Clerk Colvill (Child 42), 4, 11
  Fair Margaret and Sweet William (Child 74), 31–32, 34–35
  False Hearted Miller (Roud 263), 43
  George Collins, 2–4, 5, 11, 15, 22, 25
  Judas (Child 23), 42, 56
  Lady Alice (Child 85), 4, 11
  Lord Bateman (Child 53), 18, 113, 116
  Lord Randal (Child 12), 52
  Lord Thomas and Fair Ellinor (Child 73), 29–30
  O No John (Roud 146), 125
  Our Goodman (Child 274), 154
  Robin Hood Rescuing Will Stutly (Child 141), 133
  Sir Aldingar (Child 59), 38–41, 42–43
  Sir Colin (Child 61), 36, 37, 38
  The Baffled Knight (Child 112), 142–143
  The Battle of Harlaw (Child 163), 65
  The Berkshire Tragedy (Roud 263), 43–47, 51
  The Bold Princess Royal (Roud 528), 51
  The Bonnie Banks o Fordie (Child 14), 155–165, 169–172
  The Bonny Earl of Murray (Child 181), 147
  The Child of Elle, 122
  The Children in the Wood (Roud 288), 70
  The Cruel Miller (Roud 263), 43–47, 51
  The Cruel Mother (Child 20), 65, 130–132
  The Fatal Ramillies (Roud 1266), 52
  The Golden Vanity (Child 286), 65, 104–105
  The Gypsy Laddie (Child 200), 60
  The Holy Well (Roud 1697), 105–111
  The Jolly Beggar (Child 279), 135
  The Maid Freed from the Gallows (Child 95), 18, 52, 65
  The Marriage of Sir Gawain (Child 31), 42
  The Mountains High (Roud 397), 51
  The Outlandish Knight (Child 4), 61–62, 65, 154
  The Proud Pedlar, 64
  The Seeds of Love (Roud 3), 26
  Twelfth Day, 42, 56

Two Sisters, The (Child 10), 18, 104, 134–135
Bänkelsang, 117
Baring-Gould, Sabine, 50, 173
Barry, Phillips, 4, 16
Bateson, F. W., 5, 6, 7, 8, 9, 11, 12, 13
Bates, Sarah, 34
Beckett, Samuel, 152
Beethoven, Ludwig van, 20, 85
  Hammerklavier Sonata, 13
Bellemin-Noël, Jean, 152
Bell, John, 128
Benjamin, Walter, 117
Bennett, Sam, 142, 144, 154
Beowulf, 55
Berliner, Émile, 95
Bible, the, 53, 58, 65
bibliographic codes, 71, 82, 136
Bogatyrëv, Peter, 10–11
Bohlman, Philip, 49, 50
bothy ballads, 60
Bownd, Nicholas, 64
Brady, Erika, 95
broadsides
  and music notation, 75, 80
  black-letter, 81
  decline of, 87
  distrust of, 28, 50, 87
  mise en page, 81
  pasted on walls, 57, 70, 76, 82, 83, 96
  print runs, 29, 77
  'slip songs', 45
  Stationers' Register entries, 34
  textual variation, 51–52
  tune directions, 30, 75, 80
  typographical errors, 79
  woodcuts, 70, 82
Brompton, John, 39
Bronson, Bertrand, 30, 89
Brontë, Charlotte
  Jane Eyre, 21
Brown, Mary Ellen, 37
Buchan, David
  The Ballad and the Folk, 10, 50
Buchan, Peter, 130, 131, 132
Bunting, Thomas, 177, 178

Burstow, Henry, 33–34

Cambuslang, Lanarkshire, 57–58
Campbell, J. F., 134
cantefables, 18
Carpenter, James Madison
  and folk plays, 154
  and 'Scotticization', 160
  collecting in Britain and Ireland, 102–103, 139–140
  collecting practices, 73, 78, 102–103, 139–142, 146
  interview with Alan Jabbour, 140, 141, 146
Catnach, James, 45
Cerquiglini, Bernard, 66, 67, 68
Chambers, E. K., 40, 41, 43
Chandler, Daniel, 75
Chappell, William, 29, 30
Chartier, Roger, 54, 56
Cheap Repository Tracts, 69
Child, Francis James
  and ballad origins, 4, 37, 55
  and broadside print, 50, 90, 136
  and conjectural emendation, 133
  and 'Sir Aldingar' (Child 59), 40, 43
  and 'Sir Colin' (Child 61), 36, 37, 38
  editing principles, 130–137
  English and Scottish Ballads (1857–58), 128
Chomsky, Noam, 8, 9
Chopin, Frédéric, 14, 16, 86, 87
Christie, William, 130, 131
Christophersen, Paul, 39
Cobb, Mrs, 177, 178
Coffin, Tristram Potter, 135
Collection of Old Ballads, A, 29, 121, 122, 133
Collins, Shirley, 62
'conceptual text', 165, 166, 167
Copper, Bob, 2–3, 11
Copper family, 3, 34, 63
Cornwallis, Sir William, 69, 70, 73
critique génétique, 150–151
Culler, Jonathan, 8, 11

Dalrymple, David, 122
Dancing Master, The, 30

Davis, Arthur Kyle, Jr., and editing, 137–138
de Biasi, Pierre-Marc, 153
deictics, 61
Derrida, Jacques, 7, 74, 96–97, 99
Diceto, Ralph de, 39
Dicey company, 29, 31, 122
Dickens, Charles
  Great Expectations, 16, 21
Dixon, James Henry, 131
Donne, John, 178
Douglas, Gavin, 58
Dugaw, Dianne, 51
D'Urfey, Thomas, 122

Edison, Thomas Alva, 92, 95
Eisenstein, Elizabeth, 77
Eliot, T. S., 152
Ely Farming Memoranda, 56
England, John, 26
Entwistle, W. J., 9, 40

Ferrer, Daniel, 153
Fine, Elizabeth, 110, 112
Fish, Stanley, 60
Flaubert, Gustave, 152, 153
Flodden, battle of, 58
Foucault, Michel, 14, 21
French, 43, 56
Friedman, Albert, 122, 123, 173
Furnivall, Frederick J., 128

Galicia, Spanish, 118
Gammon, Vic, 57
Garbáty, Thomas, 41, 42
Gardiner, George B., 4
Genette, Gérard, 9
Georges, Robert, 18, 19
Grainger, Percy
  and electro-mechanical recording, 92
  and Lincolnshire singers, 110, 116
  and music transcription, 90–91, 96, 101, 111, 113
  and phonograph recording, 73, 79, 90–91, 96
  and singers' recall, 142
Graves, Robert, 129

Green, Richard Firth, 59
Greig–Duncan folk song collection, 26
Grier, James, 93
Grundtvig, Svend, 17, 127
Gypsy singers, 60

Hales, John W., 128
Hambridge, Somerset, 26
Harker, Dave, 117
Heather, Samuel, 105, 106, 110
Helmholtz, Hermann von, 99, 113
Henderson, T. F., 43, 125
Herd, David, 31, 135
Hints to Collectors of Folk Music, 111
Hogg, James, 83
Holcroft, Thomas, 70
Honko, Lauri, and 'mental text', 113, 165
horizon of expectations, 60, 63
Hughes, Thomas, 134
Hugo, Victor, 152

Innis, Harold, 74, 82
intention, authorial, 120, 139, 153, 180
International Folk Music Council, 28
interpretive communities, 60

Jabbour, Alan, 140, 141, 146
Jakobson, Roman, 10–11
James, Henry, 14
Johnson, Samuel, 123
  'Life of Milton', 151
Joyce, James, 152, 153
  Ulysses, 17, 68

Keats, John
  'Ode on a Grecian Urn', 5, 13
Keed, John, 46
Ker, W. P., 9
Khan, Ali Akbar, 86
Kidson, Frank, 26
Kinloch, George R., 133
Knight of the Burning Pestle, The, 31, 34
Knight, Stephen, 133
Krohn, Julius and Kaarle, 120

Laidlaw, Margaret, 83
langue, 8, 9, 10, 11, 19, 96

Latin, 43, 55, 56
Latin verse, 180
Levin, Richard, 33
line endings, 81, 182
literacy, 53–56, 60, 74, 96
Lloyd, A. L., 173
Lollards, 58
Lomax, Alan, 103
Lord, Albert B.
  Singer of Tales, The, 9–10, 50, 53
Lyle, Emily, 36–37
Lytton, Edward Bulwer, 21

Macqueen, Thomas, 31
Marconi, Guglielmo, 72
McEwan, Mrs Alexander, 155, 158, 159, 162, 163, 164, 165, 166
McKenzie, D. F., 33
McLuhan, Marshall, 54, 74
McShane, Angela, 59
metaphysics of presence, 97, 99, 100, 113, 116, 117, 119
Milton, John
  Lycidas, 5
modernist poetry, 65, 66
Mona Lisa, 5, 6, 13
'mondegreens', 147
Moore, Marianne, 65
Motherwell, William, 17, 28, 35, 90, 125–127, 128, 131
mouvance, 67
'murdered-sweetheart' ballads, 44
music writing, prescriptive and descriptive, 91–92, 101, 104
'musical language', 7, 97
'musicking', 7

O'Keeffe, Katherine O'Brien, 179, 180
Old English, written, 55
Old English verse, 179–181
Ong, Walter, 54, 55
operas, based on Child ballads, 18
oral-formulaic theory, 50, 52
oral tradition
  and ballad melodies, 34, 50, 52, 75, 96, 97
  as eighteenth-century construct, 35, 74

iconic status of, 27–28, 49–50, 63, 74, 98
non-falsifiability of, 32, 33, 35, 41
Osborne, Dorothy, 26

palimpsest, 150, 153, 166, 167, 168
Paris, Matthew, 39, 43
parity of ignorance, 36, 37, 41, 42, 43, 47
parole, 8, 9, 10, 11, 19, 96
Peirce, Charles Sanders, 93–94
Penguin Book of English Folk Songs, 3, 4
Pepys, Samuel, 35
Percy, Thomas, *Reliques of Ancient English Poetry*, 37, 120–123, 124, 128, 137, 173
  and 'Fair Margaret and Sweet William', 31
  and 'Lord Thomas and Fair Ellinor', 29
  and 'Sir Aldingar', 43
  and 'Sir Colin', 36
  and 'The Child of Elle', 122
  Scott's discovery of *Reliques*, 121
Percy folio manuscript, 36, 38, 40, 41, 42, 90, 121–123, 128
Peters, John Durham, 94
Phelps, Sarah, 154
phonautograph, 92, 94
phonocentrism, 7, 74, 83
Piers Plowman, 58
Pitts, John, 45
Plato, 96, 97
Poe, Edgar Allan
  'The Philosophy of Composition', 151
political ballads, 59
Popper, Karl, 32, 33
Pound, Ezra, 21
Preston, Dennis, 109–110, 112
Proust, Marcel, 152
punctuation, 80, 81, 103, 137, 138, 178–180, 181–182

Quiller-Couch, Arthur, 16, 129

Ramsay, Allan, 122
reading aloud, 53, 54, 59, 66, 70, 79, 99, 179, 180
reading communities, 54, 56, 78
Reeves, James, 125
Renwick, Roger, 20

Ritson, Joseph, 30, 122, 123, 124, 128
romances, medieval, 15, 38, 41, 58–59, 60, 62, 66, 122
Rothenbuhler, Eric W., 94
Rousseau, Jean-Jacques, 96

Sandys, William, 30
Saussure, Ferdinand de, 8, 9, 96
Scots Musical Museum, 80
Scott, David, of Peterhead, 130
Scott, Walter
  and Hogg's mother, 83
  and Percys *Reliques*, 121
  and 'Sir Aldingar', 43
  letter to Motherwell, 90, 125–126, 127
  Minstrelsy of the Scottish Border, 120, 123–126, 129, 130, 137, 147
Scott de Martinville, Édouard-Léon, 92, 94, 95
Seeger, Charles, 91–92
Shakespeare, William
  and collaborative playwriting, 21
  editing of, 123, 133
  Hamlet, 5–6, 13, 14, 16, 18, 20, 23, 67, 68, 154
  King Lear, 16, 67, 68
  Macbeth, 67
Sharp, Cecil
  and music transcription, 90, 91, 101
  and phonograph recording, 79
  and singers' recall, 142
  continuity, variation, and selection model, 4, 10, 28
  distrust of print, 28, 50
  English Folk-Song: Some Conclusions, 28
  first encounter with folk song, 26
  manuscripts, 125
Shenstone, William, 123
Shillingsburg, Peter, 133, 144, 179
Sir Gawain and the Green Knight, 62
Slovenia, 118
social theory of text, 21, 139, 145, 150
Solomon and Saturn I, 180
Sterne, Jonathan, 99
Stewarts of Fetterangus, 64
Stock, Brian, 56, 57, 58, 65, 67

Stockhausen, Karlheinz
  Klavierstück XI, 21, 86

Tanselle, Thomas, 5, 6, 174
Taylor, Joseph, 79, 113, 116
Terry, Charles, 174, 178
textual communities, 56–59
Thackeray, William, 29
Thackeray, William Makepeace, 178–179
Thomas, Keith, 55, 56
Thompson, Stith, 17
Todorov, Tzvetan, 8
Travellers, 52, 60, 63, 64, 155
Treitler, Leo, 5, 6, 18, 19, 23, 84–87
tune families, 17
type/version paradigm, xv–xvi, 17, 19, 119, 120, 137

Universal Songster, The, 4, 22

Valéry, Paul, 152
variance, 66–67, 68
Veal, Sidney, 108
versions, of literary works, 120

Waldensians, 57
Walton, Izaak
  The Compleat Angler, 64, 70
Warner, Richard, 105
Weddynge of Sir Gawen and Dame Ragnell, The, 41
White, Enos, 2–3, 4, 11, 15, 22
Whitefield, George, 57
William of Malmesbury, 38, 39, 40, 43
Williams, Ralph Vaughan, 2, 22, 173
Williams, Raymond, 34
writing, 'branchable' nature of, 98, 103

Yeats, W. B., 65, 152

Zola, Émile, 152
Zumthor, Paul, 67

This book does not end here...

At Open Book Publishers, we are changing the nature of the traditional academic book. The title you have just read will not be left on a library shelf, but will be accessed online by hundreds of readers each month across the globe. We make all our books free to read online so that students, researchers and members of the public who can't afford a printed edition can still have access to the same ideas as you.

Our digital publishing model also allows us to produce online supplementary material, including extra chapters, reviews, links and other digital resources. Find *The Anglo-Scottish Ballad* on our website to access its online extras. Please check this page regularly for ongoing updates, and join the conversation by leaving your own comments:

http://www.openbookpublishers.com/isbn/9781783740277

If you enjoyed this book, and feel that research like this should be available to all readers, regardless of their income, please think about donating to us. Our company is run entirely by academics, and our publishing decisions are based on intellectual merit and public value rather than on commercial viability. We do not operate for profit and all donations, as with all other revenue we generate, will be used to finance new Open Access publications.

For further information about what we do, how to donate to OBP, additional digital material related to our titles or to order our books, please visit our website.

Knowledge is for sharing

www.ingramcontent.com/pod-product-compliance
Lightning Source LLC
Chambersburg PA
CBHW071840230426
43671CB00012B/2021